DO YOU LIKE FOOD WITH GOOD, OLD-FASHIONED FLAVOR?

Enjoy the delights of rural American cooking with nearly 500 authentic, unusual recipes in this modern, practical adaptation of a genuine 19th century cookbook.

* How to bake your own bread, muffins, pies
* How to make jellies, marmalades, preserve fruits
* How to make your own candy
* Plus old-fashioned home remedies, beauty secrets and household hints!

Grandmother's Country Cookbook

Ted and Jean Kaufman

PAPERBACK LIBRARY

NEW YORK

PAPERBACK LIBRARY EDITION

First Printing: December, 1966
Second Printing: January, 1971
Third Printing: June, 1972

Paperback Library is a division of Coronet Communications, Inc.
Its trademark, consisting of the words "Paperback Library" accom-
panied by an open book, is registered in the United States Patent
Office. *Coronet Communications, Inc., 315 Park Avenue South,
New York, N.Y. 10010.*

CONTENTS

INTRODUCTION

Today, with our population overwhelmingly urban, it is difficult for us to realize that throughout most of the nineteenth cenutry, the United States was a country of farms and that our principal national wealth lay in the land. To own and work a farm was the ambition of most men and women of that age. Fortunately our land was so broad and extensive in area that there was room enough for all—the pioneer, the immigrant, and the hordes of restless urbanites caught up in the frenzy of the great movement of the West.

The soil was rich and the families working the land were large. Inspired by a common goal, the men, women and children all shared the long hours of backbreaking labor which the working of a farm entailed. Thousands of such unified endeavors resulted in a vast farmland filled with such plenty and abundance as few nations had ever before equaled. Agriculture was king.

With an abundant supply of foodstuff on hand, and in the presence of so many hungry mouths to be fed, it was natural that the kitchen should become the domestic focal point of farm life.

From sunup to sundown the housewife's labors never ceased; the stove's fire remained ever lit. Besides having so many voracious appetites to appease, it seems amazing—in retrospect nigh unbelievable— that she should also have found time to bear and rear so many children; to act as both doctor and nurse in emergencies; to keep the peace in a household bustling with a highly individualistic breed of men. Thus the kitchen, inevitably, played the most important part in binding the family close, and it was the mother who was truly responsible for turning the house into a home. Yet, despite her many other tasks, it was the kitchen stove, over which she reigned as undisputed queen, which occupied most of her sixteen–hour–long day.

Physically, it took strong arms and a strong back to manipulate the large wood or coal-burning stoves, and to lift and move the heavy iron skillets, pots and kettles about the room. Then, too, it took a woman of constant ingenuity and inventiveness—no matter how large her collection of family 'receipts'—to cope with converting the huge quantities of foodstuffs into abundant meals, sufficiently varied to satisfy the appetites of her menfolk, as well as to provide them daily with the nourishment their heavy toil demanded. Though the housewife might often refer to her recipes for guidance in preparing some of the dishes, likely as not she might just cook them 'by ear,' knowing instinctively, from years of experience, just how much of this or that ingredient was required without ever measuring or weighing it.

Though the country meal consisted of many courses, the individual dishes were all basically simple, but filling. Soups were substantial and satisfying. The meats were apt to be highly seasoned, but otherwise plain-cooked. Rich sauces or other culinary embellishments were not the order of the day. The vegetables, so right at hand from the ground, were, like the meats, many but plain-cooked.

Thus far we note that the country fare was ample, but not fancy. When, however, we come to bread or cakes, puddings and other desserts we find that a radical change takes place! For in preparing these dishes the country cook 'pulled out all the stops' and let herself go on a culinary rampage. These were the dishes in which she truly and creatively expressed herself and in which she excelled. As a matter of record, dishes of this sort occupied such an important place on the country table that in cookbooks circulated at the time the recipes dealing with baking, pudding and dessert-making far outnumbered all the others, and in the table of contents they always received premier listing. Perhaps the country housewife liked to bake for the same reason given by an American woman who, writing during the nineteenth century, said, "My happiest thoughts come to me while I am mixing a cake!"

Inevitably there were always two, or three, or more desserts served at the table. It might be one of each—cake, pudding and fruit dessert—or it might even be three cakes at the same time. But whatever the assortment, one or more pies would be included along with them.

Pies, first the mainstay of rural desserts, gradually caught the fancy of the people as a whole and became, in the nineteenth century, the national dish of America. But, however popular these were to become in the city, it was in the country, and more specifically on the farm, that they were served for breakfast, dinner, supper and 'in betwixt' times. In reading through some culinary writings of that century we came across the following, evidently written by a farmer's wife, in which we find that the importance of pies in the feeding of rural America was not exaggerated:

"I always calculate to bake a dozen pies of a Saturday. In haying and harvesting I make as many as thirty or forty every week. Nothing pleases our folks so much when they come in hot and tired, as a bit of pie—it don't make much difference what kind—apple, blueberry, cherry or squash—so long as it is pie."

Little wonder, then, that her menfolk readily admitted, according to an old farm saying, that "When a man can no longer enjoy his pies, his best years are gone!"

Bread also had to be baked at home, for in those days one could not simply run down to the country store and buy ready-made loaves. Therefore, it was an absolute necessity for the country homemaker to possess a thorough knowledge of bread making. And she did—for she looked upon bread baking as the true test of her culinary prowess and the culmination of her abilities as a homemaker. Moreover, she regarded the baking of bread not as a laborious task—though she made a score or more loaves weekly—but as an almost sacred duty. It was by the baking of bread that she felt she most truly carried out the words in the Bible which proclaimed, "She riseth also while it is yet night, and giveth food to her household." Thus it was that of all the old 'receipts' handed down from mother to daughter, none were more highly prized than those for breads. A number of such 'receipts' have been included in this book. Most of the recipes are practical for those who would essay this most soul satisfying of all culinary productions.

In addition to the multitude of dishes which the country housewife prepared from day to day and which contained foods 'in season,' she also had to plan ahead for the long, cold, winter months when the food would have to come chiefly from the cellar. At such times she would draw from her repertoire of inherited 'receipts,' those dealing with the pickling and preserving of all varieties of meats, fruits and vegetables. Many of these she would pickle 'as is'— a larger number she would 'lay down' as jams, jellies, marmalades, condiments and relishes. Still others she would dry out in the sun and rehydrate them when required. Among such naturally dehydrated items one especially was a common sight in most country homes of the period: dried apple slices, strung on long cords and hung along the ceilings. From this 'bank' the housewife could withdraw them, as needed, for her winter pies, sauces or whatever. Most of the pickled and preserved foods, however, were relegated for storage in cellars carefully constructed for that purpose, with their temperatures naturally regulated by the wide space left between the walls for air.

All this peeking and peering into the busy kitchen of yesteryear undoubtedly evokes a strong feeling of nostalgia for the time and period in which is predominantly flourished. This feeling will persist as you read over the recipes in this book. They are all authentic farm and country recipes and come to you, with a minimum of editing, exactly as they originally appeared in books, and manuscripts, and out of time–yellowed, food–spotted, pen and pencil scrawled pages of notebooks in the years which marked nineteenth century America.

Although these recipes are the forerunners of the more concisely written recipes of today, you will find them more fully explanatory, more unhurriedly composed, and often more elaborately descriptive than those to which we are accustomed. Be patient when you read the recipes for appearances are deceptive. You will discover after a while that despite the seemingly complex style in which they are presented, they have a quaintly charming way, all their very own, of really simplifying the preparation of the dish. These recipes, besides providing interesting reading and an insight into the goings on of grandma's kitchen, are also, on the whole, just as usable today as they were at the time of their origin. A careful perusal will unearth many useful and valuable cooking hints to the reader.

Oven temperatures were never specified in the recipes of yesteryear for two very simple reasons. First, the 'ovens' in use then were wood or coal burning stoves and had no temperature readings or controls. Secondly, the housewife reading recipes which read 'slow,' 'moderate,' 'hot,' 'quick,' or 'very hot' stove knew, by instinct born of long practice, precisely how to regulate the fire in the stove, and manipulate her pots and pans along the lidded stove top. Therefore, in order to more easily transpose the early stove heats indicated in the recipes to correspond with modern oven temperature readings, we have tabulated a 'Table of Oven Temperatures and Baking Time.' It will be found immediately following this Introduction.

While modern recipes are usually prepared to serve from four to six persons, the nineteenth century country cook, however, had most often to prepare recipes to serve not only a large family but also any number of 'hired hands' as well. Consequently, most of the recipes in this book will serve six to eight persons. Some exceptions have also been included to better illustrate the nature of 'large family' feeding of that era. To prepare fewer portions than called for by the recipe, just reduce the amount of ingredients proportionally.

Many recipes qualify certain ingredients as fresh. Among them we find fresh milk and cream, fresh eggs, fresh butter and fresh fruits and vegetables. The term was used advisedly at the time, for it should be remembered, for instance, that the cows were milked daily and due to the lack of proper refrigeration the milk would quickly sour if not immediately used. Cream not used in cooking was churned at once into butter, which was wrapped in muslin and, if no other type of refrigeration was available, laid in the cold streams which ran through most of the fields. The eggs were collected daily from the henhouse and most found immediate use; the remainder were sold. Although the fruits and vegetables were always as fresh as minutes out of the ground, or off the trees, the recipes calling for them to be fresh did so more as a caution to mother not to steal any from her preserve jars! Unfortunately, as we can not go out to milk the cow, nor gather eggs from a henhouse, nor in most cases pluck our vegetables and fruit from their source, store bought supplies must suffice us today.

It should also be borne in mind that travel in those days, whether by land or sea, was dreadfully slow. More importantly, the hardy voyager was required in most cases to provide his own 'vittels.' Thus, only foods which kept could be taken along. Some of the recipes herein will give you an idea of what types of food were best suited for that purpose, and the way in which they were prepared.

In addition to cookery recipes the cookbooks which were in circulation during the nineteenth century were also crammed full of miscellaneous information which it was thought would interest the homemaker. Adopting the style so current in the popular almanacs of the day, such information included chapters on shopping, on butchering, on general household hints, on medical remedies, and on the never omitted beauty 'secrets,' to name but a few. Although not properly categorized as recipes, we have nevertheless included some of those hints, remedies, and beauty 'secrets' in this book solely as a matter of general interest and nostalgia. We will not vouch for the efficacy of any of these so-called medical 'remedies,' but they do make good reading.

A brief explanation is due here, too, concerning

another chapter in this volume which does not properly fall within its scope. It is the one entitled, The Saying of Grace. In the era of which we write, no meal was ever begun without first invoking the Lord's blessing upon all those gathered around the table, and for the food spread so bountifully on it. The saying of grace was so widespread a custom in the country, and on the farm in particular, that it really formed an integral part of the meal. Therefore a number of renditions have been included.

It should be noted that further elaboration on the recipes, the foods, the various phases of preparation, and other such pertinent information, will be found in separate texts which precede many of the individual chapters.

In conclusion we offer, with commingled feelings of pride and humiliation, our thanks and gratitude to the many women of long ago who have so enriched us with their recipes, and without whom this book would not have been possible. In a still larger sense, theirs is a heritage which has since become a rich and noble part of our country's history.

Ted and Jean Kaufman

OVEN TEMPERATURES

The terms "slow," "moderate," "hot," and "very hot," are applied to gas and electric oven temperatures, as follows:

Slow oven ..	250° F. to 325° F.	Moderate ...	350° F. to 375° F.
Very Slow ..	200° F. to 275° F.	Hot	400° F. to 450° F.
Quick	375° F. to 400° F.	Very Hot ...	450° F. to 500° F.

To test a slow oven, place a pan sprinkled with a little flour in the oven and if the flour becomes a delicate brown within five minutes, the oven is slow, (250° F. to 325° F.) If the flour becomes a medium golden color within five minutes, the oven is moderate (350° F. to 375° F.) If the flour turns a deep dark brown within five minutes, the oven is hot (400° F. to 450° F.) If the flour turns a very dark brown within three minutes, the oven is very hot (450° F. to 500° F.) These same tests may be made with white tissue paper.

Always test your cake before removing it from the oven. Your cake is done when it has risen to its full height above the cake pan and has a delicate brown crust, and it should shrink slightly from the sides of the pan. Do not overbake as the edges and sides of the cakes will become dark and crusty. The top of the cake when pressed with a finger will spring back and leave no imprint. A cake tester or tooth pick inserted in the center of the cake should come out clean and dry. After removing sponge cakes and angel food cakes from the oven turn the pan upside down on a cake rack for an hour, until completely cold, then loosen sides with the flat side of a silver knife.

Do not remove sponge cakes and angel food cakes from the pans while still warm. These cakes are so delicate that they will not hold up on their own weight unless they are completely cold.

BAKING TIME TABLE

Angel Food Cake	330° F. to 350° F. invert pan at once cool for one hour	50 to 60 minutes
Sponge Cake	330° F. to 350° F. invert pan at once cool one hour	40 to 45 minutes
Cup Cakes	350° F. to 375° F.	25 minutes
Muffins	375° F. to 400° F.	20 to 25 minutes
Sheet cakes for Jelly Rolls	375° F. to 400° F.	12 to 15 minutes
Layer Cakes	350° F. to 375° F.	25 to 30 minutes
Loaf Cakes	350° F. over 2½ inches thick	40 to 45 minutes 1 hour
Pound Cake	300° F.	1¼ to 1½ hours
Cookies	350° F. to 400° F.	most cookies 10 to 20 minutes
Fruit, soft molasses, and chocolate cookies	325° F. to 350° F.	8 to 15 minutes
Pastry shells for pies	450° F. 375° F.	for first 10 minutes, to finish baking
Berry and Fruit Pies	450° F. 375° F.	first ten minutes, 30 to 40 minutes longer
Custard Pie in uncooked pastry shell	425° F. 350° F.	ten minutes 20 to 25 minutes longer
Baking Powder Biscuits	450° F.	12 to 15 minutes
Quick Coffee Cake	400° F.	25 to 30 minutes
Corn Bread	425° F.	30 to 40 minutes
Fruit or Nut Bread	350° F.	1 to 1¼ hours or until done
Rolls	425° F. to 450° F.	15 to 20 minutes or until golden brown
Yeast Bread	400° F. to 425° F. 375° F.	10 to 15 minutes, then 30 to 35 minutes longer
Sweet Dough	375° F. to 400° F.	25 to 35 minutes or until golden brown
Chocolate Cakes	350° F.	25 minutes for layer cakes, 40 minutes for loaf cakes
Popovers	450° F.	30 minutes, then 350° F. for 10 to 15 minutes

Prepare pans before mixing batter or dough. Use sweet butter for greasing pans for a more delicate flavor. Butter the bottom of cake pans well; butter sides sparingly. Dust pans lightly with flour. Use spring forms for sponge cakes and angel food cakes. Do not grease pans. For the batter cannot cling to the sides of the pans if greased, and the cakes will not reach their full height.

WEIGHTS AND MEASURES

One quart flour ....one pound
Two cups of butter ....one pound
One pint of liquid ....one pound
Two cups of granulated sugar ....one pound
Two heaping cups of powdered sugar ....one pound
2 to 2¼ cups firmly packed brown sugar ....one pound
3½ cups confectioners sugar ....one pound
Four cups flour ....one pound
Three and half cups Graham flour ....one pound
Five cups rye flour ....one pound
Four and half cups cake flour ....one pound
Two cups nut meats ....one pound
Two pints very finely ground nuts ....one pound
Three and a fourth cup seedless raisins ....one pound

MEASURING TABLE

Four ounces ....one fourth pound
Sixteen ounces ....one pound
Sixty drops ....one tablespoon
Three teaspoons ....one tablespoon
Four tablespoons ....one fourth cup
Eight tablespoons ....one half cup
Sixteen tablespoons ....one cup
Two cups ....one pint
Four cups ....one quart
Small wine glass ....one fourth cup
A dash ....less than one eighth
                                                        teaspoon
Saltspoon ....one fourth teaspoon

HOT BREAKFAST CEREALS

There was scarcely a country household in which some kind of mush, gruel or porridge did not form a portion of the morning meal. Unrolled oats or wheat required long cooking and were usually prepared the night before, to be reheated in a double boiler the next morning, with the addition of one half a cup of boiling water, one half a cup of hot milk, a lump of sweet butter, salt and a little sugar to taste. Served with fresh milk or thick sweet cream, with a dusting of maple sugar or a dribble of dark molasses or honey, the cereal was a satisfying and highly nourishing dish with which to start the day.

Such a cereal, combined with griddle cakes, biscuits, ham, bacon and eggs, washed down with pots of strong, hot coffee and pitchers of fresh, sweet milk was considered a simple, country breakfast! Many country kitchens also served broiled fish, hash, potatoes, home fried or mashed, chicken stewed with mushrooms, small birds, tongue, sausages, freshly made cream cheese, fresh fruit in season, relishes and a variety of rolls and muffins.

These sound like huge breakfasts—and they were. However, we must remember that a few hours of backbreaking toil on the soil, or tending to the many farm chores, was more than enough to work it off and renew appetites for the next meal.

Oatmeal Mush

Steamed or rolled oats may be prepared in the morning—if time allows—about half- to three-quarters of an hour before breakfast. Allow one cupful of oats to one quart of water and one teaspoon of salt. Stir several times, remove the cover five minutes before serving, add butter and a little sugar. Serve with fresh sweet milk, cream, maple sugar or warm honey.

Corn Meal Mush

Boil one quart of water. Stir one pint of cold milk with a pint of corn meal and a teaspoon of salt. Mix well. When the water boils, pour mixture in gradually, stirring all the time. Cover. Cook slowly for three hours over low heat, until the mush is thick and free from lumps. Beat smooth with a wooden spoon. Serve with milk or cream and sugar. Place leftover mush in a dish, which has been wet with cold water. When cold, cut into slices and dip each slice into beaten egg and flour or bread crumbs. Fry in butter until golden brown. Serve with maple syrup. For round uniform slices, pack warm mush into large baking powder tins. When cold, loosen with the flat side of a silver knife; the mush will slip out easily. Cut into slices and proceed same as above.

Indian Meal Gruel

Two quarts boiling water, one cup Indian meal (corn meal), and one tablespoon wheat flour wet up with cold water, salt to taste, one tablespoon sugar and a pinch of nutmeg. Wet the meal and flour to a smooth paste and stir into the boiling water. Boil slowly one hour, stirring up well from the bottom with a large wooden spoon. Add sugar and nutmeg. Some sweeten it but it is better with a little pepper. If a cathartic is desired, omit wheat flour altogether.

Milk and Rice Gruel

One quart boiling milk, two tablespoons (heaping) ground rice wet with cold milk and one teaspoon salt. Stir the rice paste and boil ten minutes, stirring constantly. Season with sugar and nutmeg. Eat warm with cream.
(Cream of Rice is now available in all food markets. Follow directions on the box. Serve the same as above. It is a smooth and easily digested cereal; ideal for breakfast, or even a late evening snack.)

Farina

One cup of boiling water, one cup of fresh, sweet milk, one large tablespoon of farina, moistened with a little cold water, two teaspoons of sugar or honey, a pinch of salt. Stir the farina into the boiling water, slightly salted. Boil fifteen minutes, stirring constantly, until well thickened. Then add the milk gradually, and cook gently fifteen minutes longer. Sweeten, and serve at once.

Barley

Two cups of boiling water, two tablespoons of barley, a pinch of salt, two teaspoons of sugar. Soak barley for one hour in one third cup of lukewarm water. Stir, without draining, into the slightly salted boiling water. Simmer gently for one hour, stirring often, until the barley is tender.

Barley Water

One cup of barley, six to eight cups of cold water, salt to taste. Wash barley several times in cold water. Place in top of a double boiler, add cold water and salt. Simmer gently for five to six hours until the barley is very tender. Strain and cool. If desired add the juice and grated rind of one small lemon. Sweeten with honey and chill. Reserve barley for other use. ·

Corn Porridge
(1854)

Take young corn and cut grains from the cob. Measure it, and to each heaping pint of corn allow one quart fresh sweet milk. Put the corn and milk into a pot, stir them well together, and cook them until the corn is perfectly soft. Then add some bits of fresh sweet butter dredged in flour, and allow to boil five minutes longer. Stir in at the last two egg yolks, and after three minutes remove from the fire. Take up the porridge, and send it to the table hot, and stir in some fresh sweet butter. You may add sugar and nutmeg.

(This delicious old recipe may be served also, if desired, as a luncheon or supper soup. Frozen corn kernels and even canned corn kernels may be used. Omit sugar, season with salt, freshly grated peppercorns or nutmeg. The addition of a bay leaf and a small rib of celery with the leaves on, adds extra flavor and aroma. Discard both before serving.)

Grits or Small Hominy

The small grained hominy must be washed and boiled. Use one and a half pints of water to a quart of small hominy. Boil until perfectly soft, drain it well, and send it to the table in a deep dish without a cover. Eat it with butter, sugar or molasses, cream or fresh milk, as desired. If covered, after boiling, the vapor will condense with the lid, and make the hominy thin and watery.

(Hominy is white Indian corn, shelled from the cob, divested of the outer skin, scalded in hot lye and washed in several waters. It is soaked overnight, then cooked until soft. It was, and probably still remains, an important food item in most country kitchens.)

Samp is Indian corn skinned, and then pounded or ground until it is small and finer than grits. It is cooked and used in the same manner. Samp is very tasty when eaten with cream and sugar. It was often served to invalids—made very thin and eaten as a gruel. Nourishing and most satisfying, it caused no strain upon the invalid's digestive system.

BREAKFAST MUFFINS AND BISCUITS

Country Biscuits
Plain And Simple

Three cups flour, one-and-one-fourth teaspoons soda, two-and-one-fourth teaspoons cream of tartar, one-half teaspoon salt, six tablespoons sweet butter, fresh whole milk, or half cream and half milk. Sift all the ingredients several times, this is important. Add shortening and blend well. Then use enough milk to make a soft batter. One of the secrets of making good biscuits is that the batter must be as soft as possible and still firm enough to roll out. Bake in a hot stove (400° F.) for about fifteen minutes. Open biscuit, if light and fluffy and the tops are golden, they are ready for breakfast.

(Baking powder was usually made at home by combining cornstarch, bicarbonate of soda, and cream of tartar. In 1880 the first ready-made baking powder was packed and sold in tins by the Great Atlantic and Pacific Tea Co.)

Beaten Biscuit

One quart of flour, one-quarter cup of good lard, one half teaspoon salt, one cup of cold water. Rub lard and salt into the flour and mix all with the water until a stiff dough is formed. Knead ten minutes, then beat hard with a biscuit beater or heavy rolling pin, turning the mass over and over until it begins to blister

27

and looks light and fluffy, or until, when pulling off a piece quickly, it will give a sharp snapping sound. When the dough is in this condition pull off small pieces suddenly and form it into round biscuits. Then pinch off a bit from the top of each, turn the biscuit over, then press it with the thumb, leaving a hollow in the middle. Arrange the biscuits some distance apart in the pans, prick them with a fork, and bake twenty minutes in a quick stove. They should be light and of even grain and should crack at the edges like crackers.

Potato Biscuits

Boil and mash two white potatoes; add two teaspoons of brown sugar; pour boiling water over these, enough to soften them. When tepid add one cake of yeast; when light, warm three ounces of fresh sweet butter in one pint of sweet milk, a little salt, and pour enough flour to make a stiff sponge; when risen, work it on a board; put it back in the tray to rise again; when risen, roll into cakes, let stand half an hour. Bake for twenty to twenty-five minutes in a quick stove.

Rusks For Afternoon Tea

Two cups of raised dough (when baking bread), one cup of sugar, half a cup of sweet butter, two well-beaten eggs, flour enough to make a stiff dough; set to rise, and when light, mold into high biscuits, and let rise again; rub damp sugar and cinnamon over the top and place in the stove. Bake about twenty minutes.

Aunt Susie's Rusk

One quart sweet milk, one-half cup yeast, flour for a stiff batter, make a sponge of these ingredients, when very light add one cup sweet butter, rubbed smooth, with two cups powdered loaf sugar, one egg well beaten. Flour to make a stiff dough. Knead briskly and set to rise for four hours. Then make into rolls, and let them stand an hour longer, or until light and 'puffy,' before baking. Bake in a moderate stove until golden brown. Just before drawing them from the oven, glaze with a little cream and sugar. Rusks are best eaten fresh.

Wheat Puffs

Two eggs, one pint of fresh sweet milk, one tablespoon of melted butter, one teaspoon of baking powder, one of salt, flour to thicken. Beat the eggs, add them to the milk, stir in the melted butter and the salt, and add flour to thicken to a rather stiff batter. Bake twenty minutes the same as muffins. These puffs are perfect as a snack with coffee, as they contain no sugar.

Yeast Biscuits

Dissolve one rounded tablespoon of butter in a pint of hot milk; when lukewarm stir in one quart of flour, add one beaten egg, a little salt, and a teacup of yeast; work into dough until smooth. If winter, set in a warm place, if summer, in a cool one, to rise overnight. In the morning, work the dough softly and roll out one-half inch thick and cut into biscuits; set to rise thirty minutes, when they will be ready to bake. Bake in a hot stove for fifteen or twenty minutes. These are truly delicious.

Spoon Biscuits

One quart sour milk or buttermilk, one teaspoon soda, a little salt, two tablespoons melted butter, and flour to make a stiff batter; drop in hot gem pans and bake fifteen to twenty minutes in a quick stove.

(In the old days, yeast was usually purchased from the baker or made at home from hops or potatoes. By the late nineteenth century yeast cakes had almost taken the place of baker's yeast. A few pennies worth of fresh yeast cake dissolved in warm water was equal to one cupful of homemade yeast. However, the country housewife who lived a great distance from the baker or neighbors, still resorted to her own mixture. A simple, thin batter of flour and water was placed in a warm place until it began to ferment and was full of bubbles. A pint of 'ferment' was equal to a cupful of old yeast in starting the new.)

Berry Teacakes

Little teacakes to be baked in muffin tins are made from one cup powdered loaf suger, sifted, two eggs, one-and-a-half cups of sweet milk, one heaping tea-spoon baking powder, a piece of sweet butter the size of an egg and flour sufficient to make a stiff batter. Into this batter stir in one pint of berries, any fresh variety will do. Bake in a 375° F. stove for twenty to twenty-five minutes. Serve while warm; they are a dainty addition to the tea table. Eat with fresh sweet butter.

Velvet Coffee Cakes

One quart new sweet milk, or half cream and half milk, three eggs, yolks and whites beaten separately, one scant teaspoon salt, rice flour. Mix the beaten yolks with the milk, add the salt, then the rice flour to make a stiff batter; lastly whip in the stiffened whites very lightly and bake immediately until golden brown. (Twenty-five to thirty minutes).

Rice Muffins

One pint flour, one tablespoon of sugar, one tablespoon sweet butter, one cupful of cold cooked rice, two eggs, two teaspoons baking powder, one teaspoon of salt and one half pint fresh sweet milk. Mix the flour, sugar, baking powder and salt in a sieve, and rub them through thoroughly, and beat the eggs light. Add the milk to the dry mixture, and when smooth stir in the rice. Beat again thoroughly, add the eggs, and bake quickly in a hot stove twenty-five to thirty minutes.

Cream Toast
(1820)

Slices of stale baker's bread, from which the crusts have been removed. One quart fresh sweet milk, three tablespoons sweet butter, whites of three eggs, beaten to a stiff froth, salt, and two tablespoons best wheat flour or corn starch. Boil water. Toast the bread golden brown, do not burn. Have on the stove, or hearth, a shallow bowl or pudding dish more than half full with boiling water, in which a tablespoon of butter has been melted. As each slice is toasted, dip in this for a second, sprinkle with salt, and lay in the deep heated dish in which it is to be served. Have ready, by the time all the bread is toasted, the milk scalding hot, but not boiled. Thicken this with the flour, let it simmer until cooked. Put in the remaining butter, and when this is melted, the beaten egg whites. Boil up once, and pour over the toast, lifting the lower slices one by one, that the creamy mixture may run between them. Cover closely, and set in the stove until the toast has absorbed all of the milk mixture before sending to the table.

(This was a favorite dish originated by the early settlers and served to members of the family when they suffered upset stomachs or were otherwise feeling poorly.)

Farmers Toast

Six slices baker's bread sliced one inch thick, six slices crisp broiled bacon, two medium onions, thinly sliced and sauteed in sweet butter, salt and pepper, butter, six eggs, sharp grated yellow cheese. Brandy and boiling hot water. Butter sliced bread, arrange in a buttered baking dish. Place in a hot stove until the bread is toasted a golden color. Place bacon, sliced sauteed onions on the toasted bread, break eggs over the toast, season highly with salt and pepper, sprinkle with coarsely grated cheese. Bake in a slow stove for fifteen to twenty minutes until the cheese is melted. On a cold, damp day, dip the toast quickly in boiling water, sprinkle generously with good brandy, then proceed as above. Serve with home fried potatoes.

Milk Toast

Put over the fire a quart of fresh sweet milk, put in two tablespoons cold, sweet butter, stir a heaping tablespoon flour into a half pint of milk; as soon as the milk on the fire boils, stir in the flour and the milk; let all boil up at once, remove from the fire, and dip slices of toasted bread into it. When all are used up, pour what is left of the scalded milk over the toast. Cover and send to the table.

Country Toast

To one egg, thoroughly beaten, put one cup of sweet milk and a little salt. Slice light baker's bread and dip into the mixture, allowing each slice to absorb some of the milk; then brown on a hot griddle, well buttered, or on a thick bottomed frying pan. Spread with sweet butter and serve very hot.

Quick Sally Lunn

One pint sifted flour, two teaspoons baking powder, one half teaspoon salt, two eggs, one-half cup fresh sweet milk, one-half cup melted sweet butter. Mix flour, baking powder and salt. Beat egg yolks, add the milk, and melted butter. Put the two mixtures together quickly, adding the beaten egg whites last. Fill buttered muffin tins two-thirds full, and bake fifteen minutes in a very hot stove. This makes delicious muffins. If for tea add two tablespoons sugar to the flour.

Country Wonders

Beat one egg, add one scant teaspoon salt, or to taste, and enough flour to make a stiff dough. Roll out as thin as a wafer, cut out with a large round cutter, and fry one minute in hot fat. Serve with honey or syrup, or with cream and jelly, or any delicate pudding sauce. A very good cake for Sunday breakfast.

Featherlights

Beat one egg, yolk and egg white separately, one-fourth cup sweet cream, salt to taste, one teaspoon baking powder, one-half teaspoon cinnamon, one teaspoon brandy, flour enough to roll out. Roll as thin as a wafer and cut with a pastry jagger into small squares or diamonds. Fry quickly in boiling lard. Drain on paper. Sprinkle thickly with powdered sugar.

Apple Snow Cakes
(1854)

Half a pint of milk, an egg, an apple, pared, quartered and chopped very fine; a cupful and a half of flour, one-fourth teaspoon salt, a bowl of fresh, light, fluffy, newly fallen snow. Beat the egg light and add the milk to it. Pour gradually on the flour and beat until light and smooth. Add apple and salt and, at the last moment, the fresh clean snow. Drop by spoonfuls into boiling fat and cook until a rich golden brown. Serve dusted with powdered sugar, or with warm maple syrup.

Squirrel's Tails
(1896)

To a quart of flour, that has been sifted twice, add a little salt, a piece of butter the size of an egg, then rub them well into the flour. Dissolve half a cake of yeast in a little lukewarm water, add to this warm milk to make a soft batter. Do not spare the kneading. Set to rise, covered, in a warm place. When light, add the whites of two eggs that have been beaten to a stiff froth. Let rise again. Make a sauce of one cup powdered sugar and half a cup of fresh sweet butter. Beat until light and creamy. Roll out the dough thin, cut into strips, about an-inch-and-a-half wide and six inches long. Spread the sauce on each strip and sprinkle with chopped nuts. Roll each strip up carefully, place in a buttered baking pan, let it rise again. Bake in a hot stove for twelve to fifteen minutes until golden brown.

(This late nineteenth century delicacy was first made by an ingenious lady of New England from which area many novel and delicious recipes have come.)

Apple Johnny Cake

One pint white cornmeal, two tablespoons sugar, one-half teaspoon salt, one of cream of tartar, milk enough to mix quite soft, three apples, pared and sliced. Mix in the order given. Bake in a shallow, buttered pan for thirty minutes. Cool. Break apart with a fork, serve warm with soft sweet butter and jelly.

Rice Crusts

Cook one cup of cold, boiled rice in the double boiler, in milk enough to make a thin mixture, until the rice is very soft. Add one tablespoon sugar, a little salt, one egg, and flour enough to hold together. Spread on a buttered pan, having the mixture one-third of an inch thick. Bake in a hot oven for twenty-five minutes. Split and eat with syrup. Good for breakfast.

Buttermilk Doughnuts

Two tablespoons melted sweet butter, one cup powdered loaf sugar, two eggs, three-fourth cup fresh buttermilk, one half teaspoon baking soda, three cups sifted flour, four teaspoons baking powder, salt to taste, cinnamon sugar. Blend butter with sugar, add eggs and beat until smooth. Stir soda into the buttermilk and beat well. Blend in the sifted flour, baking powder and salt, making a rather stiff batter. If dough is too soft gradually add a little more flour. Roll out

on a floured bread board about one-half inch thick
and cut out with a doughnut cutter. Drop into hot fat.
When brown, drain on paper, roll in cinnamon sugar
while still warm.

Indian Bannock

One cupful of Indian meal, one-fourth teaspoon salt,
butter the size of an egg, one cup and a half of boiling
water, one tablespoon sugar. Pour the boiling water
on the Indian (corn) meal, sugar and salt. Beat thoroughly. Add the butter, and, when mixed, pour into a
shallow buttered earthen dish. Bake in a very hot
stove for twenty minutes. For a lighter Bannock add
two egg yolks and the two whites beaten to a stiff
froth. Serve in the same dish. Dribble soft, sweet butter and warm syrup over the Bannock.

Indian Puffs

Boil one quart milk and, when it has come to a boil,
stir into it, gradually, eight large tablespoons of Indian meal, four large tablespoons of powdered sugar,
and a grated nutmeg. Stir it hard, letting it boil a
quarter of an hour after the Indian meal is in. Then
take it up and set it to cool. While cooling, beat eight
eggs as light as possible and stir them gradually into
the batter when it is quite cool. Butter some large
teacups, nearly fill them with the mixture, set them in
a moderate stove, and bake them well. Send them to
the table warm and eat them with butter and molasses, or with butter, sugar, lemon juice, and a little
nutmeg stirred to a cream.

Buttermilk Muffins

Three-fourth cup brown sugar, one egg, well beaten,

one cup buttermilk, one teaspoon soda, one-and-a-half cups sifted flour, one-half cup chopped nuts, grated rind of one small lemon. Blend all ingredients with a wooden spoon, pour batter into buttered muffin tins, three-fourth full, bake in a moderate stove, thirty minutes, until golden brown.

Rice Muffins

Mix one cup boiled rice, so cooked that the grains are distinct and separate, with two cups flour, into which four teaspoons of baking powder and a half teaspoon salt has been sifted. Beat one egg lightly, add one cup and a quarter of milk and stir into the first mixture. Add three tablespoons of melted butter, beat thoroughly and bake about twenty-five minutes in a hot, buttered gem pan.

Blueberry Muffins

One heaping cup of fresh, firm blueberries, two cups sifted flour, one-half teaspoon salt, two teaspoons baking powder, four tablespoons sweet butter, four tablespoons powdered sugar, one egg, beaten separately. Use perfect berries, firm and ripe, wash, dry and sprinkle them with a little flour. Sift flour with salt and baking powder. Cream butter with the sugar, add beaten egg yolk and milk, stir in flour mixture. Fold in egg white beaten to a stiff froth, add berries carefully, folding gently into the batter with a wooden spoon. Pour into buttered muffin tins. Bake thirty minutes, until golden brown, in a moderately hot stove.

COUNTRY BREAKFAST
AND
LUNCHEON DISHES
(1839-1883)

Sheep's Tongues, Braised

Wash, dredge six sheep's tongues with salt and flour. Brown in salt pork fat, with one to two minced onions, and put them in a pan with water or soup stock to half cover. Add one sprig of parsley, a little salt and pepper, cover and cook two hours, or until tender. Remove skins, and trim neatly at the roots. Place a mound of spinach in the center of the dish. Arrange the tongues around the spinach, alternating with diamonds of fried bread.

Lambs Tongues, Boiled

Boil six lamb's tongues in salted water, with the juice of half a lemon. Cook gently until tender. Serve cold with tartar sauce, or pickle them by covering with hot spiced vinegar.

Beef Liver

Soak beef liver ten minutes in boiling water to draw out the blood. Drain, remove the thin skin and veins. Cut into pieces for serving. Season with salt and pepper, roll in flour, and fry in salt pork or bacon fat. Drain, serve with brown gravy, seasoned with onion, lemon juice or vinegar, or spread with butter and broil quickly. Season with salt and pepper to taste.

Lambs Liver

Cut it in slices an inch thick, beat the yolks of two eggs, dip slices of liver in the eggs, cover them with cracker dust seasoned with salt and pepper, and fry them in hot drippings or half lard and butter. Serve up with hashed brown potatoes.

Calves Liver

Wash the liver in cold water before you slice it, wipe dry, then cut it in slices one-half inch thick. Season with salt and pepper and dust with flour. Melt in a frying pan good drippings or very nice lard and when hot lay in the slices. Fry very slowly until quite brown on both sides. Take out the liver and lay them side by side on a hot dish. Dust some flour into the frying pan, shake it about until well mixed with the fat, add a little hot water, boil up, stir, and pour the sauce over the liver.

Calves Heart, Braised

Wash in cold water, remove veins and arteries, and stuff with cracker crumbs seasoned with onion juice, salt, pepper and herbs. Moisten with melted butter. Lard with bacon or salt pork. Dredge with salt and flour. Fry one onion in salt pork fat or nice drippings. Brown well. Cook it as liver is cooked. (See above)

Beef's Heart

Lay the heart in cold water, with a handful of salt, for one hour, then wash it in fresh cold water and wipe it dry. Prepare the filling with a coffee cup of finely grated bread crumbs, season with salt and pepper, half a teaspoonful of sweet basil, the same of sweet marjoram and sage, all dried and powdered. Add to this a small onion, chopped fine, and a teaspoon of minced parsley. Melt a piece of butter the size of an egg, and pour over the crumbs, mixing all thoroughly together with a knife. Beat up an egg and stir in. Cut with a sharp knife a deep incision through the middle of the heart, put in the filling, pressing it down and well through it, skewer it across to prevent the filling from falling out, season it outside with salt and pepper, dust it with flour and set it in a hot oven in a small dripping pan. Baste it frequently with butter and water, and, if the heart is large, bake an hour or longer. When the heart is done, take it from the pan and add to the drippings a glass of wine, one of tomato catsup, and a little flour, and if too thick a very little boiling water. Boil up, pour over the heart, and serve the heart cut into slices.

Dried Frizzled Beef

Shave the beef as thin as paper. Melt in a frying pan a piece of butter the size of a large egg; when hot, stir in the beef and toss it about for a minute. Have ready a teacup of cream or rich milk, with the yolk of an egg beaten in it and one quarter teaspoon of mixed mustard. Dust the beef with flour, stir it about, then pour in the cream, shake it through the meat. Boil up and serve.

Toad In A Hole

Mix one pint of flour and one egg with milk enough to make a batter (like that for batter cakes, see p. 52) and a little salt. Grease dish with butter, put in lamb chops, add a little water with pepper and salt. Pour batter over it and bake for one hour.

Fricatelli

Chop raw, fresh pork very fine, add a little salt, plenty of pepper and two small onions chopped fine, half as much bread as there is meat, soaked soft, two eggs; mix well together, make into oblong patties, and fry like oysters. These are very fine for breakfast.

Ham and Eggs Fried in Gravy

Place slices of ham in boiling water and cook until tender. Put in a frying pan and brown, dish on a warm platter. Fry some eggs by dripping gravy over them until done, instead of turning. Take up carefully and lay them on the slices of ham.

Potted Beef

Boil shin of beef in sufficient water to cover it, until the meat drops from the bones, which will take five to six hours. Skim out the meat, pick out all the bones and gristle, chop in a wooden bowl until it is a paste, moistening as you chop it with some of the liquor it was boiled in. Be careful to get the marrow out of the bones, and put with the meat; when it is chopped to a paste, season highly with salt, pepper and a small teaspoon of grated nutmeg, sweet marjoram, sweet basil and a little powdered cloves. Chop all together, then press it closely into molds by pressing down with a spoon. Set in a cool place; when you wish to use it, turn it out of the mold and set it on a dish to be sliced like tongue. A very good dish for breakfast or lunch. (You will need a pint or more of liquor to moisten the meat as you chop it, but it must not be too thin. The remainder of the broth may be used for soup.)

Potted Liver

Braise calf's or lamb's liver in rich, highly seasoned soup stock. When tender, cut fine and pound to a paste, adding enough of the strained liquor, in which it was cooked, to moisten it. Add half a cup of fresh sweet butter, melted and strained. Rub all through a sieve. Pack in a buttered loaf pan or into jars and pour melted butter over the top.

Meat Souffle

Make one cup of cream sauce, and season with chopped parsley and onion juice. Stir one cup of chopped meat, (chicken, tongue, veal or lamb) into the sauce. When hot add to it the beaten yolks of two eggs, cook one minute. Set aside to cool. When cool stir in the whites, beaten to a stiff froth. Bake in a buttered dish about twenty minutes, and serve immediately. Excellent for breakfast; if for lunch, serve with hot mushroom sauce.

Stewed Sweetbreads

Wash the sweetbreads and blanch them in boiling water for a few minutes only, take them out and lay them in cold water for ten minutes; then put them in a saucepan with broth enough to cover them, stew them tender; add to them a lump of butter the size of an egg mixed to a paste with a tablespoon flour; a bunch of fresh parsley, chopped, and a large coffee cup of cream; boil three minutes; serve on hot toasted baker's bread.

(Bunch parsley: perhaps a few sprigs)

Meat Fritters

Cut any kind of cold meat into dice. Season well with salt and pepper. Make a fritter batter. Take up some of it in a large spoon, put a small spoonful of meat in the center, cover with the batter, and slide gently into the boiling fat. Cook about one minute. Drain on brown paper, and serve on a hot dish.

Fritter batter: One cup sifted flour, one fourth cup powdered loaf sugar, one half teaspoon salt, two teaspoons baking powder, one beaten egg, one third cup sweet milk, two teaspoons melted sweet butter. Sift the flour, sugar, salt and baking powder. Combine egg and milk, and add gradually to the flour mixture, stirring well until the batter is smooth and free from lumps. Blend in the melted butter. Mix well. This batter should be rather stiff.

Meat Hash

Chop rather fine any kind of cold meat; corned beef is best. To each pint add one-and-one-half pints of cold boiled potatoes, chopped fine, one tablespoon of butter and one cupful of stock; or, if no stock is on hand two-thirds of a cupful of hot water. Season with salt and pepper to taste. Put the mixture in a frying pan and stir over the fire for about eight minutes, being careful not to burn. Spread smoothly. Cover the pan and set back where the hash will brown slowly. It will take about half an hour. When done, fold it like an omelet and turn out into a hot dish. Garnish with points of toast and parsley. Serve hot. If there are no cold potatoes, the same quantity of hot mashed potatoes may be used.

A Giblet Breakfast
or
Luncheon Pie

Clean, very well, the giblets from two geese or four ducks. Put them into a stew pan with two sliced onions; a bunch of tarragon, or sweet marjoram and sage; half a dozen peppercorns; and four or five blades of mace. Add very little water; cover the pan closely and let them stew until the giblets are tender. Then take them out and save the gravy; having strained it from the seasoning articles. Make a rich paste (see p. 223), roll it out into two sheets, with one sheet cover the bottom and sides of a deep buttered dish. Put in the giblets; mixing among them a few cold potatoes, sliced, the yolks of some hard boiled eggs, coarsely chopped, and some bits of butter rolled in flour. Pour the gravy over the giblets. Cover the pie with the other sheet of paste and notch the edges. Bake in a 450° F. oven for ten minutes. Reduce heat to 350° F. and bake thirty minutes longer. Send it to the table hot. A pigeon or rabbit pie may be made in a similar manner.

Reed Birds

When cleaned, dip each bird in beaten egg yolks, then in bread crumbs or cracker dust which has been seasoned with salt, pepper and herbs, and fry a nice brown in half butter and half lard. Or, they may be broiled and served on toast with plenty of butter and salt and pepper.

Birds In A Grove

Having roasted some reed birds, larks or plovers, or any other small birds such as are usually eaten, mash

45

some potatoes with butter or cream. Spread the mashed potatoes thickly over the bottom, sides, and the edges of a deep buttered dish. Nick or crimp the border of the potatoes that goes around the edge, or scallop with a tin cutter. You may, if you choose, brown it by holding over it a salamander, or a red hot shovel. Then lay the roasted birds in the middle of the dish, and stick round them and among them, very thickly, a sufficient number of sprigs of curled or double parsley.

Stewed Pigeons

Cut a quarter of a pound of fat salt pork into strips, lay them in a stew pan with the pigeons, their liver and gizzards; brown them in this; then add two or three small onions, a bunch of parsley and thyme tied together, three cloves, pepper to taste, and boiling water sufficient to stew them; cook until tender; thicken the gravy with browned flour, and pour over the pigeons when you serve them.

Frogs

Only the hindquarters of frogs are cooked; wash and wipe them, flour, and fry a light brown in butter. Or put them in a stew pan with butter, a sprinkling of flour, and pepper and salt to taste; shake them about over the fire for a moment, then add a very little water; simmer until tender and almost dry, then add a coffee cup of cream, butter the size of an egg, a little flour and chopped fresh parsley; give a boil up and serve on thick slices of toast.

Fondue Of Chicken

One pint of cooked chicken, finely chopped; one pint of cream sauce, four eggs, one tablespoon of fresh minced parsley, one teaspoon of onion juice, salt and pepper to taste. Stir the chopped chicken into the hot cream sauce, add seasonings. Cook two minutes. Add the well beaten egg yolks, and set aside to cool. When cold, beat the egg whites to a stiff froth, and fold into the chicken mixture. Turn into a well-buttered baking dish and bake one-half hour in a moderate stove. Serve with a mushroom or cream sauce. This dish must be served the moment it is baked.

PANCAKES AND GRIDDLE CAKES

On a crisp cold morning, in the country, there is nothing to compare with hot griddle or pancakes sizzling over a wood burning fire. The countrymen, trudging into the warm kitchen in the early morning hours for their 'first' breakfast, after tending and milking the cows, were greeted with pancakes stacked high on the table, dripping with golden, melted, fresh, sweet butter and fragrant maple syrup. Without exception the favorite breakfast throughout the farmlands of America was dishes of hot, steaming wheat cakes, buckwheat cakes, griddle cakes, or corn cakes, and a variety of others to stagger the imagination.

"Some Country Rules"

Griddle cakes should be well beaten when first made, and are much lighter when the eggs are separated, beating the yolks to a thick cream, and adding the whites beaten to a stiff froth just before baking. Many of the country cooks never stir buckwheat pancakes after they have risen, but take them out carefully with a large spoon, placing the spoon when emptied in a saucer, not back in the batter. In baking griddle cakes have the griddle clean and, if the cakes stick, sprinkle on salt and rub with a coarse cloth before greasing. The griddle needs to be very hot. Iron griddles, if properly cared for, need washing very seldom. Immediately after use, they should be carefully wiped and put away, and never used for any other purpose. Never turn griddle cakes the second time after baking, as it makes them heavy. Serve the same side up as when taken from the griddle. Always mix griddle cakes in a bowl or pitcher with a lip, and beat well between each baking. Pour the batter onto the griddle; the mixture should sizzle as it touches the griddle. Pour one in the center and six cakes around it; within a few minutes they will be full of little bubbles and ready to turn, to brown then on the other side. Wipe the griddle often with a dry cloth, and grease lightly after baking. Turn the griddle frequently over the fire, or the hottest part of the stove, that the cakes may cook evenly. If you like your griddle cakes brown, add a teaspoon brown sugar to the batter.

Early Colonial Pancakes
(1802)

Pour in boiling water to one pint of Indian meal, one teaspoon of salt, small teaspoon of soda, until a little thinner than mush. Let stand until cool, then add the yolks of four eggs, half a cup of flour in which is mixed two teaspoons cream of tartar. Stir in as much sweet milk or water as will make the batter suitable to bake; beat whites well and add just before baking. Bake each separately in a small frying pan.

Apple Pancakes

Three egg yolks, two eating apples, peeled and cubed, salt to taste, one cup fresh sweet milk, two tablespoons sugar, two tablespoons butter. Sift the flour, salt and sugar into a bowl. Beat the eggs and milk together, add the flour, beating hard until smooth. Stir in the apples. Melt the butter in a heavy frying pan. Pour batter from a large spoon making small pancakes. Bake until brown, turn carefully, bake other side. Sprinkle with powdered sugar and cinnamon, or serve with warm maple syrup.

Buckwheat Pancakes

One pint buckwheat flour, one-half cup of Indian meal, one-half cup of yeast, or one-half cake of compressed yeast, one pint of warm water, one teaspoon salt, one tablespoon of molasses. Beat the batter thoroughly, and place it where it will rise overnight; it should rise and fall again by morning. In the morning add a teaspoon of finely powdered soda, stir well and fry. If the cakes are desired three times a week, fresh yeast will not be required after the first making, if a little more than a pint of batter is reserved each time and kept in a cool place and used instead of the yeast. Always put molasses in these cakes as it helps to give them a fine brown appearance in frying.

(Good old-fashioned 'risen' buckwheat pancakes! A small amount of the unused batter was saved from the previous day, ready for another batch of pancakes.)

Buckwheat Cakes With Bread

Two cups of buckwheat, two-and-a-half cups of warm water, one cup of stale bread, one cup of fresh milk, one teaspoon of salt, one-half cake compressed yeast. Dissolve the yeast in a half cup of the water, put this with the rest of the water, and pour all upon the buckwheat. Add the salt, beat well for ten minutes, cover the batter, and set to rise. Place the bread in a bowl of warm milk and let it soak overnight in a cool place. In the morning mash it fine and light, and add it to the risen buckwheat. The batter is then ready to use.

Light Bread Pancakes

Take stale bread and soak overnight in sour milk; in the morning rub through a colander; to one quart add the yolks of two eggs, one teaspoon salt, one teaspoon soda, two tablespoons sugar, and flour enough to make a batter a little thicker than buckwheat cakes (see p. 51); add last the well beaten whites of eggs, and bake a nice golden brown.

Delicate Pancakes

Beat together, till smooth, six eggs and a half pound of sifted flour, melt four ounces of fresh sweet butter, and add to the batter, with one ounce sifted, powdered sugar and a half pint sweet milk, and beat all until smooth and free from lumps. Put a tablespoon at a time into a hot, lightly buttered frying pan, spreading the batter evenly over the surface of the pan by tipping it about. Fry to a light brown, turn out on a clean cloth, keep covered until all the pancakes are done. Spread with jelly and roll up, dust with powdered sugar, serve hot.

Indian Batter Cakes

A quart of warm water or skim milk. A quart of Indian meal and a half pint of wheat flour, sifted, and a level teaspoon of salt. Pour the water into a pan; add the salt; and having mixed together the wheat and Indian meal, stir them gradually into the water, a handful at a time. It should be about the consistency of buckwheat cake or muffin batter. Beat it long and hard. If you find it too thick, add a little more water. Have ready a hot griddle, grease it, and bake the cakes on it. They should not be larger than the top of a tumbler, or a small saucer. Send them to the table hot, in even piles, and eat them with butter and molasses.

(These are the plainest sort of Indian batter cakes; but if well beaten and properly baked, they will be found very good.)

Sour Milk Pancakes

One quart sour milk, about four cups sifted flour, two teaspoons soda, dissolved in boiling water, three tablespoons molasses, salt to taste. Mix the molasses with the milk. Put the flour into a deep bowl, mix the salt through it; make a hole in the middle and pour in the milk, gradually, stirring the flour down into it with a wooden spoon. The batter should not be too thick. When all the milk is in, beat until the mixture is free from lumps and very smooth. Add the soda-water, stir up fast and well, and bake immediately.

(These cakes are simple to make and are extremely palatable. Clabbered milk is better than sour milk. Try them!)

To Make Clabbered Milk

Pour fresh sweet milk into earthenware crocks, cover, set in a warm place for twenty-four to thirty-six hours. Milk will become thick as custard, tart to the taste. Chill and serve with sugar and berries. Use also in baking in place of sour milk or buttermilk.

Grandma's Pancakes

One quart clabbered milk, if half cream, all the better; one tablespoon molasses, not syrup; two eggs beaten light; one good teaspoon soda, dissolved in hot water. Salt to taste. For a good batter, begin with three even cups of flour. Stir the molasses into the milk, then the eggs and salt. Make a hole in the flour, and mix as you would 'sour milk' cakes (See page 53). Beat in the soda last. Bake immediately on a hot griddle.

Mush Pancakes

Mold cold, boiled corn meal mush into balls, using a little flour to prevent sticking to hands, flatten them, and bake brown on a hot griddle; turn them over when one side is brown. Split and butter them and send to the table hot.

Rice Flour Batter Cakes

Melt a quarter of a pound of fresh butter in a quart of milk, but be careful not to let it begin to boil. Divide the milk equally by putting it into two pans. Beat three eggs very light and stir them into the half of the milk, with the addition of one large tablespoon wheat flour. Stir in as much ground rice flour as will make a thick batter. Then put in a small teacup of strong fresh yeast, and thin the batter with the remainder of the milk. Cover it, and set it to rise. When it has risen high, and is covered with bubbles, bake it on a hot griddle, in the manner of buckwheat cakes (see p. 51.) Send them to the table hot, and butter them.

Snow Cakes

Take less than a pint of sweet milk, warmed a little, salt to taste, one-half cup sifted flour, three table-spoons yeast, one egg well beaten. Set to rise over-night. Make a thick pancake batter, have griddle hot, gather one cup clean, fluffy, new fallen snow. Beat snow rapidly into the batter; bake pancakes at once before the lightness of the snow evaporates.

Country Flapjacks

Two-and-a-half cups sifted flour, one-half teaspoon salt, one egg, two cups sour milk, rounded teaspoon soda, one tablespoon melted butter. Beat thoroughly. Place batter in a pitcher, pour on a hot, greased griddle or in a heavy frying pan. Let butter begin to smoke before cooking the flapjacks; if large bubbles form at once on top of the flapjacks, the griddle is too hot. If the top of the cake stiffens before the underside is done, the griddle is not hot enough. Never turn a cake twice, as this toughens them. Serve at once with fresh, creamy sweet butter and warm maple syrup. For lighter cakes, separate egg, beat and fold in the stiffly beaten egg white.

Corn Griddle Cakes

One pint milk, two cups freshly grated corn kernels, a little salt to taste, one teaspoon sugar, two eggs, a teaspoon of baking powder, flour sufficient to make a good batter to fry on the griddle. Butter them hot and serve at once.

Farina Griddle Cakes

Four tablespoons farina, one quart fresh sweet milk, two eggs, well beaten, one tablespoon butter and one cup sifted flour. Scald farina overnight with a pint of boiling water, and let stand until morning. Thin with the milk, beating it gradually to avoid lumping. Next, the beaten eggs, the salt and butter, last one cup flour stirred in with light swift strokes. Do not get the batter too thick. Bake on a hot griddle at once.

Flannel Cakes

One quart of flour, sifted, two eggs, two teaspoons salt, three tablespoons yeast, one tablespoon butter, melted, and one-and-a-half pints of milk. Scald the milk and, when it has cooled, add the salt, flour and yeast. Beat the mixture until light and set to rise overnight. In the morning, add the melted butter and the beaten eggs. Bake on a hot griddle. Serve with melted butter and warm honey.

Griddle Cakes
(South Carolina)

Take a pint of milk, warmed a little, salt to taste, one-half cup flour, three tablespoons yeast, one egg well beaten, set to rise overnight. Bake on a hot griddle, turning once until both sides are golden brown. Spread with jelly or warm syrup.

Hoe Cakes

One pint of corn meal, one-half teaspoon salt. Place the cornmeal and salt into a bowl and pour sufficient boiling water to moisten the meal. After it has stood ten minutes, add cold water until the mixture drops from a spoon. Bake the same as griddle cakes on a hot griddle, or on a hoe. When done place a bit of butter on the top of each cake and serve hot.

(Hoe: A garden tool consisting of a thin flat blade made of tin or stainless steel, set across a long wooden handle.)

Huckleberry Griddle Cakes

One pint sifted flour, one-half teaspoon salt, one scant pint sour milk or cream, two eggs, well beaten, one pint fresh picked huckleberries. Sift the soda and the salt into the flour, mix thoroughly. Add the milk, and beat well, then add the beaten egg yolks, and lastly the beaten egg whites, beaten with a whisk to a stiff froth. Pick over the berries and roll them in flour, fold gently into the batter. Bake on a hot griddle lightly buttered, turn them when they are full of bubbles, and bake the other side till they stop puffing. Sour milk is best for griddle cakes, and when thickened just right, the cakes are very good without eggs.

SAUCE: Mash a pint of huckleberries, cleaned and picked over, sweeten with powdered sugar. Bring to a quick boil. Remove from fire at once. Serve as a sauce.

Raspberry Griddle Cakes

One cup sweet milk, two cups fresh picked raspberries floured, a little salt to taste, one tablespoon powdered sugar, two eggs, a teaspoonful of baking powder, flour sufficient to make a batter to fry on the griddle. Combine all ingredients, fold in the raspberries last with a wooden spoon. Butter them hot, sprinkle with powdered sugar and serve.

Rye Griddle Cakes
(Halltown, West Virginia)

Take a pint of rye flour, one-half pint Graham flour, one tablespoon sifted sugar, salt to taste, two teaspoons baking powder, one egg and one pint fresh sweet milk. Sift together rye flour, Graham flour, sugar, salt, and baking powder. Add beaten eggs and milk, mix into a smooth batter. Bake deep brown color on a hot griddle.

Slap Jacks
(1834)

Sift one pint of Indian meal, mix with four tablespoons of wheat flour, add one quart of fresh sweet milk, four well beaten eggs and a little salt. Bake small cakes on a hot griddle, stack high with fresh sweet butter. Dribble with warm syrup.

Aunt Jennie's Squash Griddle Cakes

One cup boiling milk, one cup mashed squash, one tablespoon butter, one tablespoon sugar, salt to taste, one egg, two teaspons baking powder, and one cup flour. Pour boiling milk into the squash; add the butter, sugar and salt. When cool, add the well beaten egg, then the baking powder, mixed and sifted with the flour. If too thin, use more flour; and if too thick, add a little milk. The dry mealy squash is best. Serve with soft butter.

EGG DISHES

A NOTE

Do not use a fresh egg till it has been laid ten hours, as the white does not become set or thick till then and cannot be beaten stiff. Albumen when heated becomes a dense solid; if mixed and heated with a liquid, it hardens and entangles in its meshes any solids or impurities in the liquid, and rises to the surface with them as scum. Thus the white of an egg clears soups, jellies and coffee.

FURTHER NOTES OF INTEREST

Eggs Cooked In Hot Ashes

When a wood fire burned constantly, the countryfolk would bury eggs, in an upright position, in the hot ashes upon the hearth. When a clear drop oozed out at the top of the eggshell, the eggs were fit to be eaten.

Eggs Cooked Without Fire

The most unusual method of cooking eggs is attributed to the early shepherds, who, it is said, were able to cook eggs without fire by placing them in a sling and whirling them around so rapidly that the friction of the air heated them to the exact degree of doneness!

Eggs Baked With Cheese

Take one cupful of stale cheese, cut into thin slices and arrange three-fourth cupful of it in the bottom of a buttered baking dish. Break six eggs, taking care not to break the yolks, on top of the cheese. Sprinkle with salt and pepper and dot with three tablespoons of sweet butter and the rest of the cheese. Bake in a moderately hot stove for about fifteen minutes until the whites are set and the cheese is melted. Serve hot from the baking dish.

Coddled Eggs In Milk

Six large eggs, about two-and-a-half cups of milk, three tablespoons sweet butter, salt and pepper as you like it. Scald the milk in a saucepan and add the slightly beaten eggs. Cook over hot water, stirring constantly until of a soft, creamy consistency. Add seasonings and serve on buttered toast.

Baked Eggs

Break seven or eight eggs into a buttered baking dish, taking care that each egg is whole and does not encroach upon the others so much as to disturb the yolks. Sprinkle with pepper and salt, and put a bit of butter and a cube of yellow cheese upon each. Put in stove and bake until the whites are well set. Serve very hot with rounds of hot buttered toast.

Deviled Eggs

Boil eight eggs hard, leave in cold water until they are cold. Cut in halves, slicing a bit off the bottoms to make them stand upright. Extract yolks, and rub into a smooth paste with very little melted butter, some cayenne pepper, a touch of mustard, and just a dash of vinegar. Fill the hollowed whites with this, and send to the table upon a bed of chopped cresses seasoned with pepper, salt, vinegar and a little sugar. Serve as a salad with a sauce if desired.

Egg With Mashed Potatoes

Pipe creamy mashed potato mixture, well seasoned, as a border around an individual egg dish; sprinkle with finely crushed herbs, and a mixture of minced meat or fish in the open space in the bottom of the dish; above this break two eggs. Cook in the oven until the eggs are set. Sprinkle with salt and pepper. Serve hot.

Eggs Sur Le Plat
(Eggs on The Plate)

Little stone dishes come expressly for this mode of serving eggs. Heat and butter the dish, and break into it two eggs, being careful not to break the yolks. Sprinkle lightly with salt and pepper, and drop on them half a teaspoon of sweet butter broken into little pieces. Top with a little finely chopped ham and parsley. Place in a moderately hot oven until the white is set, which will be in about five minutes.

Soft Cooked Eggs

Pour boiling water over eggs. Draw to a cool part of the stove, and let stand, covered, for ten minutes. The eggs will be creamy.

Ham and Eggs On A Bed of Rice

Serve poached eggs on thin slices of broiled or fried ham; serve up hot, on highly seasoned boiled rice, top with fresh stewed tomatoes.

Fried Stuffed Eggs

Have eggs cooked and shelled. With a tin tube, half an inch in diameter, remove a cylindrical piece of white from the pointed end of each egg; then with a small spoon empty whites of yolks. Pound the yolks with hollandaise sauce, adding cooked mushrooms, chopped fine. Fill the eggs with this mixture, and put the piece of white back in each place; roll egg in breadcrumbs and fry in deep hot fat until a pale straw color. Serve with hot tomato sauce.

Poached Egg In Meringue

Add a few grains of salt to the white of an egg, beat until dry and turn into a buttered glass or china bowl; form a nest on the top for the yolk. Set the glass on a trivit, in a covered dish of lukewarm water—let cook until the egg is set and rises to the top of the glass. Do not let the water boil around the glass.

Poached Eggs With Creamed Spinach

Cook half a peck of fresh picked spinach, drain and chop. Cook two tablespoons of flour in two tablespoons of butter, add half a cup of cream and, when well blended and smooth, add the spinach, salt and pepper as needed. Cook and stir until well mixed. Spread on rounds of toast, or fried bread and place a poached egg on top. Sprinkle the yolk with fine-chopped parsley.

Quaker Omelet

Three eggs, half a cupful of milk, one-and-a-half tablespoons of cornstarch, one teaspoon of salt, one tablespoon of butter. Put the omelet pan, with a cover that will fit closely, on to heat. Beat well together the yolks of the eggs, the cornstarch and salt. Beat the whites to a stiff froth. Add to the well-beaten yolks and cornstarch. Stir all together very thoroughly and add the milk. Put the butter in the hot pan. When melted, pour in the mixture. Cover, and place on the stove where it will brown, but not burn. Cook about seven minutes. Fold, turn on a hot dish, and serve with cream sauce poured around it. If the yolks and cornstarch are thoroughly beaten, and if, when the stiff whites are added and they are well mixed, and the pan and cover are very hot, there can hardly be any failure.

(A Quaker omelet is a handsome and a sure dish when care is taken in the preparation.)

Pannikins

Warm minced ham or tongue or veal in a thick cream sauce, and pile it in the center of a platter. Heat and butter some small earthen cups, break an egg in each and bake until the eggs are firm. Turn them out and arrange round the meat. Sprinkle with fresh minced parsley, serve up hot.

Tomato Eggs

Place a tablespoon of tomato sauce in individual molds or ramekins. Break an egg into each and sprinkle lightly with salt and pepper, a few dots of butter, and top with coarse breadcrumbs. Set the ramekins in a pan of warm water, place in the stove and bake until the eggs are set and the crumbs are delicately brown. Serve hot.

Stuffed Tomatoes With Soft Boiled Eggs

Rather than half fill the tomatoes, from which the centers have been taken, with equal parts of cooked, chopped mushrooms, trimmings and ham, moistened slightly with mushroom liquor, or the chopped tomato taken from the centers. Season the mixture with salt and pepper and bind with the yolk of an egg, if desired, before putting in place. Bake the tomatoes until tender, but retain the shape, if possible. When ready to serve, dispose in each tomato a soft boiled egg, shelled and reheated in hot water. Garnish the dish with broiled mushroom caps, from which the trimmings were taken, then place on rounds of toast. Serve with cream sauce apart, or poured over each egg.

Sunday Morning Potato Omelet

One-and-a-half cups of cold boiled potatoes, one teaspoon onion juice, two tablespoons sweet butter, four eggs, four tablespoons water, salt and pepper as you like it. Cut the boiled potatoes into small cubes, add the onion juice and turn into the frying pan into which the butter has been melted. Cook the potatoes, stirring constantly, until they are hot and slightly browned. Beat the eggs until light, add water, salt and pepper and pour over the potatoes. Let stand a few minutes; then move the pan to distribute the uncooked egg. When all the egg is cooked, turn out on a hot dish.

Corn Omelet

One pint cold, cooked corn, four eggs, half a cup of milk, one-and-a-half teaspoons of salt, a little pepper, three tablespoons of butter. Beat the eggs and add them to the salt, pepper, milk and corn. Fry like a plain omelet.

Rice Omelet

One cup boiled rice, one cup milk, one tablespoon sweet butter, three eggs, salt and pepper. Beat the eggs until light and add them to the warm rice, heated milk, melted butter and seasonings. Pour into a buttered baking dish and bake in a hot oven, folding over once. Serve with catsup or stewed tomatoes.

MILK SPECIALTIES

Koumiss

One quart fresh sweet milk, one-and-a-half table-spoons of white sugar, one tablespoon of slightly warmed syrup, one tablespoon brewers yeast or one-third cake compressed yeast dissolved in one table-spoon lukewarm water. Heat the milk to a tempera-ture of 100° F., add the sweetening and the yeast, stir thoroughly until well mixed, then turn into bottles that can be tightly corked. Let the bottles be filled within two inches of their full height. Cork and tie securely. Let stand at 60° to 70° F. temperature for twenty-four hours. Turn the bottles carefully on their sides in a cold place. The koumiss is highly charged and is effervescent, care should be taken when open-ing as the contents will foam and shoot out like champagne. It is one of the most easily digested forms of milk. Delicious when served cold.

Sour Milk
(Yogurt)

Put four quarts fresh sweet milk in a large porcelain-lined kettle; stand it over the fire for thirty minutes where it will come slowly to the boiling stage (do not boil). Take from the fire and, when cool, add four heaping tablespoons of thick sour cream or thick sour milk. On one side, gently lift the skin that has formed on top of the milk, put in the spoon and stir where the skin is lifted without breaking the rest of the

67

skin. Cover the kettle, if possible wrap it in flannel, and keep in a warm place for five to six hours. At the end of that time you will have a thick, milk jelly, like blanc mange. Keep in a cold place and it may be eaten just as it is, or serve topped with fresh berries, dusted with powdered sugar. This is another delicious home-made milk product, very easily digested. It is also an aid in intestinal upsets when eaten plain every few hours.

(With its thick, smooth custard-like consistency, yogurt may also be served as a dessert, flavored with vanilla and sprinkled with cinnamon sugar. Add fresh fruits in season and sweeten to taste with golden honey. Often served as a luncheon dish with cut up fresh garden vegetables; scallions, tiny, red radishes, minced sweet bell peppers, cucumbers, tomatoes, and highly seasoned with freshly cracked black pepper-corns and a few grains of salt. A healthful and excellent food for all members of the family.)

Sour Milk
(Our Version)

Two cups fresh milk, two heaping tablespoons plain yogurt or sour cream. Heat milk slowly, pour a few drops on wrist, when comfortably lukewarm, remove from heat at once. Pour into a wide-mouth jar, add yogurt or cream. Stir briskly with a spoon. Cover with glass cover or wax paper. Set aside in a warm place. When thickened, chill for several hours or overnight. Quick and easy method and most refreshing. Serve as above with fruit or vegetables.

Clabbered Milk

Set a china or glass dish of whole milk away in a warm place, covered. When it turns smooth and firm, but not a tough cake, like blanc mange, serve in the same dish. Cut out carefully with a large spoon and put in saucers, with cream, powdered sugar and a pinch of nutmeg to taste. It is better to set on the ice for an hour before it is brought to the table. Do not let it stand until the whey separates from the curd. Few people know how delicious this healthful and cheap dessert can be if eaten with a liberal allowance of cream and sugar, before it becomes tart and tough. There are not many jellies and creams superior to it.

Rennet

Clean the stomach of a calf (or have your butcher do it for you) as soon as it is killed, scouring inside and out with salt. When perfectly clean, tack upon a frame to dry in the sun for a day. Cut in squares and pack down in salt, or keep in wine or brandy. When you wish to use the salted rennet, soak half an hour in cold water, wash well, and put in milk to be turned, tied to a string, that it may be drawn out without breaking the curd. The liquor (rennet) sold in drug stores is sometimes good, more often worthless.

Mountain Custard

Take a piece of rennet (see above) an inch long, or a teaspoon of the wine in which the rennet is kept, and add to each quart of milk. Season with vanilla or lemon, a little nutmeg, and a tablespoon of white sugar. More will retard the formation. Set in a warm place near the fire, or on the kitchen table, closely covered. Look at it from time to time, and if, in the course of an hour, there is no sign of stiffening, add more rennet. When it is firm, like blanc mange, set it upon ice until wanted. Serve with cream and powdered sugar.

Grandma's Special Milk Drink

Place a quart of fresh sweet milk in a deep saucepan and heat slowly to a boil. Add a stick of cinnamon, broken up into pieces, and a handful of washed raisins. Simmer slowly. Serve either hot or cold.
(When milk is taken frequently and it is necessary to remove the odor of fresh sweet milk, grandma had her own time-tested remedy for improving the taste and flavor.)

To Whip Heavy Sweet Cream

Skim off cream from top of milk, place in bottles, and pack in cracked ice for several hours. The cream must be at least a day old and very, very cold, otherwise it will be difficult to whip. The reason why sweet cream so often 'goes to butter' is that it is too warm or too new.

Devonshire Cream

Put four quarts of sweet milk into an enamel basin; let stand overnight. Cover with a thin linen cloth. Next morning stand it in the back of the stove where it will come slowly to the boiling point. Remove at once to a cold place; skim off the cream that has risen to the top. Place in dishes and put in a cold place. Smooth and thick enough to use also in place of butter.

Egg Nogg

Twelve fresh eggs, twenty-four tablespoons of powdered loaf sugar, one quart fresh sweet milk, six wine glasses of good, dark rum, six wine glasses of brandy.

Beat the whites and yolks of the eggs separately. When the yolks are light and thick, add sugar gradually and continue to beat until the egg nogg is very light. Add the brandy first, then the rum, two glasses at a time, pouring into the mixture, drop by drop, then add the rest gently. Add milk slowly and turn into the punch bowl. Stir in part of the beaten egg whites, then spoon in the rest of the whites, until they float on top of the nogg. Let stand in a cool place for a few hours before serving. Nice with whipped cream folded in at the last, or float on top, sprinkled lightly with grated nutmeg.

Thickened Milk

Boil one quart of fresh sweet milk, add a very little salt, and two tablespoons of rice or wheat flour wet in a little cold milk. Stir it smoothly and let it thicken in a vessel (double boiler) of boiling water, keeping the outer sauce pan at a hard boil for half an hour. Eat with butter and sugar, or cream and sugar. For children suffering stomach disorders, boil at least an hour, stirring very often.

Summer Cottage Cheese Dessert
(1885)

Press *twice* through a fine sieve one pound fresh homemade cottage cheese. Rub until very smooth with two tablespoons thick sour cream, two tablespoons powdered loaf sugar, one tablespoon grated lemon and orange rind. Beat until very light. Fold in one-half cup whipped sweet cream and the white of an egg beaten to a stiff froth with a heaping tablespoon of powdered sugar. (Add the sugar at the end). Pack into a small stone crock or in a deep china dish.

Keep cold before serving. Pass a bowl of strawberry preserves and thick Devonshire cream. (See p. 70)

Homemade Country Cottage Cheese

Heat sour milk until the whey rises to the top. (Do not boil). Pour off the whey and put the curd in a cheesecloth bag and let it drip six hours without squeezing the bag. Put in a wooden bowl. Chop fine with a wooden spoon, salt to taste, and work to the consistency of soft putty, adding a little cream and butter as you proceed. Mold with your hands into 'pats' or balls, and keep in a cool place. It is best when fresh.

Cottage Cheese
(Our Version)

Spoon one carton of yogurt (plain) into a double thickness of cheesecloth. Pull up ends and tie tightly with a string. Hang up over a deep bowl and allow to drip for two hours. Remove cheese, place into a glass crock, beat with a fork until smooth. If desired, add one tablespoon of sour cream. Mix well. Chill.

Cream Cheese

Stir a little salt into a pan of clabbered milk. (See p. 68). Beat with a wooden spoon. Pour into a linen or cheesecloth bag, and let it drain for three days, changing the bag every day. Then pack the cream cheese in wooden cups or molds with holes in the bottom and press for two hours. Wet the molds with cold water before putting in the cheese. Wrap in soft, white paper, two or three folds of tissue paper will do, to exclude the air. They will keep in a cool place for one week.

(This is the cheese sold under the name of Neufchatel.)

Country Shmierkase

Pour four quarts of boiling water into four quarts of thick sour milk; let it stand for a moment; turn into a drain bag made from several thicknesses of cheesecloth or thin muslin; hang up to drain overnight. (Do not squeeze bag). When ready to use, empty bag; beat smooth with a wooden paddle or spoon; season with salt and freshly ground peppercorns. Keep in a cool place until needed.

SOUPS

Clear Soup Stock

(The country housewife prided herself on her stock-pot. But one had literally to be a mathematician to figure out the quantities of meat, cracked bones and vegetables that went into the pot. This was without counting the trimmings from leftovers which were saved from each meal. The pot was kept on the back of the stove, simmering slowly for hours, until a rich dark essence resulted. This formed the foundation for making soups, sauces and gravies and it was always kept on hand.

The old recipes call for pounds and pounds of meat, fowl, bones and gallons of water. This was all simmered from five to six hours until the soup stock was reduced one-third to one-half. The stock was then strained through a cheesecloth or a very fine sieve and chilled until a layer of fat congealed on top. This was removed until the stock became very clear. When thoroughly chilled it became a quivering mass of thick jelly which kept well for a week or longer. Quantities were removed for each meal, reheated, seasoned, and with the addition of fresh cooked peas, beans, noodles or rice, provided a satisfying, rich and nourishing dish.

It is interesting to read the various ingredients and the amounts used in this very old (1832) recipe for soup stock: one wonders at the size of the soup pot used to hold such a tremendous amount of ingredients!)

Use eight pounds of veal, eight pounds round of beef, half cup butter, three gallons cold water, half carrot, two large onions, half head of celery, thirty peppercorns, six cloves, one blade mace, one small piece cinnamon, four sprigs parsley, four sprigs sweet marjoram, four sprigs summer savory, four sprigs thyme, four sage leaves, four bay leaves, two egg whites, one cup cold water. Place four ounces of the butter in the soup pot, add meat, cut into small cubes. Brown over high heat stirring constantly; add one quart water and cook until the water is reduced to a brown glaze, about one hour. Add remainder of water, bring to a rolling boil, skim off top frequently, reduce heat and allow to simmer gently for six hours. Saute carrot, sliced onions and celery in remaining butter until lightly golden; add to soup pot, together with all herbs and spices. Continue to cook for one hour, salt to taste, strain through a fine sieve. Set in a cold place until next day. Skim off congealed fat. Strain soup again, being careful to discard sediment in bottom of pot. Reheat slowly. Beat the egg whites with one cup cold water; add to soup together with egg shells. Simmer slowly for twenty minutes. Strain again through a very fine sieve or several thicknesses of cheesecloth. Keep in a cold place and use as needed as a foundation for soup, consomme or gravies.

The preparation of the above recipe probably took an entire day, and how the muscles must have ached when it was finished! The following recipe, for a simplified soup stock, is our version for a quick and easy way to prepare a rich chicken broth:

6 cups clear chicken soup, canned	2 tender scallions
1 whole carrot	2 sprigs fresh parsley
2 stalks celery	2 tablespoons sherry wine
1 small young parsnip	

Scrape and wash vegetables. Bring soup to a boil, reduce heat. Add vegetables and sherry wine. Simmer gently for twenty to thirty minutes, strain soup and let cool. Chill. Remove any congealed fat. Reheat, add one cup cooked noodles, one-half cup fresh cooked peas and one tablespoon fresh minced parsley. Serve at once.

For a double rich clear soup; bring soup to a boil, reduce heat, add one-half pound soup meat, in one piece, two soup bones, and four to six chicken wings. Simmer gently for one hour, or until the meat is fork tender. Add the vegetables and wine; cook twenty minutes longer. Strain soup. Cool. Chill. Remove congealed fat. Reheat and serve as desired. May be served with carrots, peas, cooked fine noodles, boiled rice or dumplings. (Serves 6.)

Country Garden Soup

(The warmth of the country kitchen was always permeated with an appetizing aroma arising from the soup kettle which bubbled gently on the back of the stove. The steaming soup, which simmered on the stove for hours, sometimes all day, was laced with a variety of fresh garden vegetables in season. Grains, meat, cracked bones, soup greens, and many a left-over morsel, too, went into the soup pot. Favorite soup recipes were handed down through the generations, from mother to daughter and, as time went on, each improved upon the original recipe. Some of the soups were so thick that a soup spoon could stand up on end without toppling over.

Here is such a soup, a cherished country recipe which we found, yellowed with age, in a notebook dated 1852.)

Take six pounds lean fresh beef, one teaspoon salt, six quarts water, one hock cold ham, one pound cracked bones, quarter peck of tomatoes, quarter peck of okra, two sliced onions, four potatoes, cubed, one quart shelled lima beans, six ears fresh corn, pepper to taste, four tablespoons oatmeal, and a bouquet of fresh herbs tied with a string.

Cut the beef into small pieces, sprinkle with salt; place in a large soup pot and pour on the six quarts water. Add the ham hock and bones. Set over a moderate fire, and let boil slowly. Skim off top. Slice okra, tomatoes and onions in thin rounds; add potatoes and shelled lima beans. Season with pepper. Cook for three hours or longer until the beef is reduced to shreds. Grate the fresh ears of corn; add to soup together with the oatmeal and bundle of herbs. Cook one hour longer. When ready to serve, discard bones, all bits of meat, ham hock and the tied herbs. The soup when done should be as thick as jelly.

(As you can tell, this soup was hearty fare indeed, and was the mainstay of the midday or evening meal. It 'stuck to the ribs!' Here is our version of the Country Garden Soup:

6 cups boiling water or light soup stock
1 pound soup meat
1 veal knuckle, cracked
1 whole onion, pierced with 2 peppercorns
2 small carrots, sliced
1 green stalk celery with leaves, cut into half
½ small parsnip, grated
1 cup corn kernels, fresh or canned
1 cup shelled or frozen baby lima beans
2 tablespoons cream of wheat
1 tablespoon fresh minced parsley
Salt to taste

Heat water or soup stock; bring to a rolling boil. Add meat, veal knuckle and onion. Reduce heat. Cook over medium heat for one-and-one-half hours; skim top occasionally. Add carrots, celery, parsnip, corn, lima beans, cream of wheat, parsley and salt. Simmer gently for thirty minutes, or until the meat is fork tender. Remove meat. Slice and serve separately, if desired. Discard onion, bones and celery. Serve at once in warm soup bowls. Serves 6.

Country Chicken Soup

(This different and unusual recipe for chicken soup was served in many a country kitchen in the dark of winter. Its hearty and nourishing combination of ingredients and flavors, cooked together with two or three chickens, and simmered slowly for hours on top of a wood burning stove, produced a flavorful and fragrant essence, rich in protein and minerals. This soup was served as a main course.)

Take two four-and-a-half to five pound chickens, cleaned and cut into serving pieces, six slices thin ham, pinch of cayenne pepper, one small blade mace, pinch nutmeg, one head celery, cut into long bits with its tender leaves finely minced, quarter pound butter, cut in half and rolled in flour, three quarts milk, small dumplings, beaten yolks of three eggs, fresh minced parsley, dash of paprika. Wash chicken parts thoroughly in cold water. Place chicken and ham in a large soup pot. Season with cayenne, mace and nutmeg. Do not use any salt. Add celery, minced leaves, butter and milk. Boil slowly over low heat, skimming top occasionally, for one-and-one-half hours. Add dumplings rolled into small balls. Continue to cook gently until the chickens are very tender. Stir in the beaten egg yolks, over low heat, beating vigorously until completely blended. Heat five minutes longer. Cut chickens and ham into bite-size pieces, arrange in the bottom of a large soup tureen, pour soup over all. Sprinkle with fresh minced parsley and paprika. Serve at once with portions of chicken and ham in each soup bowl.

(Here, with the quantities reduced and the selection of ingredients somewhat altered, is our version of the same soup.)

3½-pound chicken	½ small tender parsnip
6 cups water	1 slice celery knob
2 carrots, cut into strips	2 sprigs parsley
1 whole onion, pierced with 2 peppercorns	1 cup noodles, cooked
	1 tablespoon fresh minced parsley
1 small celery heart, with tender leaves	Salt to taste

Clean chicken thoroughly; cut into serving pieces. Heat water to a rolling boil. Add chicken parts, carrots, onion, celery, parsnip, celery knob, and parsley. Season. Reduce heat, cover, and cook gently for one-and-one-quarter hours, or until the chicken is very tender when pierced with a fork. Remove chicken pieces to a warm platter. Discard onion, celery heart, parsnip and celery knob. Cool soup. Chill. Remove congealed fat. Reheat; add noodles and parsley. If desired, also add one cup fresh or frozen cooked green peas. This recipe serves 6.

How To Make A Bouquet of Sweet Herbs For Use In Soups

Lay a six-inch square of muslin or double thickness cheesecloth on a table. Add two bay leaves, sprig of fresh or dried marjoram, sprigs of tender celery leaves, three sprigs of fresh parsley, sprig of thyme, tender spring onions, cut into small pieces, three cloves and three peppercorns. Tie up in the muslin. Immerse in soup pot and discard when soup is done.

Farmer's Soup

Two quarts rich soup stock, eight chicken wings, eight drumsticks, eight chicken feet, scalded and skinned, one whole onion, browned in one tablespoon of chicken fat, cornmeal dumplings and toasted seeded rye bread. Bring soup stock to a rolling boil, add wings, drumsticks, feet and onion. Reduce heat, cover, simmer over low heat for one-and-one-half hours. Skim top, discard onion. Remove wings, drumsticks and feet. Trim off meat from wings and drumsticks and return to soup. Drop dumplings by teaspoonful into soup, cover, cook fifteen to twenty minutes until the dumplings rise to the top. Toast eight large slices of seeded rye bread, rub toast with a clove of crushed garlic, spread with hot goose or chicken fat , serve very hot with the soup.

Cornmeal Dumplings:

Half cup flour, half teaspoon salt, one teaspoon baking powder, one egg, a quarter cup milk or soup stock, one tablespoon grated carrot and half teaspoon parsley flakes. Combine dry ingredients, beat egg with milk, add to flour mixture, stir well. Drop by spoonsful into hot soup. Cover and cook fifteen to twenty minutes.

If you get too much salt into soup, a teaspoon of brown sugar, or one pared potato will correct matters.

Cream of Mushroom Soup

(Most of the country folk grew their own mushrooms, drying them out in the sun. They then strung the dried mushrooms on long strings and hung the fragrant necklaces on hooks in a cold, dark room where most of the food supplies were kept. Many soups, chowders and stews were enhanced with the addition of several of the aromatic, dried mushrooms. A great family favorite was a barley casserole, baked long and slowly in the oven and laced with a mixture of softened dried mushrooms, cream and sweet herbs. What a dish to serve up on a cold winter's night! Little wonder that many a gourmet treasure originated on the old wood burning stove of long ago. The following recipe, for cream of mushroom soup, was from Hopewell, New Jersey, dated 1867.)

Half pound firm, white mushrooms, four tablespoons butter, one small onion, minced, two cups light soup stock, salt and freshly ground pepper to taste, two cups scalded milk, two tablespoons flour, two tablespoons cold milk, one cup cream, scalded, two tablespoons fresh minced parsley, six dried mushrooms soaked in half cup hot water. Wipe mushrooms with a damp cloth. Do not peel. Cut into small pieces and saute in butter together with the onion for five minutes. Add mushrooms and onion to the hot soup stock. Simmer gently for fifteen minutes. Season to taste. Cool milk, stir in flour blended smooth with cold milk. Add slowly to the soup, stirring constantly until slightly thickened. Blend in cream slowly. Place over very low heat for five minutes. Add parsley and paprika. Soak ten dried mushrooms in half cup hot water for several hours. Snip with a sharp scissors into thin strips, add with liquor to soup stock and simmer gently until the mushrooms are soft. Dried mushrooms lend a piquant flavor and a tantalizing aroma to any dish.

Creamy Potato Soup

Six large potatoes, three cups hot water, salt to taste, one small celery heart with tender young leaves, minced, one small onion, minced, two tablespoons sweet butter, three cups milk, scalded, dash fresh ground pepper, two tablespoons minced fresh parsley, three hard boiled eggs, sliced, sliced dark bread, toasted, sweet butter. Wash and pare potatoes. Cut into cubes and boil in salted water until tender. Remove potatoes, mash until smooth and return to water. Add minced celery, onion sauteed in butter, milk and pepper. Cover and cook over very low heat for twenty minutes. Garnish each portion with minced parsley and sliced eggs. Serve in deep soup bowls.

Fresh Corn Soup

(Since corn grew in great abundance on the farms, the busy housewife dreamed up scores of corn recipes, so that never an ear of corn went to waste. A great country favorite was fresh corn soup which was served as often for breakfast as it was for lunch or dinner. A sense of nostalgia, hearkening back to her childhood, may well overtake many a reader as she remembers the sweet aroma of fresh picked corn still wet with the morning dew, with its silk glistening in the sunlight. The creamy smoothness of this soup, its texture enhanced with the perfume of sweet herbs and with an extra dash of this and that just for good measure, will be found to be as mouth-watering a dish today as it was in yesteryear.)

Use four tablespoons sweet butter, two medium-size onions, minced, two cups light vegetable stock, six ears fresh picked corn, three peppercorns, scant teaspoon sugar, two cups creamed corn, five cups rich milk, scalded, two tablespoons flour, a few sprigs of fresh sweet herbs and two small carrots, grated. Saute onions in two tablespoons butter until lightly golden. Do not brown. Add onions to hot vegetable stock. Simmer gently for ten minutes. Scrape corn with a sharp knife, add to the stock, together with the corn cobs, peppercorns, sugar, creamed corn and milk. Bring to a slow boil, reduce heat. Cook gently for twenty minutes. Brown flour in remaining two table-spoons butter, blend until smooth. Add slowly to soup, stirring constantly until soup begins to thicken slightly. Season with salt to taste. When ready to serve sprinkle with grated carrot.

The corn cobs give a delicious and unusual taste to the soup; be sure to discard when soup is ready to serve.

Summer Soup
(Alabama)

Two pounds lean beef, two quarts water, salt and pepper to taste, six small turnips, sliced, two young onions, sliced, three sprigs fresh parsley, one table-spoon fresh sweet marjoram leaves, one pound shelled, fresh lima beans, two tablespoons fresh or pickled nasturtium seeds, small dumplings season to taste. Wipe beef off with a damp cloth, place in water, bring to a rolling boil. Skim off top, reduce heat. Season with salt and pepper. Cook gently over medium heat until the meat is fork tender. Remove meat. Chill soup. Skim off hardened fat. Return to heat. Add thinly sliced turnips, onions, parsley, marjoram, lima beans, nasturtium seeds. Continue to cook thirty minutes longer until the vegetables are tender. Prepare tiny dumplings. Add to soup, cover, and cook ten to fifteeen minutes. Serve hot.

Grandmother's Pumpkin Soup

(In the autumn pumpkins of every size and shape were gathered and stored in the root cellar, from which they were drawn, as needed, for pies, soup and stews. The pumpkin seeds were toasted, brushed with melted butter, sprinkled with salt and served as a satisfying nibble for both the children and the grownups. On special occasions grandma prepared a velvety smooth, golden soup rich with pureed pumpkin, creamy milk, eggs, spices and herbs. Perhaps many readers may recall how the spicy fragrance of this soup perfumed the busy farm kitchen.)

Use two pounds of pumpkin, pared and cut into cubes, two cups lightly salted water, four cups creamy rich milk, scalded, three tablespoons sweet butter, one tablespoon sugar, two egg yolks, quarter teaspoon nutmeg, freshly grated peppercorns, pinch cloves, buttered toast, cut into cubes, unsweetened whipped cream. Place cubed pumpkin in a large soup kettle with the salted water. Bring to a rolling boil, reduce heat, and simmer gently for one hour or until the pumpkin is very soft. Rub through a fine sieve, return to pot, add scalded milk, butter, nutmeg, pepper and cloves. Cover and cook gently for fifteen minutes. Beat egg yolks with one-quarter cup light cream until very well blended. Add to soup, gradually, stirring constantly. Place over very low heat for five minutes. Serve in deep soup bowls with cubed, buttered toast. Garnish with a dab of whipped cream.

Grandpa's Wine Soup
(A Kentucky Recipe)

Six cups light soup stock, three tablespoons farina, two stalks celery, finely minced, one carrot, grated, one-third cup sherry wine, twelve small hard boiled egg yolks (from pullet eggs), one heaping tablespoon fresh minced parsley. Bring soup stock to a rolling boil, reduce heat, add farina slowly, stirring constantly until the soup begins to thicken slightly. Add minced celery and carrot. Cover and simmer gently for twenty-five minutes. Add sherry wine, and whole hard boiled egg yolks. Sprinkle with fresh minced parsley. Season. Serve at once in warm soup bowls. (Since this is an old Kentucky recipe, we suspect that sometimes, when no one would notice, Grandpa would substitute his favorite brand of bourbon in place of the sherry wine!)

Milk Soup With Noodles

Six cups milk, a small piece of lemon peel, two tablespoons sugar, half teaspoon salt, two tablespoons farina, two egg yolks, six ounces noodles, a quarter inch wide, boiled and drained. Heat milk to boiling point, reduce heat, add lemon peel, sugar and salt. Add farina slowly, stirring constantly. Simmer gently for fifteen minutes. Remove from heat. Beat egg yolks with a little cold milk, add slowly to soup, beating constantly until well blended. Place over very low heat; keep hot, do not boil. Have boiled noodles ready, well drained. Add to milk soup, stir with a large spoon until noodles are well dispersed in the soup. Serve at once in deep soup bowls with toasted crackers. If desired, for added flavor and aroma, sprinkle each portion lightly with a dash of cinnamon sugar.

(This is a delicious and delicate soup, quick and easy to prepare. It was often served to the ladies at quilting parties, with fresh baked bread, freshly churned sweet butter and a pot of blackberry or raspberry jam. Milk soup was also often served to convalescents in order to tease the palate, and because it is easy to digest and is extremely nourishing.)

Peas, Beans and Barley Soup

Two onions, sliced, two tablespoons butter, one tomato, sliced, two quarts cold water, two stalks celery, finely minced, two small carrots, finely minced, one cup dried lima beans (soaked overnight), half cup split green peas, half cup navy beans (soaked overnight), half cup medium pearl barley, two whole carrots, grated, one herb bouquet, salt to taste, three peppercorns, one small celery heart with tender leaves, minced, six dried mushrooms, soaked in half cup hot water for several hours or overnight, and one tablespoon fresh, minced parsley. Saute sliced onions in butter until soft and transparent; add tomato and saute until soft. Bring water to a rolling boil; add onions and tomato; reduce heat; add celery, carrots, soaked lima beans, split green peas and navy beans. Simmer slowly for two hours, or until the beans and peas are very tender. Pour soup and all ingredients through a fine sieve; rub vegetables, beans and peas with a wooden spoon. Reheat puree; add barley, grated carrots, herb bouquet, salt, peppercorns and celery. Snip softened mushrooms into thin slices with a scissors; add to soup together with their liquor. Cover and simmer gently for one hour, or until barley is soft. Discard herb bouquet. Sprinkle with fresh minced parsley and serve with hot, toasted, buttered dark bread.

Vegetable Soup
(South Carolina, 1884)

One cup minced onions, sauteed in two tablespoons butter, one cup cubed carrots, one cup cubed tender turnips, one cup minced celery, one cup minced, tender parsnip, pepper and salt to taste, two bay leaves, eight cups water, four boiled potatoes, one tablespoon minced, fresh parsley, one tablespoon butter, one tablespoon flour, toasted rounds of white bread. Add sauteed onions, carrots, turnips, celery, parsnip, salt and pepper, and bay leaves to boiling water. Cover and simmer gently for one hour. Press vegetables through a sieve and return to soup. Sprinkle with minced parsley. Melt butter in a small skillet, add flour, rub smooth, stir into soup. Stir constantly until completely blended. Simmer for ten minutes. Serve each portion with a toasted round of white bread. If desired, sprinkle with shredded, yellow, store cheese.

MEATS

Meat

In nineteenth century America most of the countryfolk did their own butchering. Sides of beef were
prepared and hung; the meat being cooled for twenty-four hours before it was cured. Fresh meat was
kept for some time, corning it slightly by rubbing all
over with salt, or it was placed in a brine of rock salt
and water, in clean, tight, hardwood barrels. Salt,
molasses, or sugar and a bit of saltpeter were the pre-
servatives commonly used by the farmer. The salt
acted as an astringent, drawing the moisture out of
the meat and hardening the muscles. Since sugar and
molasses had the opposite effect, they were always
used with the salt to counteract excessive dryness.
Saltpeter was used in small quantities to prevent the
meat from darkening and to maintain its natural red
color. Hams were placed in strong muslin sacks,
whose bottoms were heavily padded with straw. The
hams were then placed in the sacks and covered completely over with more straw. The bags were tied
tightly and hung in a cool, dry place. The muslin
sacking itself, prepared early in the season before the
flies appeared, let in the cool air and at the same time
kept the hams out of the reach of flies and insects.

The countryfolks' natural instinct and 'know-how'
kept their food well preserved during the various seasons. Hog killing time was an excuse for relatives and
friends to gather for an outdoor picnic, for which the

womenfolk prepared headcheese, sausages and pickled pig's feet. The spicy aromas of the many herbs and spices—sage, cloves, allspice, and the strong, pungent vinegar—filled the crisp country air as everyone bustled about; stirring, grinding and chopping the meat and preparing the brine.

"Want not, waste not" was not an empty adage in early America. It was a way of life. Nothing was ever wasted. The head, ears, feet, cheeks, stomach, liver, tongue and every other part of the animal was utilized, prepared and served up as good, old-fashioned, hearty dishes.

An 1875 Old-Fashioned Herb Beef Stew

Two-and-a-half pounds boneless beef, cut into cubes, three tablespoons flour, four cups boiling, good beef stock, two medium onions, chopped, one clove garlic, minced, two tablespoons fresh minced parsley, two bay leaves, two whole cloves, about two teaspoons salt, one-fourth teaspoon pepper, eight potatoes, pared and quartered, pinch ground ginger, six fresh garden carrots, cut into one inch pieces, twelve small whole white onions, one-and-one-half cups fresh green peas, three ribs of celery, cut into one inch pieces, pinch fresh or dried marjoram, pinch sage. Place meat and flour in a bowl, mix well until each cube is well covered. Heat some fat in a heavy Dutch oven, brown meat on all sides, add the hot meat stock and all the seasonings. Simmer gently for two hours or until the meat is fork tender. Add the vegetables, cook for one-half hour or until the vegetables are done. Remove stew to a warm serving dish, discard bay leaves, sprinkle with fresh minced parsley and a smidgeon of fresh dill or fresh minced celery leaves. (A fragrant and elegant stew, as appetizing and as simple to prepare today as it was in the 1800's.)

Beef Stew With Country Fresh Vegetables

Three pounds of chuck or bottom of the round, with a fair amount of fat on it. One quart beef or vegetable stock, one pound cut up white potatoes, turnips, carrots, sweet potatoes and one young fresh parsnip. Place beef stock and beef in a large kettle, simmer very slowly for two-and-one-half hours. Add all the vegetables and a little warm stock, if necessary, as there should be plenty of juice. Add a few bay leaves, a whole onion, and two ribs of celery for flavor. Cover and stew over medium heat until the vegetables are tender. Set the stew aside to cool. The next day, reheat slowly, adding a little warm soup stock. Discard bay leaf, onion and celery. Simmer until the stew is good and hot, serve over hot dumplings or hot broad noodles. The stew is better the next day as the full flavors and all the deliciousness have had an opportunity to ripen. (Do not add cold stock or water as it coagulates the fat and toughens the meat.)

Brown Stew

Put on the stove a rather thick piece of beef with a little bone and some fat; four hours before it is needed, pour on just enough boiling water to cover, then cover with a close fitting lid; boil gently and, as the water boils away, add only enough, from time to time, to keep from burning, so that the meat is tender; the water may all be boiled away, as the fat will allow the meat to brown without burning; turn occasionally, brown evenly over a slow fire; make a gravy by stirring flour and water together and adding to the drippings; season with salt an hour before it is done.

Beefsteak

Take a smooth, thick-bottomed frying pan, scald it out with hot water, and wipe it dry; set it on the stove, and when VERY hot, rub it over with a rag dipped in butter; then place your steak in it, turn often until cooked through; take up on a warm platter and season both sides with salt, pepper and butter. Serve hot. Many folks prefer this manner of cooking steak, rather than broiling or frying in a quantity of grease. If desired, have a clear glowing bed of coals; steak should be about three-quarters of an inch thick. Lay it on a buttered gridiron, turning it often, as it begins to drip. Have all the vegetables ready. Do not season until the steak is done. Spread a liberal lump of butter over it.

Beefsteak With Oysters

Broil steak in the usual way. Put one quart of oysters with very little liquor into a stew pan upon the fire; when it comes to a boil, take off the scum that may rise; stir in three ounces of butter mixed with a tablespoon of sifted flour; let it boil for one minute until it thickens; pour it over the steak. Serve at once.

Country Beefsteak and Onions

Prepare the steak in the usual way. Have ready in a frying pan a dozen sweet fresh onions, cut in slices and sauteed in beef drippings or butter until brown. Dish steak, and lay the onions thickly over the top. Cover tightly and let stand for five minutes, then send to the table at once.

Beefsteak Rolls

Prepare a good dressing, such as you would like for turkey. Take a round steak, pound it, but not very hard, spread the dressing over it, sprinkle with a little salt, pepper and a few bits of butter over the steak before rolling it up, then wash with well-beaten egg, put a little water or stock in the bake pan, lay in the steak so as not to touch the water and bake, basting often. A half hour in a brisk stove will bake it. Make a brown gravy, and send to the table hot.

Hamburgers

Procure one-and-one-half pounds of beef of the lower sirloin or upper round, remove all the fat and stringy parts. Put meat through a chopping machine and grind very fine, putting it through the chopper twice. Mix with four ounces of fine-ground suet fat, one tablespoon of salt, one-half scant teaspoon pepper, one egg, and two tablespoons chopped onion. After mixing all together, form the meat into six even balls, flatten, then roll in bread crumbs. Place in a frying pan with one ounce of butter over the fire. As soon as hot, put in the hamburgers and fry light on both sides, about three minutes. Arrange them in a hot dish, put one teaspoon flour in the pan, stir one minute, add one-half cupful of boiling water and a little beef extract, cook two minutes, then strain. Add a small piece of butter and a pinch of salt, pour over the hamburgers, and serve with mashed or fried potatoes.

Hamburger Steak

Chop, very fine, two pounds of the round of beef. Press it into a flat steak about three quarters of an inch thick, sprinkle with salt, pepper and flour, lay it on a fine wire broiler, and broil the same as beef-steak. Spread with butter and serve on a hot dish. This steak is sometimes shaped into small, thin, flat cakes and fried in a hot frying pan, a little pork fat, or butter being used to keep the meat from sticking to the pan. A gravy made by thickening the juices in the pan, a little water being added before thickening. The gravy should be poured hot over the meat.

Beef Hash

Chop cold roast beef, or pieces of leftover beefsteak; fry a small onion in a piece of butter until brown, add the chopped beef, season with a little salt and pepper; moisten with meat gravy, if you have any, otherwise sufficient water with butter; cook long enough to be hot, but not longer, as much cooking toughens the meat. An excellent breakfast dish.

Boiled Flank With Horseradish Sauce

Take a piece of the lower flank, about one-and-a-half pounds, roll up, and tie with a string; place a soup kettle, with some soup bones, over the fire, cover with cold water; as soon as it boils up, put in the flank; add one-half tablespoon salt, two onions, one leek, one stalk celery, a bouquet of herbs and spices, and one carrot, cut into pieces; cover and cook slowly for two-and-one-half hours. When ready to serve, re-move meat from the kettle to a hot dish, take off the string, and serve with horseradish sauce. Strain the broth, add some boiled rice or barley, cook a few min-utes and serve as soup. Send plain boiled potatoes to the table with the flank.

Beef A La Mode
(1880)

In a piece of rump, cut deep openings with a sharp knife, put in pieces of pork cut into dice, previously rolled in pepper, salt, cloves and nutmeg. Into an iron stew pan lay pieces of pork, sliced onions, slices of lemon, or one to two carrots and a bay leaf; lay the meat on and put over it a piece of breadcrust the size of a hand, a half pint of wine and a little vinegar, and afterwards an equal quantity of water or beef broth, till the meat is half covered; cover the dish close and cook until tender. Then take it out, rub the gravy through a sieve, skim off fat, add some sour cream, return to stew pan, and cook ten minutes. Instead of the cream, capers or sliced cucumber pickles may be added to the gravy if preferred, or a handful of grated ginger snaps or rye bread. The meat can be laid for some days before in a spiced vinegar or wine pickle.

Roast Beef Pie

Cut up roast beef, or beefsteak from a previous meal, into thin slices, lay some of the slices into a deep dish, which you have lined on the sides with rich biscuit dough, rolled very thin. Sprinkle over this a little pepper, salt, small bits of butter, a few slices of cold boiled potatoes, a little cold gravy, if you have any left from the roast. Make another layer of beef, another layer of seasoning, and so on, until the dish is filled. Cover with the paste, leaving a slit in the center, and bake a half hour or until the crust is brown and the pie is well heated.

Meat Pudding
(1896)

One pound fine-chopped lean beef, one pound fine-chopped veal, one-half pound fine-minced larding pork, one tablespoon salt, one teaspoon pepper, one-half teaspoon grated nutmeg, three well-beaten eggs, four ounces stale bread, one grated onion. Soak bread in cold water ten minutes, enclose in a towel and press out all the water. Melt one tablespoon butter in a saucepan, add the bread, stir and cook five minutes, then remove. When cold, mix in the above named ingredients, butter a pudding form or loaf pan, sprinkle with bread crumbs, put in the mixture, pack it down firmly. Close the form or cover tightly, set it in a vessel with boiling water to reach one-third up the form, cover and boil two hours. When ready to serve turn the pudding onto a dish, and serve with mushroom, tomato or horseradish sauce. If a form is not available, bake in a loaf pan.

(Meat Pudding is highly seasoned; reduce seasoning according to individual taste.)

Roast Beef With Pudding

Bake exactly as directed for ordinary roast beef for the table; then make a Yorkshire pudding, to eat like vegetables with the roast, as follows: For every pint of milk take three eggs, three cups flour, and a pinch of salt; stir to a smooth batter, and, half an hour before the meat is done, pour into the dripping pan under the meat.

To Boil A Ham

Soak in cold water overnight. Next morning, wash hard with a cloth or a stiff brush and put to boil in plenty of cold water. Allow a quarter of an hour for each pound in cooking, and do not boil too fast. Do not remove the skin until cold, it will come off easily and cleanly then, and the juices are better preserved than when stripping hot. Send to the table with dots of pepper or dry mustard on top, a tuft of fringed, white, writing paper twisted about the shank, and a garnish of parsley. Cut very thin when serving. To glaze the ham (a cold, boiled one, from which the skin has been taken, as above), brush all over with beaten egg. To a cup of powdered cracker allow enough rich milk or cream to make a thick paste, and work in a teaspoon of melted butter. Spread this evenly a quarter of an inch thick over the ham, and set to brown in a moderately hot stove.

Ham Baked In Apple Cider

Scrape and wash ham thoroughly in cold water, soak overnight in cold water. Rinse carefully in the morning and place on the stove in a large kettle with sufficient water to cover. Bring slowly to the boiling point, skimming off the scum as it appears. Then add six cloves, six allspice berries, and one red pepper pod. Simmer, but do not boil rapidly, until the ham is so tender it may be pierced with a fork. Keep the ham covered with water all the time. When tender, remove the kettle from the stove and let the ham cool in the liquor. Then drain it and trim off all the surplus fat, the skin and all uneven pieces. Pour one-and-one-half quarts of sweet apple cider over the ham and let it soak for eight hours or overnight. Wipe dry, stick in whole cloves to make a pattern, brush lightly with beaten egg and sprinkle generously with a mixture of bread crumbs and brown sugar. Place the ham in a baking pan, pour cider about it and bake in a slow stove until it is neatly browned. This takes from one to two hours, depending upon the size of the ham. Baste frequently with cider during baking.

Lamb Chops Broiled In Paper Cases
(1889)

When intended to be served at a luncheon as an *entrée*, lamb chops are broiled in paper cases in the following manner: Mold and cut sheets of thick, white, writing paper so that when opened they will be heart shaped, making each sheet nine by four-and-a-half inches in size. Dip the cases in olive oil or melted butter, being careful that no part remains unoiled. Have the chops cut from the ribs, trim all the fat and scraps off bones, adding salt and pepper. Dip in melted butter, then place each chop on one side of a paper, with the bone towards the center, fold the paper together, and roll edges to keep them closed. Broil eight minutes over a moderate fire. Serve on a dish in the papers in which they were broiled.
(The success of paper broiling lies in getting every part of the paper well oiled. The broiler should be turned almost constantly while the chops are cooking.)

Crown of Lamb

Season a nice crown of lamb with pepper and salt; set it in a roasting pan; pour over two ounces of fresh melted butter; put one onion in the center; place in a medium hot stove. Roast thirty minutes; then add one cupful of good stock; baste frequently till the roast is done, about two hours. Shortly before serving, place meat on a hot dish; free the gravy from fat; mix one tablespoon cornstarch with one-half cupful of stock or water; add it to the gravy and cook a few minutes; strain and pour some sauce over the meat.

Garnish with fresh cooked peas, carrots, potato balls and small white onions. Serve the rest of the sauce in a boat.

Country Lamb Stew

Prepare two-and-one-half pounds of lamb from the forequarters, cut into two-inch pieces; place in a covered saucepan, cover with boiling water; add two scant tablespoons of salt, and a small teaspoon pepper, two fine-cut white onions, and cook forty minutes. Then add one quart peeled potatoes; when nearly done, melt one ounce of sweet butter in a saucepan, add one tablespoon of flour, cook a few minutes until creamy, stirring well; add it to the stew, and cook till done. Serve on a warm dish.

For a delectable sauce, strain the gravy, mix in the yolks of two eggs with one-half cupful of cream, add it to the sauce, remove from the fire; add the juice of one-half lemon and a little grated nutmeg. Pour the sauce over the meat and serve hot.

Roast Lamb

The best roasts are the fore and hind quarters. Lamb will not keep like mutton and it should be used not later than three days after killing. Like veal, it should be thoroughly cooked. If the roast is from the breast, make a stuffing as directed for stuffed veal (see recipe, p. 104) and fill the pocket made for stuffing. Wipe the meat, dredge with flour, salt and pepper, place a cupful of water in the bottom of the roasting pan and roast the lamb on a rack, basting often, allowing fifteen minutes to the pound. Brown well last few minutes. Serve hot on a warm platter. Send to the table with a separate dish of mint sauce.

Mint Sauce:

Pick the leaves from mint stalks until there is a half pint. Wash the leaves, drain well and place in an earthenware bowl. Then, using a knife and fork, cut the leaves into very small pieces, or snip them fine with a sharp scissors. Do not use a wooden bowl as half the mint will be absorbed by the wood. When the mint is well chopped, stir in half a tablespoon of sugar, mix thoroughly and pour in half a pint of hot vinegar. Cover tightly and serve after a few minutes. Some cooks pour the vinegar on cold and serve the same after it has stood for one hour. This is a matter of taste. Mint jelly is also very good to serve with the lamb.

Boiled Leg of Mutton With Caper Sauce

Put the mutton in a kettle, pour over it boiling water, sufficient to cover, and add a cupful of washed rice, which will render the mutton whiter and even more tender. When the water boils, skim it carefully and allow it to boil rapidly fifteen minutes; then set the kettle where the boiling will be gentle but constant and, if the meat is desired rare, allow fifteen minutes to each pound.

Caper Sauce:

Two tablespoons of flour, one tablespoon of lemon juice, three tablespoons of capers, one-half cupful of butter, one pint of boiling water, pinch pepper and half a teaspoon of salt. Beat the flour and butter to a cream and add the boiling water gradually, stirring all the time, until heated to the boiling point; then put in the seasoning, lemon juice, and capers, and serve, either by pouring it over the leg of mutton or else in a separate dish. Another way of browning, dredge well with flour when done, season, place on a meat rack in a dripping pan and brown a half hour in a very hot stove.

Roast Little Pig
(1889)

The little pig should be about three weeks old. Draw and scrape it, clean well. Cover the point of a skewer with a piece of soft cloth, and work the wooden skewer in the ears to clean them. Clean the nostrils the same way, also the vent of the tail. (If squeamish have the man of the house do it!). Scrape the tongue, lips and gums with a sharp knife, wipe them with a soft cloth and take out the eyes. Wash the pig well with plenty of cold water, wipe dry, and rub a tablespoon of salt inside the pig. Make a nice stuffing of three pints soft bread crumbs, three tablespoons of salt, one-half teaspoon of pepper, one tablespoon of powdered sage, three tablespoons of fresh sweet butter and three tablespoons of finely chopped onion. Mix all together, first rubbing the butter into the crumbs, then adding the seasoning. Fill the body with the stuffing. Press the fore feet forward and the hind feet backward, and skewer them to position. Force the mouth open and place a small block of wood between the teeth. Butter two sheets of paper and pin them about the ears. Sprinkle the pig with salt, rub all over with soft butter, and dredge with flour. Then place it in a roasting pan and cook at least three-and-a-half hours. Baste every fifteen minutes with butter or salad oil, sprinkle with salt and flour after each basting. Water should not be used if the surface of the meat is desired crisp. Remove the paper from the ears the last half hour. When ready to serve, remove the block of wood from the mouth, inserting a small ear of corn or a small lemon. Serve apple sauce with this dish. In carving the roast pig, the head is cut off first, the meat split down the back, the hams and shoulders taken off and the ribs separated. A portion of dressing is served each person.

Apple Dressing For Roast Little Pig:

Pare and cut into quarters about eight large, greening apples, remove the core; place the apples in a large kettle over the fire; add one cupful of water and cook till tender, but not broken. Then remove; when cold, add flour, four ounces of baker's white bread, picked into small pieces, without the brown crust; dry five minutes in the stove; add one-and-one-half tablespoons powdered loaf sugar, one-half ounce sweet butter, a little lemon juice and two eggs. Mix well together. Heat until thickened. Use as a dressing or sauce.

Baked Little Pig With Golden Corn Stuffing
(Nashville, Tennessee, 1885)

Take a young, little pig about six weeks old, nicely prepared and cleaned; score skin in squares, and rub lard all over it; make a dressing of two quarts of cornmeal, salted as for bread, and mix to a stiff bread with boiling water; make into pans and bake. After this is baked brown, break it up and add one quarter pound fresh sweet butter, pepper to taste and thyme. Fill the little pig till plump, sew it up and place it on its knees in the pan, which fill with as much water as will cook it. Baste frequently with gravy, also two red pepper pods. Turn while baking, the same as turkey, and continue to baste till done. Some use turkey dressing instead of the above.

Cornbread Stuffing:

Use two eggs, one-and-one-half cups of fresh sweet milk, one large cup of corn meal, one-half cup of wheat flour, one-and-one-half tablespoons of melted butter, two teaspoons baking powder and one-half teaspoon salt. Beat the whites and the yolks of the eggs separately. Sift the flour and the meal together, add baking powder and sift again. Place the milk in a large mixing bowl. Add to it the beaten yolks, salt, one tablespoon sugar, if desired, then the meal and flour. Mix very thoroughly together and, when well beaten, stir in the beaten egg whites. Bake half an hour in a well-buttered pan. Cool. Break up and use as stuffing; also very palatable as bread. Serve warm with fresh sweet butter.

Pork
(1880)

A pig should not be allowed to eat anything for twenty-four hours before being killed. After the pig is butchered, great care should be used to keep the pork from tainting; it spoils more readily when fresh, than any other meat. Cook all kinds of pork thoroughly. When underdone it is not only unpalatable, but exceedingly unwholesome. During the butchering time fresh spareribs, chine, steak, with other succulent bits, are welcome upon the choicest bill of fare. The rest of the animal, ham, shoulders, and middlings are consigned to the smokehouse. Young pigs, under six months, are highly esteemed. The meat is fine and sweet, unless too fat, and nearly as delicate as that of chicken. Salt pork, bacon and ham are less objectionable than fresh pork; in fact, salt pork and bacon should always be kept on hand in the kitchen to use in cooking other meats. There is no part of the pig that is not used; consequently, to the poor man, it is a very profitable animal. Pork requires a great deal of cooking, for, when underdone, the danger from eating it is very much increased. However, the countryman keeps the animal well fed on corn, allowing them an abundance of water, and they are generally so cared for, diseased meat is an impossibility.

Broiled Pork Steak

When pork is to be broiled, it should be cut very thin, indeed, salted and peppered quite well. Many cooks wrap greased paper around the meat. The broiling of pork is a very delicate operation, since the meat must be thoroughly cooked. For fried pork chops, melt drippings in a heavy frying pan. Dust well with salt, pepper and flour. Fry slowly on both sides until a fine brown. Thicken gravy in the pan as directed for roasts and pour over the chops. Serve with thick slices of juicy apples poached in a simple sugar syrup. Add a few drops of cranberry juice or beet juice for color.

Roast Veal

Wipe the meat, dredge with flour, season with salt and pepper, and place in a pan, pouring a little water in the bottom of the pan. Roast from twenty to thirty minutes, for every pound of veal. Baste every twenty minutes with a half pint of warm broth into which has been melted a full teaspoon of butter, using the liquid in the bottom of the pan for basting as soon as there is sufficient. Make a gravy the same as you do for any roast, using the liquid in the pan. Strain the sauce, season, and pour over the meat.

Roast Breast of Veal

Prepare the breast of veal for filling. Season with salt and pepper, stuff the breast with a veal or sausage forcemeat, and sew it up; then lay it in the roasting pan, spread two ounces of butter on the top, lay three slices of larding pork underneath the veal, set it in a hot oven and roast until the meat has obtained a nice brown, basting often with the gravy; then add one cupful of water, boiling hot, or good stock if you have some. Continue to roast and baste until the meat is done, which will take a small breast one-and-one-half hours, for a large one, two hours. Ten minutes before the veal is taken out from the oven, add one cupful of sour cream; a few minutes before serving, lay the meat on a warm dish, remove fat from gravy, mix one tablespoon of cornstarch with one-half cup of cold water, add to gravy, stir briskly and cook a few minutes longer. Add sufficient boiling water or broth to make a pint of sauce, cook three minutes; strain, pour two tablespoons over the veal and serve the remainder in a sauce bowl.

Veal Cutlets, Fried

Select two pounds veal from the leg, cut it into six even slices; fry four ounces fine-cut larding pork light brown, put in the cutlets; fry light brown on both sides. Arrange them in a warm dish when tender. Mix one ounce of butter with one-half tablespoon seasoned salt. Spread it over the cutlets and serve with boiled potatoes. Or if desired, dip the seasoned cutlets in fine bread crumbs or crackercrumbs and beaten egg, then in bread crumbs again. Brown thoroughly on both sides.

Veal Hash

Chop remnants of cooked veal very fine; add to one pint of chopped veal, one pint fine-chopped, cold, boiled potatoes. Place a saucepan with one ounce of butter and two tablespoons fine-chopped onions over the fire, cook five minutes; add one tablespoon of flour, stir and cook three minutes; then add one cupful broth, one even teaspoonful of salt, one-half of pepper; add the meat and potatoes, stir and cook five minutes. Serve on a hot dish. Lay six poached eggs in a circle around it; sprinkle one tablespoon of fine-chopped fresh parsley over the hash and serve very hot.

Veal Loaf

This may be served cold for luncheon or tea, or hot with a sauce made from veal stock or tomatoes. It is also delicious sliced cold for picnic sandwiches. Two-and-one-half pounds veal, one-half pound of salt pork, two teaspoons of salt, one-half teaspoon of pepper, one teaspoon of finely chopped onion, one-half cupful of cracker crumbs, one-quarter cupful of stock or water, one egg, two tablespoons fresh butter, and one-half teaspoon of sage. Chop the veal and pork very fine and add all the other ingredients, except the butter. Mix well together with the hands or a large wooden spoon. Butter a small pan or deep pie pan and press the mixture into it like a loaf, making it about three inches high. Cook for two hours in a rather hot stove, basting with another half cupful of stock in which the butter has been melted. Serve with the natural gravy.

Jellied Veal

Any cheap cut of veal will do for this dish, which is very nice for luncheon or supper. Take three pounds of veal, one tablespoon of finely chopped onion, one-half tablespoon sage or any other fresh or dried herb available, salt and pepper to taste. Cut the meat in pieces, and stew slowly in a little water. When very tender take it from the kettle and chop it fine. Then return the meat to the kettle with the water it was cooked in, add salt and pepper, the sage and onion, and a bit of chopped celery and parsley, if it is to be had, chopping all the vegetables very fine. Cook ten minutes and pour into a square tin. When cold, cut into slices and serve. Care should be taken not to use too much water in cooking the veal.

Veal and Ham

These are often dressed together. Heat the frying pan hot and fry the ham, use no fat unless very lean. When the ham is cooked, place it on a serving dish, and cook the veal in the juices left from the ham, frying without covering until it is a deep brown. Place them on a platter, add a little water to the gravy in the pan, season with salt and pepper, and pour it without thickening over the meat. The gravy will scarcely need any salt, unless the ham is very fresh.

VARIETY MEATS

Variety Meats

The country and farm folk of America were a God-fearing people. They read their Bible religiously and, besides the spiritual solace they obtained from the Scriptures, they found in it many hints and remedies which they applied to their daily living. In Deuteronomy certain foods were recommended: "Butter of kine, and milk of sheep, with fat of lambs, and rams the breed of Bashan and goats, with the fat of kidneys, and wheat." The fat of kidney, or kidney suet as it is now called, was found to be especially good to relieve constipation.

It is interesting to note that many of the foods mentioned in the Bible, which today are proclaimed the most nutritional, such as the variety meats, butter, milk and honey, were used constantly by the country and farm folk and may have brought them a long and healthy life.

Early American Jerky

Jerked meat is beef or venison dried naturally in the sun. It can only be made during hot, dry, sunny weather. The meat is cut into strips and hung to dry from racks in the sun, a method also common to explorers and travelers on long journeys. The jerky was usually stored in the supply closet and often used to flavor soups, baked beans and other dishes. Its strong concentrated flavor and odor was not objectionable and although the jerky itself was unattractive, it was appetizing and highly nutritious. This method of preparation was also used by the American Indians, the early American settlers and the frontiersmen. Jerky's long lasting qualities and freedom from spoilage made it a necessary protein food item for those making extended sea voyages.

Calf's Head

Preparing a calf's head for cooking, stewing, baking or boiling is definitely not a task for the squeamish. It takes a stout heart and strong nerves for one to remove the tongue, eyes, brain, jaws and teeth; withal it is really a job for a professional butcher. However, in the country and on the farms the countryfolk had to do their own butchering and so the majority of cook books published in the nineteenth century, gave extensive directions on butchering and preparing various carcass for the kitchen use. "Waste not, want not," being the motto of every frugal housewife, it followed that a use was found for literally every part of an animal.

As a matter of historical interest, if not of immediate practical use, we are including this old recipe in every detail so that the reader may have a better idea of what the housewife on the farm had to contend with in preparing her 'vittels.' Besides using the regular cuts of meat, the housewife also prepared good nourishing meals from the head, tongue, heart, liver, kidneys and brains of the carcass. Meat was corned, pickled, dried, smoked or potted. The sausage grinder was constantly busy as the children fed the machine and watched streams of red meat and fat pour into pans, ready to season and pack into containers, cloth bags or skins, to be sliced as needed or even frozen in the winter. There was never a dull moment in the country kitchen; everyone worked hard and long during the summer and the bulging, well-stocked, food larders showed the results of their labors.

TO CLEAN A CALF'S HEAD

Place the head in warm water for five minutes; then lift it out and powder the hair with pulverized resin. The resin is not indispensable, but it does facilitate the operation. Have ready a large kettle of scalding water and, after using the resin, plunge the head into the kettle, covering every part. Raise it after one minute, hold it by the ears, and carefully scrape off all the hair. Then lay the head on a board, saw it in halves lengthwise through the skull, and take out the eyes, brains and tongue. Scrape the ears, nasal and throat passages well, scalding them perfectly clean and remove the gristle that is around the nose. Break the jaw bone, remove the gum and teeth, and lay the head in a large panful of water to soak.

STEWED CALF'S HEAD

Put the head in slightly salted water; add pepper, four tablespoons butter, an onion studded with cloves and fresh parsley. Boil until the meat is tender; then take it up and drain well. Score the top a little, rub it over with melted butter, dredge with flour and place it in the oven in a large baking pan to brown. When browned, pour over the head the following sauce:

Brain Sauce: Clean the brains, remove the membranes, and soak in cold water. Put them into a pint of cold water with one tablespoonful of lemon juice and a half teaspoon salt. Boil ten minutes; then plunge into cold water. Make one pint of drawn butter sauce; flavor with lemon and parsley, add the brains chopped fine, and serve while hot.

Calf's Head Cheese

One calf's head, cleaned and scalded, one teaspoon salt, one teaspoon summer savory, one tablespoon chopped parsley, one teaspoon chopped onion, one teaspoon sweet marjoram, one-fourth teaspoon black pepper, and one teaspoon sage. Place the calf's head in enough hot water to cover it and simmer until the meat will leave the bone. Take out the head very carefully on a skimmer, remove the bones, chop the meat and add all the seasonings. Have ready a small bag made of several thicknesses of cheesecloth, pack the mixture into it, tie the bag tightly, and hang away to cool. When cold, turn the bag wrong side out, off the meat. Serve cold for lunch or tea, cutting the cheese into thin slices. Spread each slice with prepared mustard.

More Head Cheese

This recipe is made of the head, ears and tongue, seasoned highly. Boil the cleaned head in salted water until very tender. Skim out the head, place in a colander to drain, and remove all the bones with a knife. Cut the ears rather fine and place them with the head meat. Season the whole with pepper, salt, sage, sweet marjoram, and any other sweet herbs available, adding also a little powdered cloves. Mix the mass well together, taste to see if properly seasoned, and pack it tightly into a bowl, interspersing the layers of meat with slices of boiled tongue. Press the meat into a compact shape, and cover it with a plate upon which place a heavy weight. [Allow to stand for three days to ripen, then cut into slices, dip in beaten egg and cracker crumbs and fry. This mode produces a very pleasant breakfast dish.] Serve with vinegar or mustard, if preferred.

Jellied Calf's Feet

Three pounds calf's feet, split in half, three quarts water, one large onion or four to six spring scallions, chopped, four stalks celery, four cloves, four peppercorns, two bay leaves, three teaspoons salt, two cloves garlic, crushed, half teaspoon black pepper. Some horseradish sauce. Boil water, add cleaned feet, onions, celery, spices, salt, pepper and bay leaves. Simmer gently until the meat is tender and falls away from the bones. Cut meat into serving pieces, arrange in a crock or porcelain-lined loaf pan. Alternate slices of meat with sliced hard boiled eggs, if liked, until the dish is filled. Skim grease from broth, add crushed cloves of garlic, salt and pepper. Boil about twenty to thirty minutes until reduced to half. Strain broth over meat. Cool. Place in a cold place overnight until jellied. Cut into thick slices and serve with horseradish. A pleasant breakfast or tea dish.

Dried Beef

Fifty pounds of beef, one quart salt, one ounce saltpeter, and molasses. Cut meat into large three to four pound pieces. Place salt and saltpeter in a large pan over a slow fire and leave until hot. Add molasses until the mass is thick and smooth like brown sugar. Rub each piece of beef with the mixture and pack into large stone jars; add a piece of wood or large platter between, then a heavy stone weight on top of the meat. Let stand for two weeks, turning and basting every few days. The mixture will dissolve forming its own liquid. Let stand for six weeks, then remove from stone crocks and drain well. Hang up behind the kitchen stove for two weeks until the beef has dried thoroughly.

Potted Beef
(1883)

Two pounds lean beef, one tablespoon butter, one-fourth pound of butter, salt to taste, cayenne, pounded mace and black pepper. Procure a nice piece of lean beef, as free from gristle, skin, etc. as possible, and put into a jar (if at hand, one with a lid) with one teaspoon water. Cover it closely and put the jar in a saucepan of boiling water, letting the water come within two inches of the top of the jar. Boil gently for three-and-one-half hours, then take the beef and chop it very small with a chopping knife, and pound it thoroughly in a mortar. Mix with it, by degrees, all or a portion of the gravy that will run from it, and add a little clarified butter. Add the seasoning, put in small pots for use, and cover with a little butter, warmed and poured over it. If much gravy is added to it, it will keep but a short time; on the contrary, if a large proportion of butter is used, it may be preserved for some time.

Beef Heart, Stewed

Wash the heart well, and cut into squares a half an inch long. Stew them for ten minutes in enough water to cover them. Salt the water slightly, to draw out the blood, and throw it away as it rises in scum to the top. Take out the meat, strain the liquor, and return the chopped heart to it, together with a sliced onion, a large spoonful of catsup, some parsley, a head of celery, chopped fine, cayenne pepper, and a large lump of butter. Stew the meat until very tender, then add a tablespoon of browned flour to thicken. Boil up at once and serve.

Beef Tongue

Soak overnight in cold water after you have washed it well. Next morning, put it into a pot with plenty of cold water, and boil slowly until tender throughout. This you can determine with a fork. Leave in the liquor until cold. Pare off the thick skin and gristle and cut in round slices. Dish for tea, garnishing with fresh parsley.

(Boiled tongue was often served, sliced cold, for breakfast or tea, and was in great demand for sandwiches, for which it was held in even greater esteem than ham. Various herbs and spices were added to the boiling water to impart special flavors; a few cloves and allspice, a blade of mace and laurel perfumed the air as the tongues simmered long and slowly over a wood burning fire scented with juniper twigs.)

Pickled Beef Tongues

Trim roots neatly. Rub with salt and let stand twenty-four hours. For each tongue mix together three tablespoons salt, three tablespoons sugar, one teaspoon saltpeter and one-fourth teaspoon pepper. Rub tongue thoroughly with the mixture and lay it in an earthenware crock. Rub every day for a week, then add another tablespoon of salt. It will be ready to eat or smoke in another week if turned every day.

Potted Chicken, Partridge, Quail, Grouse or Wild Pigeons

Pluck feathers, draw, wash and clean well. Rub with a mixture of one tablespoon salt, one-half teaspoon white pepper, one-fourth teaspoon mace, and one-fourth teaspoon allspice. Rub birds inside and out with the spice mixture. Pack close together in a large baking dish or earthenware crock, dotting each bird with fresh butter. Make a mixture of flour paste and cover crocks with paper to seal well. Bake until thoroughly cooked, time depending on the size of the birds. Remove cover from crock, let stand until the birds are cold. Scrape off gravy and fat, cut the meat off the bones and pack in small sterilized jars. Top with melted, warm, clarified butter, covering each layer and top with it. Cover the jars well, set in a cool place and the meat will keep perfectly for several weeks.

Potted Ham
(1854)

Take some cold ham, slice it, and mince it small; fat and lean together. Then pound it in a mortar; seasoning it, as you proceed, with cayenne pepper, powdered mace and powdered nutmeg. Then fill with it a large deep pan and set it in an oven for half an hour. Afterwards, pack it down hard in a stone jar and fill up the jar with lard. If sufficiently seasoned, it will keep well in winter and is convenient to use for sandwiches or on the tea table. A jar of this will be found useful to travelers going to remote places.

Hash
(1880)

The author of this late nineteenth century recipe for hash, starts with the following comment: "Mother's hash doesn't taste of soap grease, rancid butter, spoiled cheese, raw flour, boarding house skillets, hotel coffee, garden garlic, bologna sausages, or cayenne pepper; neither is it stewed and simmered and simmered and stewed, but is made so nicely, seasoned so delicately, and heated through so quickly, that the only trouble is, *there is never enough to go around.*" Here is her recipe:

Cold meat of any kind will do, but corned beef is best. Always remove any surplus of fat and bits of gristle, season with salt and pepper, chop fine, and to one-third of meat add two-thirds of cold, chopped, boiled potato, and one onion, chopped very fine. Place in the dripping pan, dredge with a little flour, and pour in at the side of the pan enough water to come up level with the hash. Place in a moderately hot stove, do not stir; when the flour is a light brown and has formed a sort of crust, take out, add a lump of butter, stir it through several times, and you will have a delicious hash. When ready to dish, run a knife under as you would an omelet, and serve hot with catsup.

Beef Hash

To two parts of cold roast or boiled corned beef, chopped fine, put one of mashed potatoes, a little pepper, salt, milk and melted butter. Turn all into a frying pan and stir until it is heated through and smoking hot; but not until it browns. Put into a deep dish and, if stiff enough, smooth, as you would mashed potatoes, into a hillock. Or you can cease stirring for a few minutes and let a brown crust form on the under side; then turn out whole into a flat dish, the brown side uppermost. Or mold the mixture into flat cakes, dip these in beaten eggs and flour and fry in hot drippings. A little catsup and mustard is an improvement to plain cold beef, thus hashed.

Baked Liver

Have a whole calf's liver larded; in the bottom of a baking dish make a bed of vegetables, finely chopped, consisting of cabbage, turnip and onion; put a bay leaf or two slices of salt pork, on top of all place the liver; add water enough to cover vegetables, place in the oven, let bake for one hour, slowly, then take out the liver; add enough water to what is left in the pan to make gravy, let come to a boil on top of the stove, then strain and pour over the liver.

Potted Liver

Braise a calf's or lamb's liver in rich, highly seasoned stock. When tender, cut fine and pound to a paste in a mortar, adding enough of the strained liquor in which it was cooked to moisten it. Add half a cup butter, melted and strained. Rub all through a sieve, pack in jars and pour melted butter over the top.

Pickled Pigs Feet and Ears

Clean the feet and ears well; cover them with cold water, slightly salted, and boil until tender. Pack in stone jars while hot and cover while you make ready to pickle. To half a gallon of good cider vinegar allow a cup of white sugar, three dozen peppercorns, a dozen blades of mace, and a dozen cloves. Boil this one minute, taking care that it really boils, and pour while hot over the warm feet and ears. It will be ready to use in two days and will keep in a cool, dry place two months. If you wish it for breakfast, make a batter of one egg, one cup milk, salt to taste, and a teaspoon butter, with flour enough to make a thin muffin batter; dip each piece into this and fry in hot lard or dripping. Or dip each piece in beaten egg, then in pounded cracker, before frying. The pig's feet are especially good eaten cold.

(Several earthenware crocks of pickled pig's feet were always put down in a dark, cool spot in the cellar. It was a favorite dish for the menfolk in the family, and very popular among the farm hands. This staunch and hearty dish was often served cold, or fried in batter, with steaming bowls of new boiled potatoes swimming in little puddles of fresh-churned sweet butter.)

Country Scrapple

Scrape and thoroughly clean a hog's head; then split it, take out the eyes and brain. Clean the ears; scrape and scald them well. Put all on to boil, in plenty of cold water, and simmer gently for four hours, until the meat will easily slip from the bones. Lift out the meat and bones into a colander; remove bones and chop meat fine. Skim off every particle of grease from the water in which the meat was boiled and return chopped meat to the kettle and water. Season highly with pepper and salt and such powdered herbs as may be preferred. Now take a large wooden spoon or paddle and stir constantly, meanwhile adding enough corn meal and buckwheat flour, in equal quantities, to make soft mush. Cook slowly for one hour, stirring frequently, as the mush will scorch easily. Pour the mixture into dishes and keep in a cool place, slicing as needed.

To Cook Scrapple:
Cut it into rather thin slices. Dip each slice in flour and fry until brown. Drain well before serving.

Old-Fashioned Country Scrapple
A Quick and Easy Recipe

Add one-and-one-half cups cornmeal to four-and-one-half cups of boiling salted water, very slowly, stirring constantly. Boil three minutes, then place in a double boiler and cook slowly for two to three hours. Stir two cups of sausage through the mush, cook twenty minutes longer then empty into a pan moistened with cold water. When cold and firm, cut in slices, dip in flour and brown in fat.

Potted Tongue

Chop and pound cooked tongue together with any leftover cooked veal or chicken in equal quantities. Remove all gristle and skin and pound till free from any fibre; reduce to a paste. Season highly with salt, black pepper, cayenne, and made mustard; moisten with a little warm butter. Pack closely in small stone or earthen jars. Put the jars in a steamer and heat for half an hour. Then press the meat down again and cover with hot melted butter. This will keep for some time and may be sliced or used for sandwiches.

Sweetbreads, Larded and Baked

When the sweetbreads have been cleaned, put them in warm water to draw out the blood and to improve the color. Draw through each four very thin strips of pork about the size of a match, drop them into cold water for five to ten minutes, then in hot water and boil twenty minutes. Take out, spread with butter, dredge with flour, salt and pepper, and bake twenty minutes in a quick oven. Serve with green peas, well drained and seasoned with salt and butter, heaped in the center of the dish. Lay the sweetbreads around the peas and pour a cream sauce around the edge of the dish. Garnish with parsley.

Broiled Honeycomb Tripe

Cut tripe into serving pieces; roll in very fine toasted bread crumbs, or flour. Dip in melted butter, then roll again in bread crumbs. Broil four to five minutes on both sides. Season with salt and pepper to taste. Serve with mustard.

Bologna Sausage, Cooked

Two pounds each of lean beef, veal, pork, fat salt pork (not smoked), one pound beef suet, ten teaspoons powdered sage, one ounce marjoram, parsley, savory and thyme mixed. Add two teaspoons cayenne pepper, and the same of black, one grated nutmeg, one teaspoon cloves, one minced onion, and salt to taste. Chop or grind the meat and suet; season, and stuff into beef skins; tie up; prick each in several places to allow the escape of steam; put into hot, but not boiling, water and heat gradually to the boiling point; cook slowly for one hour. Take out the skins and lay them to dry in the sun upon clean, sweet straw or hay. Rub the outside of the skins with oil or melted butter and hang in a cool, dry cellar. If you mean to keep it more than a week, rub pepper or powdered ginger upon the outside; you can wash it off before sending it to the table. This is eaten without further cooking. Cut in round slices and lay sliced lemon around the edge of the plate, as many like to squeeze a few drops upon the sausage before eating.

GAME

Furred and Feathered

Note: To keep game from tainting, draw as soon as they come into your possession. Rinse with soda and water, then with pure cold water; wipe dry and rub lightly with a mixture of fine salt and black pepper. If you must keep them some time, put in the cavity of each bird a piece of charcoal; hang them in a cool, dark place with a cloth thrown over them. Small birds, unless there are a great many of them, may be kept in the icebox after they have been drawn, washed and wiped. The charcoal is an admirable preventive of decomposition.

Venison is one of the most easily digested of meats. The meat should be of a fine grain and nicely covered with fat; the dark color of the meat should be a rich reddish brown. The flavor may be objectionable to the uninitiated, but to the gourmet it is a special treat. Keep it hung in a cool, dark cellar, covered with a cloth. Use as soon as you can conveniently. If the venison is young, the hoof will be slightly open; if old, the hoof will be wide open. Venison, like all game, is not usually fat enough and is enriched by larding or placing slices of fat salt pork or bacon over it. The fat and juices are sometimes kept in by a thick layer of flour paste. Venison should always be wiped before cooking, as hairs are often found clinging to the meat. The haunch, leg and saddle are usually roasted. In roasting the saddle, the flank may or may not be removed. When retained, a few stalks of celery may be rolled in each flank; these are then trussed or skewered close to the backbone. Thus treated, the saddle presents a good appearance. But the flank is much more edible when it is stewed, or made into a ragout; the roast requires longer cooking. To serve, cut the meat parallel to the backbone, then turn the knife and separate the slices from the bone below. Cut the tenderloin beneath the same way, the roast being reversed upon the serving dish. Serve with currant jelly and an endive or escarole salad. Rings of tart apple, cooked in syrup, make an attractive garnish for roast venison. The haunch and other parts of the venison should be soaked in a good marinade (see p. 126) for several days, to tenderize the meat and remove much of its gaminess.

The tame rabbit is rarely if ever eaten. The wild hare, even if a day old, exactly corresponds to the rabbit of the northern fields: when fat and tender may be made in a variety of excellent dishes. Hares are unfit for eating in the early spring.

Haunch of Venison

If the outside be hard, wash off with lukewarm water; then rub all over with fresh butter or lard. Cover it on top and sides with a thick paste of flour and water, nearly a half inch thick. Lay upon this a large sheet of thin, white, wrapping paper, well buttered, and above this thick foolscap. Keep all in place by greased pack thread; then put down to roast with a little water in a dripping pan. Let the fire be steady and strong. Pour a few ladlesful of butter over the meat now and then, to prevent the paper from scorching. If the haunch is large, it will take about five hours to roast. About a half hour before you take it up, remove the papers and the paste, and test with a skewer to see if it is done. If the skewer passes easily to the bone, through the thickest part, set it down to a more moderate fire and baste every few minutes with Claret wine and melted butter. At the last, baste with butter, dredge with flour to make a light froth, and dish. It should be a fine brown by this time. Twist a frill of fringed paper around the knuckle.

Venison Shoulder

This is also a roasting piece, but many be cooked without the paste and paper. Baste often with butter and water, and towards the last, with Claret wine and butter. Do not let it get dry for an instant.

Venison Sausages

Five pounds lean venison, two pounds fat salt pork, five teaspoons powdered sage, four teaspoons salt, four teaspoons pepper, two teaspoons cayenne pepper, one small onion, and juice of one lemon. Chop the meat very small, season, and pack in skins or small stone jars. Hang the skins, or set the jars, tied down with bladders, in a cool, dry place. Fry as you would other sausages. These sausages are very highly seasoned; if desired, you may reduce seasoning according to taste.

Venison Gravy

Put in a saucepan a pound or so of scraps of raw venison left from trimming the haunch, a quart of water, pinch of cloves, a few blades of mace, half a grated nutmeg, cayenne pepper and salt to taste. Stew slowly to one-half the original quantity. Skim, strain, and return to the saucepan after you have rinsed it with hot water. Add three tablespoons butter and thicken with browned flour. Send to the table in a tureen. *Always* send around currant jelly with venison.

Cooked Marinade For Venison

One quart water, one pint good vinegar, two-and-a-half tablespoons salt, one tablespoon peppercorns, a blade of mace, two tablespoons butter, six sprigs of parsley, one tablespoon mixed herbs, two onions sliced, one large carrot sliced, one-half cup of wine. Put all ingredients, except the wine, over the fire; let it boil up once, then simmer gently for half an hour. Use at once, strain and pour over venison in a deep vessel; add wine, letting stand for three to four days, turning meat in the marinade often.

Venison Steaks

These are broiled rare the same as beefsteaks. Lay the steaks on bars and broil rapidly, turning often, not to lose a drop of juice. These will take three or four minutes longer than beefsteaks. Have ready in a chafing dish a piece of butter the size of an egg for each pound of venison, a pinch of salt, a little pepper, a tablespoon of currant jelly and a glass of Claret wine for every four pounds. If you have no chafing dish, heat in a saucepan. If you wish a plainer dish, omit the wine and jelly.

Hashed Venison

The remains of cold roast venison, especially a stuffed shoulder, may be used for this dish. Slice the meat from the bones. Put these, with the fat and other scraps, in a saucepan with a large cup of cold water, a small onion, minced, fresh parsley and thyme, salt and pepper, and three or four whole cloves. Stew for one hour. Strain and return to the saucepan with whatever gravy was left over from the roast, a tablespoon currant jelly, a tablespoon of tomato or mushroom catsup, a teaspoon of anchovy sauce, and a little brown flour. Boil for three minutes, lay in the venison, cut into slices about an inch long, and let all heat over the fire for eight minutes; do not allow the hash to boil. Stir frequently and, when smoking hot, turn into a deep, covered dish. Send to the table.

Stewed Rabbits With Onion

Clean a pair of nice rabbits; soak in cold salt water for an hour to draw out the blood; put on in a large saucepan with cold water enough to cover them; salt slightly and stew until tender. (Have the menfolk or hired hand skin the rabbit for you). Slice into another pot half a dozen young onions and boil in very little water until thoroughly done. Drain off the water, stir the onions into half a cup of drawn butter, pepper to taste and, when it simmers, add the juice of a lemon. Cut off the heads of the hares, lay hares in a hot dish and pour over them the onion sauce. Let the dish stand in a warm place, closely covered, five minutes before sending to the table.

Country Herbed Rabbit Stew

Having cleaned, washed, and cut up the rabbits, lay the pieces in cold water to soak out the blood. Then wash them through another water. Season them with a little pepper, some powdered mace and nutmeg, and the yellow rind of a lemon, grated. Put them into a wide-mouth jar, adding some chopped celery, sweet marjoram and tarragon leaves. Intersperse them with a few thin slices of cold ham, or smoked tongue, a teacup of water and two glasses of white wine. Cover the jar closely so that none of the flavor escapes with the steam. Set it over the fire in a large kettle of cold water and let it stew slowly for two hours. When nearly done, add some pieces of butter rolled in flour.

Brunswick Stew
(1880)

The large gray squirrel is seldom eaten in the north, but is very popular in the southern states. It is generally barbecued (the same as rabbits), broiled, fricasseed or, most popular of all, made into a Brunswick stew. This recipe is named for Brunswick County, Virginia, and is a famous dish:

Two squirrels, three if small, one quart of peeled and sliced tomatoes, one pint butter beans or limas, six potatoes, parboiled and sliced, six ears of fresh corn cut from the cob, one-half pound butter, one-half pound fat salt pork, one teaspoon ground black pepper, a half teaspoon cayenne pepper, one gallon of water, one tablespoon salt, two teaspoons white sugar, one small minced onion. Put on the water with the salt in it and boil five minutes. Put in the onions, beans, corn, pork (or bacon) cut into shreds, potatoes, pepper and the squirrels, which must first be cut into joints and laid in cold water and salt to draw out the blood. Cover closely and stew very slowly, for two-and-one-half hours, stirring frequently from the bottom. Then add the tomatoes and sugar, and stew an hour longer. Ten minutes before you take it from the fire, add the butter, cut into bits the size of a walnut and rolled in flour. Give a final boil, taste to see that it is seasoned to your liking, and turn into a nice soup tureen. It is eaten from soup plates. Chickens may be substituted for the squirrels.

Roast Pheasant

Clean, truss and stuff the pheasants as you do chickens. [Wash the inside of all game—prairie fowls in particular—with soda and water, rinsing out carefully several times with fair water.] Roast at a hot fire, baste with butter and water until brown; sprinkle with salt, dredge lightly at the last with flour to froth the birds, and serve hot. Thicken the gravy with browned flour, boil up and serve in a boat.

Quail Roasted With Ham

Clean, truss and stuff as you do chickens. Cover the entire bird with thin slices of corned ham, cover with a sheet of white paper, and secure the slices of meat with pack thread. Stitch the papers on and keep them well basted with butter and water, so that they will not burn. Roast three-quarters of an hour, if the fire is good. Remove the papers and meat. Before sending to table, brown quickly. This is the nicest way of cooking quail.

Wild Roast Duck

Nearly all wild ducks are liable to have a fishy flavor, and when handled by inexperienced cooks, are sometimes uneatable. Before roasting them, parboil them with a small carrot, peeled. This will absorb the unpleasant taste. An onion will have the same effect, but the carrot is preferable. After parboiling throw away the carrot (or onion), lay in fresh water for a half hour; stuff with bread crumbs seasoned with salt, pepper, sage and onion, and roast until brown and tender; basting for half the time with butter and water, then with drippings. Add to the gravy, when you have taken up the ducks, a tablespoon of currant jelly and a pinch of cayenne pepper. Thicken with brown flour and serve in a tureen.

Roast Snipe or Plovers

Clean and truss, but do not stuff. Lay in rows in the dripping pan, or tie upon a spit; sprinkle with salt and baste well with butter and water. When they begin to brown, in about ten minutes, cut as many rounds of bread without crusts as there are birds. Toast quickly, butter and lay a bird upon each in the dripping pan. When the birds are done, serve upon toast, with the gravy poured over it. The toast should lie under the birds while cooking for at least five minutes, during which time the birds should be basted with melted butter seasoned with pepper. The largest snipe will not require more than twenty minutes to roast.

Ortolans, Reed Birds, Rail & Sora

These may be roasted or broiled. A good way is to roll an oyster in melted butter, then in bread crumbs seasoned with pepper and salt, and put into each bird before roasting. Baste with butter and water three times. Put the rounds of toast underneath, and baste freely with melted butter. They will require twenty minutes to cook and will be found delicious.

CHICKEN, TURKEY, DUCK AND GOOSE

Fried Chicken

Cut the small chickens in four or six pieces, dip each piece hastily in cold water, then sprinkle with salt and pepper and roll pieces in flour. Have some sweet lard heated very hot in the frying pan and fry the chicken until every piece is a rich brown hue on both sides. Take up, drain well, and arrange pieces on a warm platter, setting the dish in a hot place to keep the meat from cooling while the gravy is being prepared. Pour out of the pan all but one tablespoon of the fat and stir into the pan a cup of sweet milk. When the liquid is hot and well stirred, thicken to a rich cream with a tablespoon of flour rubbed smooth in a tablespoon of butter. Boil three minutes, stirring constantly, season with salt and pepper, and pour the gravy over the chicken. Lard burns too quickly, but lard is decidedly to be preferred for this purpose. Fried chicken is a standard dish in the country home and this method of making it is the most simple.

Broiled Fillets of Chicken Breasts

Remove the bone from the breasts and thighs. Rub well with butter, season well with salt and pepper, cover with a fine cracker dust. Broil about ten minutes on both sides.

Devilled Chicken

Boil a chicken until tender in boiling salted water. When cold, cut at the joints, baste with soft butter, and broil until brown. Or cut any cold boiled or roasted chicken at the joints, rub with salt and butter, and broil till warmed through. Pour hot tartare sauce over them. Or make incisions in the flesh, and rub with mustard and cayenne pepper before broiling.

Roast Chicken With Giblet Sauce

Prepare the same as roast turkey. (See recipe p. 135), using but half the amount of stuffing and allowing but fifteen minutes cooking to the pound. Baste every ten minutes, else the chicken will be dry and disappointing. Chickens may be filled with chestnut stuffing the same as turkey. Use giblet gravy sauce (See p. 136).

Boiled Chicken With Celery Sauce

In the winter there is no better way to prepare chicken than to boil them whole and, when serving, pour over them a delicious celery sauce (recipe below). The chickens should be stuffed, well-sewed and pinned in a wet cloth (with skewers) that has been generously sprinkled with flour. They are then plunged into a large kettle of boiling water which should not cease boiling until the chicken is done. Allow twenty minutes a pound. A large, tough chicken may be made very palatable this way. For flavor place several fresh garden soup greens into the water. This chicken is also very tasty served cold on a hot summer day.

Celery Sauce:

One head of fresh celery, one pint sweet milk, salt and pepper to taste, two tablespoons flour, four tablespoons sweet butter. Cut the celery fine, with a few tender leaves. Place in a saucepan with just enough water to cover. Cover the pan and simmer gently. When it has boiled an hour, mix the butter and flour together and add them to the celery; also adding the milk, salt and pepper. Boil two minutes to a smooth cream, stirring all the time. Serve in a gravy boat.

Baked Chicken
Camping Party Style

Do not remove the feathers from the chicken. Take out the entrails and the crop, making the incisions as small as possible, and cut out the vent. Rinse inside. Stuff with half the stuffing as directed for the roast turkey, or sew up the body securely with the stuffing. Cover the chicken with wet clay, spreading it a half inch thick. Bury the chicken in a bed of hot ashes; place coals on the top and bake an hour and a quarter, if the bird weighs two pounds. The feathers will peel off as the cake of clay is removed, leaving the flesh quite clean. This is an especially good dish for the hungry camping party.

Sauteed Chicken

Disjoint a full grown chicken. Wash and wipe dry. Marinate the pieces—i.e., pour over three or four tablespoons of oil, dust with salt and pepper, strew with sliced onion rings and add the juice of a lemon. Let stand several hours, or a full day. Half an hour before serving cut a slice of salt pork in bits and try out the fat; remove the onions and pieces of chicken

on a cloth, dip them in milk and flour them well, then
saute them in hot fat until golden brown on all sides.
Serve piled on a napkin-lined plate, with bread or
celery sauce in a boat. Or separate a hot boiled cauliflower into flowerets and arrange around the chicken.
Pour a cream sauce over the whole, well-seasoned, or
serve the sauce apart. A fowl a year old should be parboiled in seasoned hot water before sauteeing.
(In reading through nineteenth century cookbooks,
one becomes bewildered at the hundreds of dishes
that are prepared from cooked chicken. Most of the
cooked entrees are prepared from the breasts alone
and are called fillets. There is no doubt that chicken,
however prepared, was a favorite food in the country
kitchen.)

Smothered Chicken

This is one of the most delicious ways of cooking
chicken. Clean, take off the neck, and split chicken
down the back, wiping it with a damp cloth. Season
inside and out with salt and pepper, and dredge on
all sides with flour. Lay the chicken, with the inside
down, in a small baking tin, adding a cupful of water.
The pan should be but a *little larger* than the chicken,
otherwise the gravy will evaporate too quickly. Cook
slowly for one hour, basting every ten minutes after
the first twenty minutes of baking. Should the chicken
be decidedly lacking in fat, add a small tablespoon of
butter. There will be plenty of gravy in the pan to
baste if the pan is small. When done, place the chick-
en on a hot platter and thicken the gravy in the pan
with a little flour, after adding another half cup of
water. Season with salt and pepper to taste. Pour the
gravy over the chicken and serve at once. The secret
of success in this kind of roasting is the frequent basting and not having the stove too hot.

Roast Turkey
(1889)

Singe and clean turkey; wash inside with cold water and a little lemon juice or salt to freshen. Dry, work hand gently under the skin on the breast to lift the skin from the flesh, working through the cut made by taking out the neck; take care not to break the skin. Put a thin layer of dressing (see recipe below) between the skin and flesh; and place the rest of the stuffing lightly in the body, being careful not to pack it at all. When the breast is stuffed, draw the skin of the neck over on the back and fasten it with a skewer to the back. Turn the tips of the wings under the back and fasten them in that position with a skewer, running it through the wings and body. Make an incision in the skin, near the opening where the entrails have been taken out, and insert the drumsticks in the holes, tying them together after they are so placed. Sew up the vent where the stuffing was put in. Moisten the skin of the bird with a little water and sprinkle it with salt, pepper and flour. The moisture helps retain the seasoning on the bird. Place the turkey on a dripping pan in the stove, adding a very little water to the pan, and roast, allowing twenty minutes to the pound. After it has roasted for twenty-five minutes, baste it with fat and water in the pan, and baste frequently, every fifteen minutes, until baked enough. Frequent basting is the secret of success in roasting fowl. If basting is done every ten minutes, it will not be too often, but it should be done at least every fifteen minutes. There is enough fat given off from the turkey for use in basting. Brown the turkey well the last few minutes, place on a platter, remove strings and skewers, and place in the oven while gravy is being prepared.

Giblet Gravy:

Place the giblets, the heart, the liver, the gizzard and the neck, which has been cut off, in a saucepan and cover with cold water. Simmer slowly and, when tender, remove neck and chop the giblets fine, saving the water in which they have cooked. When the turkey has been lifted from the pan, pour off all but three tablespoons of the fat, place the pan on top of the stove and, when the gravy boils, stir in two tablespoons of lightly browned flour. Cook two minutes and add the water in which the giblets have been cooked, pouring it in gradually so as not to thin the gravy too much. Put in lastly the chopped giblets and season to taste with salt and pepper. Serve hot in a gravy boat.

Stuffing:

Four cups of stale bread grated, two tablespoons butter, one tablespoon chopped fresh parsley, two teaspoons salt, half teaspoon pepper, one teaspoon chopped onion, one teaspoon chopped celery, one teaspoon summer savory (herb), half teaspoon thyme, two eggs, one cup fresh sweet milk. Pour the milk on the crumbs, and cover tightly for an hour; then add the rest of the ingredients, omitting onion if objectionable. Stuff the turkey.

Cranberry Sauce:

One quart cranberries, one pint water, one pint powdered loaf sugar. Pick over and wash the berries. Place in a stew pan with the water and sugar, and cook slowly for twenty minutes. Rinse a mold with cold water, pour in the stewed berries and set them away to cool. When wanted for serving time, turn out upon a flat dish, cut off a thick slice and send to the table.

Roast Turkey With Chestnut Stuffing

Draw and clean the turkey as previously described. Shell and blanch fifty large chestnuts and boil them a half hour in water enough to cover. Drain off the water, and add to the nuts three tablespoons butter, one tablespoon salt (scant), and half a teaspoon of pepper. Mix well and place them in the turkey. Truss and roast the fowl as directed in the preceding recipe. When done serve with:

Chestnut Sauce:

Thirty large chestnuts, one pint water, one teaspoon salt, one-fourth teaspoon pepper, one tablespoon sweet butter, one tablespoon of flour. Shell and blanch the chestnuts, boil until tender, drain thoroughly and mash them smooth with a potato masher. Add the water a little at a time, rub the mixture through a fine sieve and cook gently in a saucepan for half an hour. Place the butter in a frying pan and, when hot, add the flour. Cook until the flour is a dark brown, stirring constantly, then add the chestnut mixture. Cook for three or four minutes, then serve hot in a gravy boat.

Roast Duck

Pick, singe, remove crop, entrails, oil bag, legs and pinions from duck. Wipe, truss, dredge with salt, pepper, butter and flour. Stuff with apple, prune, onion or celery stuffing. Ducks and geese have a strong flavor and are improved considerably by stuffing the body and craw with apples, cored and quartered. The apples absorb the strong flavor and should later be discarded. Lay in a small roasting pan with an herb bonquet, some sliced onion rings, a stalk of celery with some leaves on it, and two or three cloves for aroma. Lay bacon strips across the breast if butter is not used. Start roasting in a hot stove, add a half cup orange juice or hot cider to the pan. Baste often, add more orange juice, warm cider or, if desired, wine. Skim off fat. Roast until tender, skim off fat from pan gravy, strain and thicken gravy. Prick duck with the sharp tines of a fork to release fat while roasting. Serve with dried fruit compote or plump, golden apple fritters.

Roast Goose

Stuff cleaned goose with a sage, onion, chestnut stuffing, or fill goose with small, juicy, whole apples and plump prunes. Since the meat of the goose is dry, it needs a moist stuffing. The stove should be hot. Baste often with hot wine or apple cider, every ten minutes to prevent the meat from drying. Place a small piece of ginger root in the roasting pan to add a spicy aroma to the goose. Roast in a pan to fit the goose closely, skim the fat often and save for other use. The goose liver is rich and is nice for *pate de foie gras,* or slice and saute a few minutes on each side with onion rings: makes an excellent onion dish.

(A nice in between snack, which we tasted in a number of country kitchens, was toasted rye bread dipped into hot goose fat and then salted liberally. Mid-morning, or mid-afternoon such a snack has the same effect as a cup of hot bouillon: arousing the taste buds and stimulating the appetite!)

FISH AND SEAFOOD

A Note About Fish

"Fish is a delicious adjunct to any dinner table. However, it requires nice and careful cooking; for if it is not perfectly fresh, perfectly cleaned and thoroughly cooked, it is not fit to appear on the table. Salmon is the richest of fish, being even richer than meat. The way fish is cooked depends largely on what kind of fish it is. Only ones, such as salmon and mackerel are best broiled or baked. White fish such as halibut, cod or haddock, are more dry and may be fried or sauteed. If cooked in water or milk they are best served with rich sauces, and if baked, they must be basted frequently with melted butter.

"The use of fish has in its favor its generally admitted wholesomeness. Much stress has been laid upon its great value as brain food, on account of its phosphorus. Were this argument sound, those who subsist almost entirely on fish ought to be persons of marked intellectuality, which is far from being the case."

—An Early 19th Century Cookbook

Fillet of Flounder With Green Peas

Dress and cut three flounders into a dozen fillets; dip the fillets in melted butter; sprinkle with salt, pepper, lemon juice and a pinch of rosemary. Fold each fillet around a bit of pared potato (this will keep the fish in desired shape). Arrange in a baking dish, half cover with hot fish stock, made of the trimmings. Cook in the stove for ten minutes. Dress the fillets, one overlapping another in a circle, with green peas, seasoned with salt, pepper and butter, in the center of the circle. Sift a cooked egg yolk, mashed fine, between the fillets. Thicken the stock with a little flour and butter for the sauce. Remove the potatoes before serving.

To Cook Frogs Legs

The hind legs of frogs are the only part used for food. They are stripped of the skin carefully to avoid tearing the tender flesh. Wash the legs in cold water and dry them well on a napkin or towel. Season with salt, pepper and lemon juice. For six legs, thoroughly beat up one egg and season it with salt and pepper; dip the legs in the egg, then in dried bread crumbs, plunge them into boiling fat, and fry for five minutes. They can be sauteed in a frying pan, but are not so nice as when cooked with plenty of fat. Frogs legs are delicious served for breakfast or luncheon with tartar sauce.

Another way: Simmer the frogs legs with fresh herbs and season well. Serve with Hollandaise sauce, or thicken the liquor it was cooked in with egg yolks. Or boil and serve with seasoned tomato sauce.

Baked Halibut

Select a solid piece of halibut weighing about three pounds; let stand in a marinade of equal parts of oil, lemon juice, salt, a dash of paprika, a little onion juice and one-half cup wine, for an hour. Drain well. Brush over with sweet butter; bake about forty minutes, until the flesh separates readily from the bone, basting every ten minutes with a mixture of butter and white wine. Remove skin, after sliding the fish onto a warm serving dish. Serve with any of the sauces for baked fish. The addition of a few fresh green herbs from the garden adds a little more pep to the fish while baking. There is a choice of fragrant herbs such as basil, dill, marjoram, tarragon, and rosemary; all fish are greatly improved by it.

Baked Salt Mackerel

Wash a salt mackerel well and soak it overnight in three quarts cold water, laying it with the skin side upward. In the morning lay the fish on its back in a shallow baking tin (not too large) and pour over it a pint of sweet milk. Bake twenty minutes in a hot stove, stirring into the milk, at the end of fifteen minutes, a tablespoon of flour and butter, and a sprinkling of pepper, all rubbed together into a smooth paste. Serve with the thickened milk poured around the fish. This makes a very palatable Sunday breakfast dish.

Broiled Mackerel With Green Butter

Cut off the fins, split, dress and, if convenient, remove the backbone; broil in the usual manner; dish on a hot platter, or on a platform of mashed potatoes shaped exactly to the fish. Spread over the fish a partly melted butter and minced parsley sauce, or green butter. (Mince parsley and cress very fine and combine with soft fresh sweet butter). Garnish with sliced lemon and sliced cucumbers. Excellent luncheon dish.

Fried Perch

Clean, wash and dry fish. Lay them in a large flat dish, salt and dredge with flour. Have ready a frying pan of hot dripping lard or butter. Put in as many fish as the pan will hold without crowding and fry a light brown. Send up hot in a chafing dish. Lay the head of each fish to the tail of the one next to it.

Fried Smelts

Clean, wash and dry smelts. Roll in seasoned flour. Beat one egg slightly, add two tablespoons water. Dip floured smelts in egg, then in seasoned fine bread crumbs. Fry in deep hot fat until a golden brown. Drain on a white blotter or paper. Serve with tartare sauce and lemon.

To Boil Salmon

A salmon weighing seven or eight pounds will require an hour to cook. Wash the fish well; lay it on a trivet in a fish kettle, with plenty of cold water and a tablespoon of salt; simmer gently to keep it from breaking; when done, lift out carefully on the trivet and set it to drain; then slip it off onto a hot platter or fish dish and make an egg sauce. Pour on or coat salmon with the sauce, serve remainder in a boat. Recommended served cold for luncheon or tea. Garnish with thin lemon slices, crisp cress and parsley. For a more flavorful and delicate tasting salmon make a court bouillon using the following recipe:

Court Bouillon for Boiling or Poaching Salmon:

Liquid enough to cover fish. One sliced onion, one small clove garlic, one sliced carrot, half stalk celery sliced, six to ten peppercorns, salt, bouquet of herbs (bay leaf, parsley, thyme and rosemary tied in a little thin muslin bag). A fish head and bones for the bouillon adds a more delicate flavor. Add one small cup white wine or the juice of a small lemon to the cold water. Bring all ingredients to boil and simmer for one-half hour, strain through a cloth or fine sieve. Return to fish kettle and boil again. Wrap fish in a cloth or lay on a trivet or rack, simmer until done. If the fish is served hot, make a rich sauce from the reduced liquid with lemon juice, plenty of fresh sweet butter, minced herbs and egg yolk for thickening. A good, strong court bouillon, made with several heads and bones and boiled down, will jelly when chilled. It forms a natural aspic and is grand on a hot day with fillets of fish imbedded in it, with a garnish of pickled, sliced cucumbers and greens surrounding it.

Baked Salmon Trout

Having cleaned the trout, wash in weak salted water, dry it in a cloth and rub inside and out with a seasoning of cayenne pepper, powdered mace, nutmeg and a little salt mixed well together. Then lay it in a deep baking pan, turn the tail around into the mouth, and stick bits of fresh butter thickly over the fish. Put it into the stove and bake it well, basting it with the liquid that will soon surround it. When you suppose it to be done, try it by sticking down to the backbone a thin bladed knife. When you find that the flesh separates immediately from the bone, it is done sufficiently. Serve it up with lobster sauce.

Broiled Shad Roe

Let the delicate shad roe stand in marinade for an hour. Broil very slowly about ten minutes, basting several times with melted butter. Serve with melted butter and minced parsley sauce. Garnish with lemon quarters.

Trout Broiled on Sticks

Sharpen and trim hardwood sticks, push through the cleaned trout, push one end of the stick upright into the ground. Surround with the hot embers, broil until crisp and brown. If desired, rub the trout with a little butter. Season and serve with lemon wedges.

Brook Trout

Clean the trout, wash quickly and wipe them dry. Dip them in beaten egg yolk; roll them in cracker dust seasoned with salt and pepper. Have ready a pan with hot lard, butter or drippings, and fry them brown on both sides.

Lake Trout

This fish may be boiled or broiled. To boil a lake trout, lay the cleaned fish in a fish kettle with boiling water to cover it; add salt and a wine glass of vinegar: a fish of four or five pounds will require twenty minutes. Serve with egg sauce, or drawn butter with chopped parsley. The remains of a boiled trout may be seasoned with cayenne pepper, covered with vinegar and a little sugar and, after standing in a cold place for a few hours, served cold. It is a nice relish for tea.

Salt Fish Souffle

Two cups finely chopped cooked salt fish, two cups mashed potatoes, three-fourth cup of milk or cream, four eggs, salt, pepper and two large tablespoons of sweet butter. Mix mashed potatoes and fish thoroughly, add butter, seasoning and hot milk or cream. Have two eggs well beaten, stir into the mixture, and heap this into a buttered baking dish. Place in a hot stove for ten minutes. Beat the whites of two remaining eggs into a stiff froth, add salt, then the beaten yolks. Spread this over the fish mixture. Return to the stove and brown nicely.

Baked Mashed Potatoes and Fish Casserole

Two cups flaked cooked fish, one cup egg sauce (see fish sauce recipes, p. 149), one quart fluffy mashed potatoes, one tablespoon butter, salt and pepper to taste. Place one-half of the fluffy mashed potatoes on the bottom of a buttered baking dish; season the fish with salt and pepper, mix with a little sweet cream, and lay it upon the potatoes. Add the sauce to the top of the fish and spread the other half of the mashed potatoes on top. Cover with a thin layer of butter and bake for twenty minutes in a hot stove until the top browns nicely. The sauce is very simple to make.

Cod Fish Balls

One quart raw sliced potatoes, one large cup of salted fish, one egg, two tablespoons of sweet cream, salt and pepper to taste. Pick all the bones from the fish, shredding the latter finely, and slowly boil the fish and potatoes together in plenty of water, until the potatoes are soft. Mash both together and beat until fine and light. Then add the seasoning, butter and milk, and the egg well beaten, mixing all thoroughly with a spoon. Have plenty of very hot fat in the frying pan and into it drop the mixture, a tablespoonful at a time. Do not use hands to form balls, as is sometimes done, and do not flour the cakes. Made this way they will be found to be very delicate and light; in fact, cooks who have tried this method will never return to the old way of making it.

Fried Eels

Skin the eels, cut them into four-inch-lengths, and season with salt and pepper. Roll them in salted corn meal and fry brown on both sides in butter.

Cocktail of Little Neck Clams in Tomato Cups

Peel and scoop out the centers of small round tomatoes; chill thoroughly on ice together with a half dozen little neck clams for each tomato. Mix one tablespoon of lemon juice, one tablespoon of mushroom catsup, five or six drops of Tabasco sauce, a dash of paprika, and one-fourth teaspoon salt, and pour one-and-a-half tablespoons of the mixture over the clams in each tomato.

Clam Pie

Take a sufficient number of clams to fill a large pie dish when opened. Make a nice paste in the proportion of a pound of fresh butter to two quarts of flour. Paste for shellfish, meat or chicken pies should be rolled out double the thickness of that intended for fruit pies. Line the bottom and sides of your pie dish with paste. Then cover the bottom with a thin beefsteak divested of the bone and fat. Put in the clams and season with mace, nutmeg, and a few whole peppercorns. No salt. Add a spoonful of butter rolled in flour, and some hard boiled yolks of eggs crumbled fine. Then put in enough of the clam liquor to make sufficient gravy. Put on the lid of the pie, (which like the bottom crust should be rolled out thick), notch it handsomely and bake it well. It should be eaten warm.

Soft Shell Crabs
(1880)

Lift the shell at both sides and remove the spongy substance found on the back. Then pull off the 'apron', which will be found on the under side and to which is attached a substance like that removed from the back. Now wipe the crabs and dip them in beaten egg and then in fine bread crumbs. Fry in boiling fat from eight to ten minutes, the time depending on the size of the crabs. Serve with tartare sauce. Or, the egg and bread crumbs may be omitted. Season with cayenne and fry as before. When crabs are cleaned and seasoned with salt and cayenne, they are then dropped into boiling water for one minute, taken up, and broiled over a hot fire for eight minutes. They are served with maitre d'hotel butter or tartare suace. (See pp. 150, 152).

Broiled Lobster

Split the meat of the tail and claws and season well with salt and pepper. Cover with soft butter and dredge with flour. Place in the broiler and cook over a bright fire until a delicate brown. Arrange on a hot dish, pour a butter sauce around it and serve at once.

Stewed Lobster

The meat of a two-and-a-half pound lobster, cut into dice; two tablespoons of butter, two of flour, one pint of stock or water, a speck of cayenne, salt and pepper to taste. Let the butter get hot and add the dry flour. Stir until perfectly smooth, then add the water gradually, stirring all the while. Season to taste. Add lobster; heat thoroughly and serve.

Fried Oysters

Use for frying the largest and best oysters you can find. Take them carefully from the liquor, lay them in rows upon a clean cloth, and press another one on top to absorb the moisture. Have ready some crackers crushed fine. In the frying pan, heat enough nice butter to cover the oysters entirely. Dip each oyster into the cracker, rolling them completely. Drop them carefully into the frying pan and fry quickly to a light brown. If the butter is hot enough they will soon be ready to take out. Test by putting one oyster in before you risk the rest. Do not let them lie in the pan an instant after they are done. Serve dry and let the dish be warm.

Roasted Oysters on Toast

Eighteen large oysters, or thirty small ones, one teaspoon of flour, one tablespoon of butter, salt, pepper, three slices of toast. Have the toast buttered and on a hot dish. Put the butter in a small saucepan and, when hot, add the dry flour. Stir till smooth, but not brown; then add the cream, and let boil up once. Put the oysters (in their own liquor) into a hot oven for three minutes; then add them to the cream. Season, and pour them over the toast. Garnish the dish with thin slices of lemon and serve very hot. Nice for lunch or tea.

Stewed Oysters

Drain the liquor from two quarts of firm and plump oysters, mix with a small teacupful of hot water, add a little salt and pepper, and set over the fire in a saucepan. Let it boil up once, put in the oysters, let them boil for five minutes, or less, not more. When they 'ruffle' add two tablespoons of butter. The instant the butter is melted and well stirred in, put in a large cup of boiling milk and take the saucepan off the fire. Serve with oyster or cream crackers, as soon as possible. Oysters become tough and tasteless when cooked too much, or let to stand too long after they are withdrawn from the fire.

To Pickle Oysters

Two hundred large oysters, half a pint of good vinegar, half a pint white wine, four teaspoons of salt, six teaspoons of whole black peppercorns and a little mace. Strain the liquor and add the above ingredients. Let boil up once and pour off the liquor, which, as well as the oysters, should then be allowed to get cold. Put into a jar and cover tight. The oysters will keep for some time.

Sauces For Fish:

Basic White Sauce

One quart milk, four tablespoons fresh sweet butter, four tablespoons flour, a small slice onion, two sprigs of parsley, salt and pepper to taste. Put the milk, onion and parsley on in the double boiler. Mix the butter and flour together until smooth and light. When the milk boils, stir four tablespoons of it into the butter and flour; when well mixed and creamy, stir it into the boiling milk. Cook eight minutes, stirring constantly. Strain and serve.

Allemande Sauce

One pint white sauce, the yolk of six eggs, the juice of half a lemon, one tablespoon mushroom catsup, one of butter, half a cupful of cream, salt and pepper, and a grating of nutmeg. Let the sauce come to a boil. Place the saucepan in another of boiling water, and add the seasoning except the lemon. (Keep the water hot, but not boiling). Beat the yolks of the eggs and the cream together and add to the sauce. Stir three minutes. Take off, add the lemon juice and strain.

Cream Bechamel Sauce

One pint of white sauce, one pint of rich cream, salt and pepper. Let the sauce and cream come to a boil separately, then mix them together, and boil up once. Strain and serve hot.

Beurre Noir

Two tablespoons of sweet butter, one of vinegar, one of chopped parsley, one teaspoon lemon juice, half teaspoon of salt, one-quarter teaspoon of pepper. Put the butter in the frying pan and when very hot, add the parsley, and then the other ingredients. Boil up once. This sauce is for fried and boiled fish, and it is poured over the fish before sending to the table.

Maitre D'Hotel Butter Sauce

Four tablespoons butter, one tablespoon vinegar, one tablespoon lemon juice, half teaspoon salt, one-quarter teaspoon pepper, one teaspoon chopped fresh parsley. Beat the butter to a cream, and gradually beat in the seasoning. This sauce is spread on fried or broiled fish instead of butter.

Celery Sauce

Cut the tender parts of a head of celery *very fine*. Pour on water enough to cover them, and no more.

Cover the saucepan and set where it can simmer for one hour. Mix together two tablespoons of flour and four tablespoons of butter. When the celery has been boiling for one hour, add to it the butter and flour and one pint of milk or cream, salt and pepper to taste. Boil up once and serve hot in a boat.

Hollandaise Sauce

This is one of the best sauces for fish. Take one-half cup of fresh sweet butter, one-half cup of boiling water, juice of one-half lemon, one-quarter teaspoon pepper and one teaspoon salt, yolks of three eggs. Beat the butter to a cream with a silver spoon; add the yolks of the eggs, one at a time, and beat well; then add the lemon juice, salt and pepper. About five minutes before serving, add the boiling water, a little at a time, drop by drop, stirring well. Place the bowl in a saucepan of hot water and stir rapidly until the sauce thickens like boiled custard. Serve at once. (In all sauces make sure that the flour and butter has cooked well together before adding the liquid. The butter should be very hot before the flour is added to it. Be certain that the creamed butter and flour has cooled before adding the liquid to the thickening.)

Mustard Cream Sauce

This is excellent served with baked crabs or roast clams and is a dainty addition to fish. Use one cup fresh sweet milk, one teaspoon mustard, three table- spoons butter, one tablespoon flour, salt and pepper to taste. Heat the milk in a double boiler. Beat the butter, flour and mustard to a cream, and gradually pour upon the cream the boiling hot milk, a little at a time. When well mixed, return all to the boiler, add the salt and pepper, boil three minutes, and serve hot.

Oyster Sauce for Boiled Fish

One pint fresh small oysters, one-third cup sweet butter, three tablespoons flour, one cup of milk, salt and pepper to taste. Heat the oysters in their own liquor to the boiling point. Remove them from the fire after they have boiled up half a minute, skim them, drain off the liquor into another stew pan. Rub the butter and flour to a cream. Add the milk to the oyster liquor and, when heated to boiling point, stir in the creamed flour and butter. Let the liquid boil up once, season with salt and pepper. Add the oysters and serve as soon as the latter are heated.

Supreme Sauce

Add to one pint of white sauce three finely chopped mushrooms (firm white ones), the juice of half a lemon, and one tablespoon butter. Simmer all together for ten minutes. Rub through a fine strainer.

Tartare Sauce

The yolks of two uncooked eggs, half cup of oil, three tablespoons vinegar, one tablespoon mustard, one teaspoon sugar, one-quarter teaspoon pepper, one teaspoon salt, one teaspoon onion juice, one tablespoon chopped capers, one tablespoon chopped cucumber pickles. Make the same as mayonnaise dressing. Add the chopped ingredients the last thing. An excellent sauce to be used with fried and boiled fish.

VEGETABLES AND SALADS

Vegetable Hints

NEW POTATOES are best baked.

OLD POTATOES are improved considerably by being soaked in cold water several hours before peeling, change water.

FULL GROWN POTATOES may either be boiled or baked.

ONIONS should be soaked in warm water for one hour before cooking to remove rank flavor.

HORSERADISH TOPS are considered choice greens.

PEAS should not be shelled until just before time for cooking.

A little sugar added to TURNIPS, BEETS, PEAS, CORN, SQUASH and PUMPKIN is an improvement, especially if the vegetables are of poor quality.

A piece of RED PEPPER size of a fingernail, dropped into meat or vegetables, will aid in killing unpleasant odors.

Small size WHITE TURNIPS contain more nutrition than large ones.

Wash LETTUCE and SALAD GREENS, leaf by leaf, in warm water first, then place in cold water at once. They will be crisp and firm.

Garden Greens

The leaves and stalks of young beets, milkweed, dandelion, and narrow dock are useful as food in the early spring, chiefly for the water and alkaline salts which they contain. They should be picked over and washed carefully, cooked in boiling salted water until tender, then drained and seasoned with salt and fresh melted butter. Vinegar is often used with them as a desirable condiment. Dandelions should be cooked in plenty of water, but other tender greens may be cooked, like spinach, in their own juices.

Stewed Asparagus

Break the stalks into one inch lengths, placing the tough ends that are not fit to serve on a plate by themselves; and wash all well. Tie the tough pieces in a piece of cheesecloth and lay them with the tender asparagus in a kettle; and stew slowly until the asparagus are tender, usually thirty minutes; the water should be diminished by this time to a quantity to keep the asparagus from burning. Remove the cheesecloth and throw away its contents. Season remaining asparagus with butter, salt and pepper, and serve at once. The tough stalks, which are usually thrown away, will be found to impart considerable sweetness to the juices in the kettle, and by tying them in a cloth, they may be readily removed when no longer required.

Creamed Asparagus

Cook as directed for stewed asparagus (see above) —boiling water down until not more than a cupful remains. To this add one cup of cream or rich milk, thicken with a tablespoon of flour, rubbed to a paste with a little cold milk. Add butter, salt and pepper, and serve at once. If desired, serve on thick slices of buttered toast; thicken sauce a little with an extra teaspoon of flour.

Asparagus Patties

Make a sauce of three tablespoons each of butter and flour, and a half cup each of chicken broth, cream and the water in which a bunch of asparagus has been boiled. Add the beaten yolks of two eggs, a teaspoon of lemon juice, salt and pepper, and a bunch of hot asparagus, cut into small pieces and cook until tender. Serve in hot puff-paste shells.

To make paste shells: One half cup sweet butter, one cup boiling water, one cup sifted flour, and three large eggs. Set saucepan containing butter and water over the fire; when the mixture boils sift in one cup flour and beat vigorously. When the mixture shrinks from the side of the pan, remove from heat and beat in the eggs, one at a time until thoroughly blended. Drop from a tablespoon onto a buttered baking sheet about two inches in diameter, placing them about two inches apart. Bake thirty minutes in a quick oven (375° to 400° F.) until golden brown.

Lima Beans

If the green beans are fresh picked, put one pint of them into just enough boiling water to cover, and cook slowly until tender. Drain off water and add one cup of milk or cream, a small piece of sweet butter, and salt and pepper to taste. Let the beans simmer a moment in the milk or cream, and serve. If dried lima beans are used, soak twelve hours in plenty of cold water; and when boiled, half a teaspoon of soda should be added to the water.

String Beans in Milk

Break off a little from each end of the pod to remove strings from fresh garden string beans. Break pods into one inch lengths and place in a kettle of boiling salted water; cook until tender. Drain off water, add milk to nearly cover them, and heat slowly. When hot, stir into the milk a little flour, made into a paste with a small quantity of cold milk, using enough flour to make the milk creamy. Boil two minutes, stirring all the time; add a lump of fresh sweet butter, salt and pepper to taste. Serve hot.

Boiled Beets

Select small, young beets. Wash them, being careful not to break the skins. Leave, on the end of the root, about one inch of the top. Cook them in boiling water without salt, until they are tender. When they are done, put them in cold water and rub off the skins. Slice the beets, dress them with vinegar, or season with butter, salt and pepper.

Boston Baked Beans
(1890)

This recipe has been successfully used for many years and does not require hours of long baking, the work is easily and quickly done:

Do not soak the beans overnight. Place a quart of pea beans over the fire, cover them with cold water, and slowly bring the water to a boil. Then set the kettle where the beans will just bubble, but will at no time boil hard. When they have cooked this way for fifteen minutes, add a four-inch-square of salt pork to the kettle and simmer gently with the beans until they may be pierced with a pin, but are not at all broken. Then turn the beans into a colander to drain. Place together in a coffee cup two large heaping tablespoons of molasses, a teaspoon of salt and pepper to taste, and fill the cup with some hot water in which the beans were boiled. Place the beans in the bean pot, which should be of earthenware with a narrow mouth and bulging sides, turn over them the cupful of seasoning and stir until thoroughly mixed. Cut the rind of the pork in small squares, sink the meat in the beans, leaving only the rind exposed. Add more bean water, until the rind is covered, and bake two hours, raising the pork during the last three-quarters of an hour, to brown and crisp the beans on top.

(Excellent baked beans have been prepared this way for many, many years, by many country housewives. This is a very fine recipe and does not require more than two hours of baking. Bake longer, until bubbly, if desired, but start early enough before supper.)

Cabbage in Milk

Chop fresh cabbage fine, having soaked it for one hour before chopping. Cook until tender in plenty of salted water, usually forty-five minutes if the boiling is slow. Drain well, cover with milk and, when hot, thicken to a cream with a little flour, rubbed smooth to a paste with a spoonful of butter. Boil one minute, stirring well, and add salt and pepper. Serve hot. This is the most delicious way of cooking cabbage.

Cabbage Hot Slaw

Chop the cabbage fine, after soaking it one hour in cold water, and place it in a kettle with a cupful of vinegar. Cover the kettle and set it where the cabbage will slowly stew for two hours, stirring often, adding a little more vinegar as that in the kettle evaporates, but only keeping the moisture in the kettle to keep the cabbage from burning. Should the vinegar be very strong, weaken it with a little water. When the cabbage is tender, add a little butter, salt and pepper, and serve hot. The slaw, when cooked, should be a delicate pinkish shade. It requires constant attention while cooking.

Boiled Carrots

Wash and scrape tender, young carrots; if small, boil whole; if not, cut into half-inch slices. Add salt to freshly boiling water and cook slices until soft. Add a pinch of sugar for added sweetness. Drain and serve them in a white sauce, or seasoned with butter, salt and pepper. If desired, mash the carrots smooth, add a lump of sweet butter, salt, pepper, and a tablespoon of heavy sweet cream. Pile hot on a dish, press down the center with a large spoon, filling cavity with melted sweet butter.

Baked Cauliflower

Boil the vegetable tender in salted water, drain well, remove from kettle, tear clusters of flowers from the stems. Place a layer of these clusters in a baking dish. Have ready a sauce made of two tablespoons butter, one tablespoon flour, one pint sweet milk, salt and pepper to taste. Heat the butter, add the flour, and when the mixture froths and is smooth, add the milk and seasoning. Moisten the layer of cauliflower in the baking dish with a few spoonsful of sauce, and sprinkle over it some grated cheese. Then arrange another layer of cauliflower and the rest of the sauce. Sprinkle thickly with grated cheese and bread crumbs. Bake twenty minutes and serve in the same dish.

Stewed Celery

Wash and scrape the stalks, and cut them into one-inch pieces; soak an hour in cold water. Drain and place celery in a stew pan, with boiling water to cover; let it simmer slowly for one-half hour, by which time the water should be reduced as to measure not quite a cupful. Add a cup of cream or milk and, when the liquid boils, thicken it to a cream with a little flour rubbed smooth in a tablespoon of butter. Add the salt and pepper to taste.

Corn

The time needed to cook corn varies with its age and freshness. Tender, fresh picked corn should cook in fifteen minutes, merely simmering for that length of time; but old corn often requires half an hour. Corn may be boiled either with or without the husk. If without the husk, strip off all of the outer covering, and remove every particle of the silk. If the husk is left on, strip off the outer leaves, pick off all the silk, and recover the ears with the leaves turned back, tying it at the top with a bit of thread. Place the corn in a large stew pan and cover with boiling water, but do not add salt as this would harden the corn. When done, remove from fire; spread a napkin on a flat dish and lay the corn upon it, drawing ends of the napkin up so as to cover the corn; serve at once. When boiled in the husk, drain the corn well before serving and break each cob from the stem. Send to the table in the napkin, but do not remove the husks.

How to Eat Corn

"Score every row of kernels with a sharp knife; then butter the corn lightly, dust it with salt, and with the teeth press out the center of the grains, leaving the hulls on the cob. It is usually considered *inelegant* to eat corn from the cob, but this method is the least troublesome."

—An Old Cookbook

Stewed Cucumbers

Pare and quarter the cucumbers and remove the seeds. Place a tablespoon of butter in a frying pan, add a small onion cut into slices, and fry brown; then put in the cucumbers and fry them until a light brown. Remove from pan and add to the gravy a tablespoon of flour, mixing it smooth. Pour half a pint of stock or water, stirring continually, and add salt and pepper to taste. Now return the cucumbers to the pan and stew gently for twenty minutes. Serve on toasted white bread.

Dandelions

These are not fit to eat after they blossom, as they then become bitter and stringy. Cut off the roots. Pick the greens over carefully, cover with boiling water, salted, and boil slowly for one hour. When done, lift them into a colander, press them to drain out all the water, and chop coarsely. Then add a tablespoon of butter, salt and pepper to taste, and serve. They are eaten with a little vinegar sprinkled on each dishful.

Stuffed Egg Plant

Cut the plant in two parts lengthwise and scoop out the meat, leaving the rind about half an inch thick, that the shape may be firm. Chop the pulp fine, season it with salt and pepper and a tablespoon of butter, and cook in a frying pan for ten minutes, stirring well; then add a scanty half cup of water and a cup of bread crumbs. Sprinkle the interior of the shells with salt and pepper, and fill them with the mixture. Spread a cupful of crumbs on the surface of the mixture, place the two pieces of plant in a baking dish or deep pan, and pour enough hot water into the pan to come half-way up the sides of the plant. Bake an hour and serve hot on a napkin. The egg plant will be found very delicate and it may be served either as a vegetable or an entrée.

Kale

This is cooked and served the same as spinach; or it may be tied in a bundle, boiled like asparagus and served on toast with a generous allowance of butter. It may also be boiled in a bundle and drained well, after which milk will be added and thickened to a cream with a little flour, the whole being seasoned with butter, salt and pepper.

Baked Mushrooms

Choose the large, firm, white mushrooms, but if the round, button mushrooms are obtainable, they are much to be desired. Peel them, cut off the stalks close to the top, and do not wash them unless they are soiled. Place them upside down on a pie dish, sprinkle with salt and pepper, and put a tiny bit of butter in each upturned cup. Bake fifteen minutes in a quick stove, basting twice with a little melted butter. Serve hot, pouring over them whatever juice may be on the dish.

Simple Stew of Mushrooms

Clean a pint of firm white mushrooms, cut them in rather small pieces, and put them in a stewpan with a tablespoon of butter and a little salt and pepper. Let them simmer ten minutes and serve. Wild mushrooms are delicious cooked in this way.

Okra

Boil the young pods, in enough salted water to cover, until tender. Drain thoroughly and, when dished pour over them a sauce of three or four tablespoonsful melted butter, a tablespoon vinegar, salt and pepper to taste. Heat to boiling before covering the okras with it.

Okra Saute

Chop a peeled onion, a clove of garlic, and half a red or green sweet pepper pod, and saute in a little sweet butter without browning. Add six or eight fresh ripe tomatoes, peeled and quartered; let simmer one-half hour, then add a dozen boiled okra pods. Cover the pan and simmer until the mixture thickens. Season with salt, pepper, a little sugar and lemon juice. Serve on thick slices of buttered toast.

Baked Onions

The large Spanish onions are far milder and more delicate than the usual winter varieties. Wash the onions clean, trim the bottoms, *but do not peel,* and boil for an hour in slightly salted, boiling water. If the onions are desired very mild, change the water twice during the time, replenishing with more hot water. Having drained them well, take each onion separately, wrap it with a square of buttered paper, twisting the paper at the top to keep it closed. Place the onions in a baking pan and bake an hour in a slow oven. When done, remove the papers carefully, peel onions and place them in a serving dish. Pour melted butter over them and dust with salt and pepper.

Creamed Onions

Peel the onions and boil for one hour in salted water. Drain well and cut each onion in four parts, over which pour a cream sauce made of two tablespoons butter, one tablespoon flour, one pint fresh sweet milk, salt and pepper to taste. Rub the butter and flour to a cream; heat the milk, and when it boils, add the butter and flour. Stir the sauce until a creamy consistency, and flavor with salt and pepper.

Fried Parsnips

Scrape the parsnips and boil them gently until tender, usually an hour. Drain. When cold, cut them into long, thin slices. Season each slice with salt and pepper; dip the slices in melted butter and then in flour; and fry in hot lard or butter until both sides are browned. Drain well and serve hot.

Parsnip Fritters

Three large, tender, young parsnips, three tablespoons flour, one tablespoon melted butter, two eggs, one cup sweet milk, one teaspoon salt. Boil the parsnips until tender, grate fine or mash them smooth, pick out the fibrous parts. Beat the eggs light and stir them into the parsnips, beating hard until the whole is well mixed. Then add the butter and then the milk, salt and flour. Mix well. Fry like doughnuts or on a hot griddle.

Green Peas

Peas are fresh when the pods are green, crisp and plump. The fresh pods are sweet and full of flavor. Wash the pods before shelling, then the peas will require no washing. Put the peas into a colander and sift out the fine particles. Boil the pods ten minutes, skim them out and add the peas. Boil fifteen minutes, or till tender. When nearly done, add the salt. Let the water boil nearly away, and serve without draining, except when the peas are to be served as a garnish. Season with butter, cream, salt and a little sugar. Old peas should be cooked until tender, drained, mashed, and rubbed through a sieve, and served as a vegetable or made into a purée.

Poke Stalks

When the young stalks are not larger than a man's little finger and show only a tuft of leaves at the top, a few inches above the ground, is the time to gather them. They are unfit for table use if they are larger and older. Scrape the stalks but do not cut off the leaves. Lay in cold water, with a little salt, for two hours. Tie in bundles, as you do asparagus, put into a saucepan of boiling water and cook fast for three-quarters of an hour. Lay buttered toast in the bottom of a dish, until the bundles are ready, and pile the poke evenly upon it, buttering well and sprinkling with salt and pepper. This is a tolerable substitute for asparagus.

Potato Fritters

Five cold, boiled potatoes, five tablespoons sifted flour, two eggs, one-half cup milk, one teaspoon baking powder, salt and pepper to taste. Grate potatoes into a large bowl. Mix the flour, baking powder and salt well together, and add the potatoes, mixing as lightly as possible. Add the milk and the eggs, well beaten. Have ready a kettle containing boiling lard to the depth of three inches. Drop in the mixture by spoonsful, and fry about eight minutes. Drain well and serve. The fat should be so hot that blue smoke rises from the center of the kettle. Serve at once.

Potato Omelet

Nine potatoes of medium size, one-fourth teaspoon pepper, half cup of hot milk, three tablespoons sweet butter, enough salt to taste. Pare and boil the potatoes, mash them fine and light, add salt, pepper, two tablespoons of the butter, and gradually the hot milk, beating all the time. Put the remaining spoonful of butter in a large frying pan and, when hot, turn in the potatoes, spreading them smoothly. Cover the pan and set it where the contents will brown slowly and evenly. When done (ten minutes), fold the potatoes the same as an omelet, turn them out upon a hot dish and serve.

Baked Pumpkin
(1825)

Choose the richest pumpkin you can find; take out the seeds, cut in to quarters or eighths, pare and slice lengthwise half an inch thick. Arrange in layers—

not more than two or three slices deep—in a shallow but broad buttered baking dish. Put in a *very* little water in the bottom, and bake very slowly until not only done, but dry. It requires a long time, for the heat must be gentle. Butter each strip on both sides when you dish, and eat hot with bread and butter for tea. This is a very palatable dish to those who are fond of the flavor of pumpkin.

Stewed Pumpkin

Cut in two, extract the seeds, slice and pare. Cover with cold water for an hour. Put over the fire in a pot of boiling water and stew gently, stirring often, until all breaks in pieces. Drain and squeeze, rub through a colander, then return to the saucepan with a tablespoon sweet butter and salt to taste. Stir rapidly from the bottom until very hot. When dishing, round into a mound, with little 'dabs' of pepper or nutmeg on top.

Radishes

Wash and lay the fresh picked radishes in ice water as soon as they are gathered. Cut off the tops when breakfast or supper is ready, leaving an inch of the stalk on; scrape off the skin if you choose, but the red ones are prettier if you do not; arrange in a tall glass or round glass saucer, the stalks outside, the points meeting at the center. Lay cracked ice around them and send to the table. Good radishes are crisp to the teeth, look cool, and taste hot. Serve little salt dishes on the side, with bread and butter sandwiches cut in fancy shapes.

Some Chitchat on Radishes

"A housewife was entertaining, and engaged a young lady who 'only hired out in the best of families as a professed cook.' She arrived in the afternoon, and was told that tea would be a simple affair: bread and butter, cold meat, cake and a *dish of radishes*, which were brought in from the garden as the order was given. The lady was summoned to the parlor at that moment, and remarked in leaving.

'You can prepare those radishes now Bridget.'

"A while later the hostess peeked into the kitchen attracted by the odor of hot fat. The frying pan hissed on the fire, the contents was a half pound of butter, and the 'professional' stood at the table with a radish topped and tailed in one hand; a knife in the other. " 'I'm glad to see ye, mam,' " thus she greeted the lady of the house. " 'Is it paled or unpaled ye'll have them radishes? Some of the quality likes 'em fried wid the skin on—some widout. I thought I'd wait and ask yerself.' " —A 19th Century Cookbook.

Fried Salsify or Oyster Plant

Boil, scrape off the skins, cut into slices, and fry like parsnips. Salsify fritters are made the same like parsnip fritters.

Spinach

Pick over, trim off roots and tough leaves; wash thoroughly, lifting spinach from one pan of water into another so that the sand may be left in the water and changing water until it is clear. Put the spinach in a large kettle without water. Place it on the stove where it will cook slowly until the juice is drawn out, then boil until tender. Drain and chop fine. Season with a lump of butter, salt and pepper, and a little, thin, white sauce. Heat again and serve on toast dressed with mashed hard boiled eggs.

Fried Squash

Unless the squash is very tender, pare thinly, cutting away little of the outer rind. Cut into slices one-fourth inch thick. Sprinkle each slice with salt and pepper, dip into beaten egg and then in finely crushed cracker crumbs. Fry in hot frying pan until crisp and brown. Drain well and serve hot. They are delicious sprinkled with powdered sugar or syrup, and taste like fritters.

Succotash
(1815)

This may be made by mixing equal quantities of shelled beans and corn, cut fresh from the cob by scoring each row and pressing out the pulp with the back of the knife, leaving the hulls on the cob. When the beans are nearly soft, add the corn, cook fifteen minutes. Add cream, butter, salt and sugar to taste.

Scalloped Tomatoes

Season one quart fresh tomatoes with one teaspoon salt, pepper to taste, a half cup of powdered sugar, and a few drops of onion juice. Butter a deep dish and sprinkle with fine cracker crumbs. Pour in the tomatoes. Moisten one cup of cracker crumbs with a half cup of melted sweet butter. Spread over top and brown in the oven. Raw tomatoes sliced may be used in layers, alternating with the crumbs and seasonings.

Boiled Turnips

Wash and pare the turnips and cut them into one-inch slices; add salt to freshly boiling water and cook slices until they are soft. Drain and mash them smooth, adding butter, salt and pepper. Serve the mashed turnips at once on a hot dish.

Sidney Smith's Winter Salad

"Two large potatoes, passed through a kitchen
  sieve,
Unwonted softness to the salad give;
Of mordant mustard add a single spoon—
Distrust the condiment which bites too soon;
But deem it not, though made of herbs, a fault
To add a double quantity of salt;
Three times the spoon with oil of Lucca crown,
And once with vinegar procured from town.
True flavor needs it, and your poet begs
The pounded yellow of two well boiled eggs.
Let onion atoms lurk within the bowl,
And half suspected, animate the whole;
And lastly, on the favored compound toss
A magic teaspoon of anchovy sauce,
Then, though green turtle fail, though venison's
  tough,
Though ham and turkey are not boiled enough,
Serenely full, the epicure shall say,
'Fate can not harm me—I have dined to-day.'"

—Buckeye Cookery
(1885)

Vegetables used for salads are boiled asparagus;
cabbage, red and white; lettuce; chicory; boiled cauliflower; celery; potatoes; dandelion; watercress; scallions; radishes, red, black and white; red and green
peppers; cucumbers; and a variety of leafy greens.
Prepare carefully by freshening in cold water, clean-
ing them carefully from all foreign matter. Dry carefully in a towel and avoid, as much as possible,
crushing the tender leaves, as it causes them to wilt.
Shred with the fingers instead of with a knife. Cover
with a 'dressing', which consists chiefly of oil, vinegar,
salt, pepper, and mustard mixed in various proportions. All the ingredients of the dressing should be

of the very best. In preparing the dressing, powder the hard boiled eggs, either in a mortar or by mashing with the back of silver spoon, (if raw eggs are used, beat well and strain) add seasoning, then the oil, a few drops at a time, and, lastly and gradually, the vinegar. Always use the freshest olive salad oil, not the common sweet oil; if it cannot be obtained, cream or melted sweet butter is a good substitute and by some considered even more palatable, but when used should be added last of all. When making chicken salad use the oil off the water in which the chickens were boiled. It is much nicer to pick the meat or cut it with a knife instead of chopping, always removing the fat, gristle and skin. Season to taste and garnish with greens, tomatoes and crisp celery. To crisp celery, lettuce, cabbage and all vegetables for use in salads, put in ice water for two hours before serving. Salads should be served the day they are prepared. Vegetable salads should be stirred as little as possible in order that their freshness may be preserved until they are served. Turkey, chicken, fish, and potato salads may be formed in an oval mound, garnish the top with slices of cold boiled eggs and, around the bottom, small sprigs of crisp celery, parsley, tiny red rose radishes, and small tomatoes. Set in a cold place till needed.

(Because an abundance of fresh garden vegetables were served with every meal, salads as a special course did not play an important roll. However, greens were freshly picked and dressed with a 'good' oil dressing or with homemade mayonnaise. Cold slaw, plain, or creamed with eggs, sweet cream, vinegar, herbs, and seasoned highly with black pepper and ground mustard, was served frequently at luncheon or supper. Chicken, turkey, fish and potato salad was company fare, and the country housewife had dozens of 'receipts' for each one.)

DESSERTS AND PUDDINGS

Since dessert was the last part of the meal, it was always, and in areas still is considered of great importance to the daily fare. The country housewife prided herself on the variety of 'receipts' she had for desserts, puddings and 'fancies.' They served not only one dessert but several at each meal; if the meal was good, they crowned it with success, if not, the desserts still overshadowed the meal. In any event, the dessert never failed to send the family, especially the children, away from the table in a happy frame of mind.

Beautiful puddings, floating islands, a snow-drift of beaten egg white, light as air, on a sea of custard and flavored with rose water were great family favorites. The more delicate dainties, topped with soft clouds of whipped cream and perfumed with orange flower water, were reserved for a company 'collation.' Needless to say, the country housewife excelled in 'nice cookery' and her skill, in whipping up tender, puffy souffles, cakes, popovers and pies, was well known throughout the American countryside.

In nineteenth century America there seemed to have been a mania for pies. Though often served at luncheon or tea, in most rural areas pie was the pièce de résistance at every meal and was served even at breakfast. Nothing pleased the menfolks more, especially after coming in hot and tired from haying and harvesting, than a nice slab of fresh fruit pie in season, or any kind of pie, but pie it had to be! A child might refuse lunch, but he always had room for a piece of pie. A toothsome mince pie made with a delicious mixture of homemade mincemeat, laced with wine or brandy was a luscious treat for Thanksgiving and Christmas. Fine golden pumpkin and apple pies were made by the dozen. However, an Indian pudding was also a prime favorite. The golden meal, cooked long and slowly, with rich fresh cream or milk, thick dark molasses and a breath of fragrant spices, topped with homemade vanilla ice cream, was perfection itself. Since corn meal was one of the most important staples in those days, Indian pudding and many corn meal dishes constantly appeared on the table. The following chapter contains a variety of delectable desserts, made in various ways from old nineteenth century 'receipts.'

Note: Refined granulated sugar was not available in the early nineteenth century. Sugar was bought in cone shaped loaves, each loaf weighing about three pounds. The loaf sugar was broken up into pieces, crushed and finely powdered when required for baking and for desserts. Small pieces were broken up and used to sweeten beverages. The countrywoman often claimed that her secret for making cakes light as a cloud was the finely powdered sugar she labored over for hours; crushing and pounding it in a mortar until it was as fine as flour.

An Ambushed Trifle
(1854)

A round, stale spongecake, one pint fresh sweet milk, one teaspoon cornstarch, one cup sweet jelly or jam. Crabapple is very nice. Three eggs beaten very light, a few grains of salt, vanilla or lemon flavoring, two tablespoons powdered sugar. Cut the top from the cake in one piece and lay it aside. Scoop out the inside of the cake, leaving the sidewalls and a bottom about one inch thick. Coat these walls with the jelly. Scald the milk; beat the eggs with the sugar and stir slowly into the milk when it is almost boiling. Crumb the cake which you have scooped out very finely, and beat into the hot custard. Return to the fire and cook stirring all the while until smooth and thick; then add the cornstarch which has previously been wet with a little cold milk. Cook a minute longer and take from the fire. When nearly cold, flavor and fill the cake with it. Cover the inside of the lid which you have set aside with jelly, fit neatly into its place; brush the whole cake with white of egg, sift powdered sugar thickly over it, and set in a cool, dry place until wanted. A simple, delightful dessert.

Apple Flame

Eight apples, two cups of loaf sugar, broken up and powdered, one cup water, raspberry jam, rum or brandy. One cup whipped sweet cream. Pare and core apples; boil sugar and syrup together for ten minutes; arrange apples in a buttered baking dish two inches apart. Add syrup; cover and bake until the apples are tender. Be careful to preserve the shape of the apples. Remove from the dish and boil syrup until thick; fill cavities with jam, pour syrup around them and, just before sending them to the table, pour over them brandy or rum. Light with a match and serve. Top with beaten and flavored sweet cream.

Steamed Blueberry Dumpling

Four cups blueberries, two cups sifted powdered loaf sugar, one teaspoon vinegar, one tablespoon sweet butter, two cups sifted flour, four teaspoons baking powder, one of salt, three-fourth cup fresh milk. Mix flour, baking powder and salt; add butter, mix until mealy; add milk. Put sugar and berries and vinegar in bottom of buttered baking dish. Cover with the flour batter and steam in stove for forty-five minutes. Serve in dish in which it is cooked. Any fresh berries in season may be used in place of the blueberries.

Canary Cream

Put a pint of fresh sweet milk into a saucepan with a little sugar and the grated rind of half a lemon. When boiling, pour it slowly upon the beaten yolks of three eggs, beating vigorously. Return it to the stew pan and stir it over a *slow fire* till the eggs thicken, be very careful that it does not curdle. When cool, stir in a small glass of sherry or brandy to flavor it. Fill tart shells with mixture or serve cold in custard cups.

Tapioca Cream

Soak overnight two tablespoons tapioca in one-half cup milk (enough to cover), bring one quart milk to a boil, beat well together the yolks of three eggs, half a teacup of powdered sugar and one teaspoon lemon or vanilla flavoring, add the tapioca and stir the whole into the boiling milk. Let boil once, turn into the dish and immediately fold in the whipped whites. Let stand in a cool place until cold. Dot with jelly.

Lemon Puff

Ten eggs, yolks mixed thoroughly with the juice of two lemons and the grated rinds, one cup of powdered and sifted loaf sugar, three tablespoons of water. Place in a double boiler, cook until smooth and very thick. Then add the whites, beaten stiff, and stir the whole together lightly. Pile into china cups or parfait glasses. Cool.

Taganrok

Add to two cups of cooked farina or hominy one cup of powdered loaf sugar, pinch salt, one tablespoon sweet butter, one cup washed and dried currants and stoned raisins, mixed, juice and grated rind of one fresh lemon, two tablespoons nice wine, and the stiffly beaten whites of three eggs. Blend gently with a wooden spoon. Pour into a mold lined with strips of angelica. Bake thirty minutes in a moderately hot stove. Serve cold garnished with cherries.

Baked Custard

Four eggs, one quart fresh, sweet milk, one-half teaspoon salt, two-thirds cup of sugar, sifted, grated nutmeg. Beat the eggs, both the yolks and whites together, add them to the milk, stirring it by degrees; then put in the salt. Stir the nutmeg into the sugar so that it will be well distributed, and add this also, beating well. Let the whole stand ten minutes until the sugar is dissolved; then pour the mixture into a pudding dish and bake. Baked custard should never boil, but the heat should be moderate. When a silver knife blade inserted into the custard will come from it clear and not milky, the custard has baked enough. When the nutmeg is mixed with the sugar, it will be found to distribute evenly through the milk, and will not float on top.

Frozen Custard

One quart of rich cream, six egg yolks, one-half pint of powdered and sifted loaf sugar, and one tablespoon vanilla. Put all but a half pint of cream on the fire in a double boiler, add the sugar and stir well. Beat the yolks of eggs until very light, and add to them the half pint of the cold cream; and when the cream in the boiler is boiling, stir the eggs and cream into it *very* slowly. Stir constantly until the mixture thickens, remove from the fire and, when cool, add the vanilla and place on ice; also place cracked ice around the dish until frozen.

Gelatine Custard

Soak half an ounce of gelatine for three or four hours in a pan of cold water. Have ready a quart of milk. Boil half a pint of it, add a bunch of fresh clean peach leaves or a handful of bitter almonds and a stick of cinnamon, broken into pieces. When the milk is highly flavored, strain the milk into a pan that contains the rest. Beat four eggs very light and mix them gradually with the milk, adding, by degrees, the gelatine, (well drained) and four heaping tablespoons of sifted sugar. Set it over a slow fire and boil it gently, stirring constantly. As soon as the gelatine is dissolved and thoroughly mixed, the custard will be done. Transfer to a deep dish or to cups and set on ice, in a cold place, till wanted.

Indian Puffs

Boil a quart of sweet milk and, when it has come to a boil, stir into it, gradually, eight large tablespoons of Indian meal, four large tablespoons of powdered loaf sugar, and grated nutmeg. Stir it hard; let it boil a quarter of an hour after all the Indian meal is in. Then take it up and set it to cool. While cooling, beat eight eggs as light as possible and stir them, gradually, into the batter when it is quite cold. Butter some large teacups; nearly fill them with the mixture; set them in a moderately hot stove and bake them well for about thirty minutes. Send them to the table warm and eat them with butter and molasses; or with fresh sweet butter, powdered sugar and lemon juice stirred to a cream.

Rice Balls with Custard

One cupful of rice, two-and-a-half cups of fresh milk, salt to taste, jelly for decorating. Wash the rice well and soak it in water, to cover, for an hour. Pour off the water, add the milk, cook for an hour in a double boiler; then put in the salt, and cook half an hour longer. Dip small custard cups into cold water, fill them with the cooked rice, and set them where they will become cold. At serving time turn the mounds of rice out onto a flat dish, and after putting a bit of jelly on them pour about them a soft custard sauce.

Soft Custard Sauce: One quart fresh sweet milk, four egg yolks, one-half cup of sifted powdered sugar, one tablespoon cornstarch, one teaspoon vanilla, pinch of salt. Beat the egg yolks light and add to them two tablespoons of the milk mixed with the cornstarch. Place the rest of the milk on the fire in a double boiler and, when it is hot, stir in the mixture of egg and cornstarch. Cook the whole gently for five minutes, stirring well. Then remove the custard from the fire, add the salt and, when cold, flavor with the vanilla. This is a cheap custard but it is much richer with six eggs; then the cornstarch is omitted. The rice may be served hot and the custard sauce cold, if desired. The rice balls may be sweetened with a little powdered sugar and flavored with rose water for a sweeter dessert.

Floating Island

Make a meringue of four egg whites beaten to a stiff froth and four heaping tablespoons of sifted powdered sugar, add one teaspoon vanilla. The meringues may be poached in water or milk; drop from a large spoon when milk is hot enough. Poach gently. When done, place in a large dish of soft custard, with a teaspoon of currant jelly on top of each island.

Syllabub

Two cups fresh sweet cream, two tablespoons lemon juice, one cup sifted sugar, one cup good sherry wine, pinch of cinnamon, grated rind of one fresh lemon. Whip cream, fold in powdered sugar, add other ingredients. Serve in frappé glasses. Garnish with bits of red cherries.

Chocolate Balls

One-third cup sweet butter, one cup sifted powdered sugar, one-half cup milk, two squares grated chocolate, two-and-one-quarter cups sifted flour, three teaspoons baking powder, four egg whites and a pinch of salt. Cream butter, add chocolate and sugar, flour, baking powder and salt. Add milk, beat well, cut and fold in beaten egg whites. Pour into popover cups and steam forty minutes in stove. Serve with chocolate sauce.

Apple Sponge

One-fourth cup sifted sugar, one-fourth cup fresh milk, one cup flour, sifted, two teaspoons baking powder, pinch salt, and five sliced juicy apples. Beat eggs; add sugar, flour, baking powder and salt, and milk. Beat well, add apples, pour into buttered baking dish and bake in a moderately hot stove for one hour. Serve with a soft custard sauce.

Hidden Mountain

Six eggs, a few slices of citron, sugar to taste, three-quarters of a pint of cream, a layer of any kind of good jam. Beat the whites and yolks separately, then mix them and beat again. Add the citron, the cream and sugar. When well beaten, put in a buttered pan and fry. Cover with the jam and garnish with slices of candied citron. To be eaten cold.

Prune Whip

Sweeten to taste and stew three-quarters of a pound of plump prunes; when *perfectly cold,* chop well and add the whites of four eggs, beaten stiff; stir all this together till light; put in a buttered dish and cover with good cream.

Pink Cream

Mix one pint fresh sweet cream with a half pint of raspberry jelly and beat until stiff. Serve in glass dish. Keep cold until needed.

Lemon Butter

Three lemons, a pound-and-a-quarter of powdered and sifted loaf sugar, two ounces of sweet butter, six eggs; beat the butter, sugar and eggs together, then add the juice of the lemons and the rind of one; set the vessel in another of boiling water and stir until it begins to thicken; take it from the fire, stir until cool, and pour into a glass bowl. Set aside to cool. Keep in a cold place.

Heavenly Hash

Strain the juice of one pint cherries or red raspberries and place in a sauce dish with alternate layers of sliced bananas, sprinkling each layer with one tablespoon of finely powdered sugar. Pour cold, soft custard over the fruit, covering with two egg whites beaten to a stiff froth with one cupful of powdered and sifted sugar. Place in a hot oven for one minute, to color the meringue, if desired. Serve cold.

Rosettes

Take four eggs, two tablespoons of powdered sugar and a few grains of salt; beat them together; then add one pint of milk and flour enough to make a batter like that used for griddle cakes (see p. 56); dip hot rosette iron in batter and fry in hot fat; serve with a garnish of currant jelly and top each with whipped cream.

Cherries with Crust

Cut rings from slices of brioche, or white baker's bread, half an inch thick. Soak these in egg yolk, beaten and diluted with milk or cream, and mixed with sugar and a grating of orange rind. Dip in macaroon crumbs, and then in bread crumbs. Saute in clarified sweet butter. Mask with marmalade and sprinkle with chopped almonds. Dress crown-shaped, one overlaying the other, with stewed cherries in the center. Thicken the cherry syrup with cornstarch or arrowroot for a sauce. A topping of whipped cream is very nice with this dessert.

Compote of Chestnuts

Forty large chestnuts, sugar syrup to cover, small piece vanilla bean, grated rind of half a lemon or orange. Put the blanched chestnuts in a large saucepan, cover with the syrup, add the vanilla bean and lemon or orange rind. Simmer twenty minutes or until tender, then drain. Pour the syrup over the chestnuts and dispose in a serving dish. The chestnuts keep their shape if fresh.
Note: To freshen hard and dry chestnuts, soak in lemon juice a few hours before cooking them.

Crème Du Thé
(Tea)

One pint rich cream, whipped light, one-half package gelatine, soaked in a cup of fresh milk, one large cup of strong mixed tea—the best quality, one cup finely pulverized loaf sugar and the whites of two eggs. Dissolve the soaked gelatine and the sugar in the boiling tea, when you have strained the latter through a fine piece of muslin, let it cool. Whip the cream and the whites of eggs in separate vessels. When the gelatine is perfectly cold, beat it by degrees into the whites until it is a firm froth. Fold in the whipped cream. Rinse a mold in cold water, fill it with the mixture, and set it in a very cold place, or on the ice for eight to ten hours. Send around a pitcher of thick sweet cream to serve with it.

Crême Du Café: Is made the same way as the Crême Du Thé, but substitute a large cup of strong black coffee instead of the tea. It is a good plan to make both at the same time, giving your guests their choice of tea or coffee.

Wine Fritters

Beat six eggs till very thick and smooth, about ten minutes. When they are well beaten, beat into them gradually six tablespoons of sweet Malaga or Muscatel wine and six tablespoons of powdered sugar. Have ready a sufficient number of milk biscuits, split in two. Soak in a bowl of sweet wine for five minutes and drain on a sieve. Put some fresh butter or lard into a frying pan and, when it boils and has been skimmed, dip each piece of split biscuit into the batter of wine, eggs and sugar. Fry them brown. When done, take them up with a perforated skimmer and drain them well from the grease. Strew thickly with powdered sugar.

Chocolate Charlotte

Lay in a deep dish or pan a half pound of baker's chocolate macaroons and pour on sufficient white wine to cover them well. Let them stand until entirely dissolved. Whip to a stiff froth a pint of rich, fresh sweet cream, sweetened to taste with powdered sugar and flavored with rose or lemon. Have ready a large, circular, almond sponge cake with the inside cut out, so as to leave the bottom and the sides standing in the form of a mold, not quite an inch thick.

Ornament the edge with a handsome border of whipped cream. In the bottom of this mold put the dissolved macaroons; over them a thick layer of jelly, whipped smooth, made of some very nice fruit or berries; and fill up with the whipped cream, heaping it high in the center. This is a very fine Charlotte and is easily made. No cooking required after the materials have been collected.

(A delicious and handsome dessert borrowed from a very old recipe.)

Chocolate Ice Cream

Chocolate used for this purpose must neither have any sugar or spice in it, unsweetened chocolate is best. For each quart of fresh sweet cream, scrape down three ounces of chocolate. Put it into a saucepan with half a pint of hot water for each ounce and mix it to a smooth paste with a spoon. Place it over hot coals and, when it has come to a boil, take it off the fire and set it to cool. When it has cooled, stir the chocolate into the cream and strain it well. When strained, add gradually for each quart of cream, three-quarters of a pound of loaf sugar, powdered and sifted, and give the whole a boil up. Then put it into the freezer.

Coffee Souffle

Three tablespoons of butter, three tablespoons sifted flour, one cup black coffee, pinch salt, the yolks of three eggs, the whites of three eggs, one-third cup powdered and sifted sugar. Make a sauce of the butter, flour and coffee; melt the butter and in it cook the flour until it is frothy, then add the coffee gradually and stir until thick and smooth. Remove from the fire, add the sugar, salt, and the yolks of eggs beaten until thick and smooth. Fold in the whites of eggs beaten to a stiff froth. Pour the mixture into a buttered baking dish and bake twenty-five minutes in a moderately hot stove. Serve with coffee sauce.

Ice Cream Cake

Make a good sponge cake, bake half an inch thick in jelly pans and let them cool perfectly cold; take a pint of the thickest fresh sweet cream, beat until it looks like ice cream, make very sweet, and flavor with vanilla; blanch and chop a pound of almonds, stir into the cream, and put between layers. This is the queen of cakes. Keep cool. Use same day.

Toad in a Hole
(Ice Cream Cake)

One-fourth pound fresh butter and powdered sugar, half pint milk, half pound sifted flour, six eggs, one glass wine, grated nutmeg; mix and bake quickly in iron gem pans. They raise light with hollow centers. When cold, cut a round hole in top (as you would plug a melon). Fill with ice cream just before serving, so that it will not have time to melt. Top with favorite berry sauce.

Moonshine

This dessert combines a pretty appearance with a palatable flavor, and is a convenient substitute for ice cream. Beat the whites of six eggs in a broad plate to a very stiff froth, then add gradually six tablespoons of powdered and sifted loaf sugar, (to make it thicker use more sugar, up to a pint), beating not less than thirty minutes, and beat in one tablespoon of preserved peaches, cut up into tiny bits, (or one cup jelly) and set on ice until thoroughly chilled. In serving, pour in each saucer some rich cream, sweetened and flavored with vanilla, and on the cream place a liberal portion of moonshine.

PUDDINGS

No ingredient of doubtful quality should enter into the making of puddings. Suet and milk must be perfectly sweet and fresh, since it may sour or curdle in the slightest degree, and may ruin the pudding with a most unpleasant flavor. Dried currants such as sold in the stores must be washed in several waters and dried between towels before using. Almonds and spices should be very finely pounded, as well as the loaf sugar, and rind of oranges and lemons rasped or lightly grated. Puddings are either baked, boiled, or steamed. Rice, bread, custard, and fruit puddings require moderate heat; batter and cornstarch, a rather quick stove. Add a pinch of salt to all puddings. Boiled puddings are lighter when boiled in a pudding cloth and allowed full room to swell. Pudding cloths should never be washed with soap, but in clear, cold water, dried as quickly as possible and kept in a place free from odors.

While the country cook had a large repertoire of pudding 'receipts' from which to draw, one of her best and a great family favorite was made from golden corn meal, cooked long and slowly in a pudding bag; often laced with good brandy and fragrant spices. The addition of plump raisins, dates and currants made it a very special dessert. Here is an early 'receipt' (1834) for a Fine Indian pudding, together with our modern and more simplified version.

Fine Indian Pudding
(1834)

Take a pound of raisins and cut them in half, having first removed the seeds, then spread them on a large dish and dredge them with fine wheat flour, turning them about, that both sides are well floured. Boil a quart of rich, fresh sweet milk and, when it comes to a boil, take it off the fire and set it to cool. Transfer the half of this milk (one pint) to another pan and, while it is still warm, stir into it a half pound of sweet butter, cut into bits and one small cup good, dark molasses, mixed with the grated rind of a large lemon or orange and also the juice. Add a teaspoon of powdered cinnamon and nutmeg, mixed, and a glass of brandy. Beat eight eggs very light and when it is quite cold, stir the eggs gradually into the other pint of milk. Then mix the ingredients of both pans together and add eight large tablespoons of Indian meal, or enough to make a thick batter. Lastly mix in the floured raisins, a few at a time, stirring the whole very hard with a wooden spoon. Have ready over the fire, a large pot of boiling water. Dip a square pudding cloth into it; shake it out; spread it open over the inside of an empty pan, and dredge it with flour; pour the batter into it and tie firmly, leaving room for the pudding to swell. Plaster a small lump of flour-and-water dough over the crevice of the tying place, to assist in keeping the water out, which, if it gets in, will render the pudding heavy. Put it in a pot of boiling water and boil steadily for six hours, turning frequently in the water. It can scarcely be boiled too long. Keep at the fire a kettle of *hot* water to replenish the pudding pot as it boils away. Do not take up the pudding till immediately before it goes to the table. Dip it into cold water, then turn it out of the cloth upon a serving dish. Eat it with wine sauce, or with butter, sugar and nutmeg. If enough of the pudding is left over, it may, the next day, be tied in a cloth and reboiled for one hour.

(A long and complicated recipe. However, here is a more simplified and delicious Baked Indian Pudding.)

Indian Pudding
(1966)

Boil two cups milk, stir in one-quarter cup yellow corn meal, cook ten minutes on top of the stove, then add one-half cup dark molasses, one-half cup brown sugar, one-half teapsoon cinnamon, pinch nutmeg, salt to taste, one-half cup plump seedless raisins and two to three tablespoons of brandy. Mix well with a wooden spoon, then add two cups milk and one well-beaten egg. Pour into a buttered ovenware pudding dish and bake in a preheated 250° F. oven for half an hour. Stir and add another cup of milk and continue baking, at least another hour-and-a-half. Serve with vanilla ice cream, flavored lightly with brandy or rum.

Birthday Pudding
(1875)

Beat to a stiff froth the whites of eight eggs. Then beat into them half a pound of powdered and sifted loaf sugar, a teaspoonful at a time. Stir into a pint of rich cream or melted vanilla ice cream a wine glass-ful of rose water, or two tablespoons of extract of roses. Stir the beaten eggs and the sugar into the milk, alternating with four ounces of sifted flour, a spoonful at a time. Beat the whole very hard, put into a deep dish, well buttered, and set it immediately into a rather quick stove, bake it well. Serve it up cold and eat with butter and white sugar, beaten to a cream and flavored with rose water. This pudding will be found to be very white and delicate. Delicious and more digestible than pie "without which father wouldn't think he could live."

To Ornament Pudding: Place six sweet almonds, blanched whole and split in half, on the center of the pudding so as to form a star. Lay others like rays diverging from the star and place still others in a circle near the edge of the pudding.

A delicious and handsome pudding as good today as it was in 1875.

Family Pudding

One quart milk, four eggs, one cup very fine, dry bread crumbs, one-half cup strawberry jam, one-half cup sifted sugar. Butter a pudding dish, sprinkle the bottom with bread crumbs, pour over these a half cup jam, wet with a little milk. Heat the quart of milk until *near* boiling, take it from the fire and add, gradually, the beaten yolks and sugar. At the last fold in lightly beaten whites. Heat this by degrees, stirring it constantly until it begins to thicken. Put it, spoonful by spoonful, upon the layer of bread crumbs, taking care not to disturb these, and, when all is in, bake until set and very lightly browned. Eat cold. Thick cream is very good with this.

Batter Pudding

One pint fresh sweet milk, four eggs, whites and yolks beaten separately, two even cups of sifted flour, pinch soda, salt to taste, one tablespoon sugar. Combine all ingredients. Bake in a buttered dish, three-quarters of an hour until lightly browned. Eat hot with a rich fruit sauce.

Gooseberry Pudding
(1875)

One pint ripe gooseberries, eight slices stale baker's bread, one cup sweet milk, one-half cup sifted powdered sugar, one tablespoon melted butter. Stew the gooseberries ten minutes, very slowly in a little water, careful not to break them. Cut slices of bread to fit pudding dish and toast to a very light brown on both sides. (Cut off all the crusts before toasting.) Dip each slice, while hot, into milk and spread with melted butter. Cover the bottom of the dish with them. Put next a layer of the gooseberries, sprinkled thickly with sugar, more toast, more berries, and so on, until the dish is full. Cover closely, bake in a moderately hot stove for twenty-five minutes. Turn out upon a hot dish and pour over it a good pudding sauce. This is also considered a good wholesome breakfast dish. In this case, omit sauce, sift powdered sugar over the top, and eat the same.

(If fresh gooseberries are not available, they may be purchased canned or preserved in fine food stores.)

Hasty Pudding

One heaping cup Indian meal, one-half cup sifted flour, one quart boiling water, one pint fresh milk, one tablespoon sweet butter, salt as you like it. Wet up the meal and flour with the milk and stir slowly into the boiling water. Boil hard for half an hour, stirring almost constantly from the bottom with a wooden spoon. Put in salt and butter and simmer ten minutes longer. Turn into a deep, uncovered dish and eat with sugar and cream, with a light dash of nutmeg. Children like it.

Lemon Meringue Pudding

One quart fresh milk, two cups bread crumbs, four eggs, one-half cup sweet butter, one cup powdered and sifted loaf sugar, grated rind and juice of one large lemon. Soak the bread crumbs in milk; add beaten egg yolks, with the butter and sugar rubbed to a cream, also add the lemon. Bake in a buttered dish until firm and slightly brown. Draw to the door of the stove and cover with a meringue of the whites whipped to a stiff froth with three tablespoons of sifted sugar and a little lemon juice. Brown very slightly; sift powdered sugar over it; eat cold.

Macaroni Pudding

One cup macaroni, broken into one inch pieces, one quart fresh milk, four eggs, one-half lemon, juice and rind, two tablespoons sweet butter, pinch salt, three-fourth cup sugar, powdered. Simmer macaroni in half the milk until tender. While hot, stir in the butter, yolks well beaten up with the sugar, the lemon and, lastly, the whipped whites. Bake in a buttered mold about one-half hour or until nicely browned. Serve with favorite sauce. Currant jelly warmed with butter and pale sherry beaten smooth is very good with this.

Mothers Souffle Pudding
(1852)

Take eight rusks or sugar biscuits; lay them in a deep dish and pour over a pint of fresh milk, sufficient to soak them thoroughly. Cover the dish and let stand for an hour-and-a-half before dinner. In the meantime, boil half a pint of milk with a small bunch of clean peach leaves and a small stick of cinnamon, broken up. Boil this milk slowly (keeping it covered) and, when it tastes strongly of flavoring articles, strain it and set it away to cool. When cold, mix it into another pint of milk, stir in a quarter of a pound of loaf sugar, powdered and sifted. Beat eight eggs, very light, and add them gradually to the milk, so as to make a rich custard. After dinner has commenced, beat and stir the soaked rusks very hard until it becomes a smooth mass and then, by degrees, add it to the custard. Stir the whole until thoroughly mixed. Set the dish into a brisk stove and bake the pudding rather more than ten minutes. The yeast in the rusks will cause it to puff up very light. When done, send it to the table warm, with powdered sugar sifted over it. Serve with thick sweet cream, sweetened and flavored with rose water and grated nutmeg.

Plum Pudding
Genuine
(1869)

Soak one pound of stale baker's bread in a pint of hot milk, let stand until cool. When cold, add to it one pound of powdered loaf sugar and the yolks of eight eggs, beaten to a cream, one pound stoned raisins, one pound currants, washed, dried and floured, one-quarter pound of citron, cut into slips and floured, one pound of beef suet, chopped finely and salted, one glass wine, one glass brandy, grated nutmeg, one tablespoon mace, cinnamon and cloves mixed; beat the whole well together and, as the last thing, add the whites of eight eggs, beaten to a stiff froth; pour into a clean pudding cloth, previously scalded and dredged with flour; tie the cloth firmly, leaving room for the pudding to swell, and boil steadily for six hours. Serve with wine or brandy sauce. It is best to prepare the ingredients the day before and cover them closely.

Raspberry Pudding

Fill a deep dish with a quart of ripe raspberries, well mixed with flour or four to five tablespoons powdered sugar. As you put in the raspberries, mash them slightly with the back of a wooden spoon. Beat six eggs as light as possible and mix them with a pint of cream or rich milk and four more tablespoons of powdered sugar, adding some grated nutmeg. Pour this over the raspberries. Pour into a well-buttered earthenware pudding dish. Set the dish immediately into a moderately hot stove and bake the pudding about a half hour. When done, set the dish on ice or where it will become quite cold before going to the table. Serve hot or cold with pudding sauce, or with fresh sweet butter, powdered sugar and lemon juice beaten to a cream.

Rhubarb Pudding

Prepare young, tender, spring rhubarb as for pies (see p. 235); cover the bottom of a buttered pudding dish with slices of bread and butter; cover with the rhubarb, cut into short pieces; sprinkle thickly with sugar; then another layer of bread and butter; and so on until the dish is full. Cover and steam, while baking, for a half hour. Remove the lid and bake ten minutes or until browned. Eat with a warm or cold strawberry sauce.

Strawberry Sauce: Clean one pint fresh strawberries, put in a saucepan with sugar, cook up for ten minutes, thicken with a little arrowroot or cornstarch.

Rice Pudding

One quart fresh sweet milk, three eggs, well beaten, four tablespoons sifted sugar, one scant tablespoon butter, pinch salt, one small cup boiled rice, one-half teaspoon rose water and a teaspoon lemon juice. Drain the boiled rice, stir into the milk. Beat the eggs, rub the butter and sugar together, and add the rose water and lemon juice. Mix all up well and bake in a buttered dish half an hour in a pretty quick oven. Serve with thick clotted cream.

Sauces For Puddings And Desserts:

Cold Brandy Sauce

Two cups of sifted powdered loaf sugar, half a cup of fresh sweet butter, one wine glass of brandy, cinnamon and nutmeg, a teaspoon mixed. Warm the butter slightly and work it to a light cream with the sugar; then add the brandy and the spices; beat it hard and set aside in a cold place until wanted.

Rose Brandy for Pudding Sauce

Gather the petals of red roses while the dew is on them and, as soon as they are open, put them in a wide-mouthed bottle. When the bottle is full, pour in the best French brandy. It will be fit for use in three or four weeks. Use as a flavoring mixed with soft custard or as a favorite pudding sauce.

Cream Brandy Sauce

One cup water, one cup sifted sugar, one-third cup sweet cream, three egg yolks, two tablespoons brandy, few orange rind gratings. Cook sugar and water ten minutes. Meanwhile, beat yolks, add cream, brandy, pinch salt and orange rind gratings. Add sugar and water slowly and beat until the mixture thickens. Serve hot or cold.

Coffee Sauce

One-half cup sugar, two eggs, few grains of salt, three-fourth cup black coffee. Cook in a double boiler until the mixture thickens. Chill. Add beaten cream and serve cold.

Chocolate Sauce

Two ounces of chocolate, one cup powdered sugar, one-half cup water, two tablespoons sweet butter, pinch salt, one teaspoon vanilla. Cook all ingredients, except vanilla, ten to twelve minutes; add vanilla. Beat well; serve hot or cold. This sauce is especially good served with ice cream but is also good with any dessert. Blend with whipped cream for a chocolate cream sauce.

Sauce for Plum Pudding
Superior

Cream together a cup of powdered sugar and a half cup of fresh sweet butter; when light and creamy, add the well beaten yolks of four eggs. Stir into this one wine glass of wine or brandy, a pinch of salt and a large cupful of fresh sweet cream or rich milk. Beat this mixture well, place this in a saucepan over the fire, stir until it cooks sufficiently to thicken like cream. Be sure *not* to let it *boil*.

Rum Sauce

One-half cup powdered sifted sugar, two egg yolks, two egg whites, three tablespoons rum and one-half cup sweetened whipped cream. Mix sugar, yolks of eggs and rum, then the stiffly beaten egg whites. Cook gently until thickened, add the whipped cream when cool. Chill.

Rich Wine Sauce

One cup of fresh sweet butter, two of powdered loaf sugar, half a cup of good wine. Beat the butter to a cream. Add the sugar gradually and, when very light, add, a little at a time, the wine, which has been made hot. Add a scant teaspoon of grated nutmeg. Place the bowl in a basin of hot water and stir for two minutes. The sauce should be smooth and creamy.

CAKES

Colonial Thanksgiving Cake
(1899)

Two cups bread dough (from bread baking), one-half cup fresh sweet butter, two cups loaf sugar, finely powdered, two eggs, one-fourth teaspoon powdered cloves, one-half teaspoon of mace and nutmeg, one cup stoned raisins, one-fourth cup sliced citron. Take the dough, when it is ready for shaping into loaves, add the other ingredients and mix and beat with the hands, as in making brioche. The beating is not done with the side of the hand, but with the tips of the fingers and directly towards the body. Turn into a tube cake pan and, when light, (it should not be quite double in bulk) bake in the stove at a temperature a little lower than for bread. When cold, pour a maple frosting over the cake and decorate with pecan or hickory nuts and ornamental frosting.

(For delicious cakes and bread, treat flour with a 'light' hand. Scant the flour in all recipes—use less in the beginning until the texture and 'feel of the dough' is just right. A delicate touch, light as a cloud with flour, and a strong hand to beat the eggs should bring forth beautiful cakes and bread.)

Election Cake
(1802)

Five pounds of dried, sifted flour, two pounds fresh-churned sweet butter, two pounds loaf sugar, broken up and powdered in a mortar and pestle, cup-and-a-half distillery yeast or twice the quantity of home-made yeast, four fresh eggs, half a cup of wine or brandy, half an ounce of nutmeg, and two pounds dried fruits, a quart fresh sweet milk. Rub the butter very fine into the flour; add half the sugar, then the yeast, then half the milk, scalded and cooled to luke-warm, then the eggs well beaten, the wine and the remainder of the milk. Beat thoroughly and let rise overnight. In the morning stir in the sugar, spices and fruit. Mix well using the hands if necessary. Let rise three or four hours till very light. Place in buttered bread tins lined with buttered paper. Cover and let rise again until double in bulk. Bake in a moderately hot stove until golden brown, about fifty minutes.

Grandmother's Molasses Cake
An old, old recipe

Cut one-quarter pound of fresh butter into a pint of dark molasses. Warm it sufficiently to soften the butter and make it mix easily. Stir it well into the molasses and add a tablespoon of powdered cinnamon. Beat three eggs very light and stir them, very gradually, into the mixture, in turn with barely enough of sifted flour (not more than a pint-and-a-half) to make it about as thick as pound cake batter. Add, at the last, a small or level teaspoonful of pearlash, or a full one of soda, dissolved in a very little warm water. Butter small cake tins, or pattypans, put in the batter and set them immediately into the stove, which must not be too hot as all the cakes made with molasses are peculiarly liable to scorch on the outside.

(Cake is often spoiled by looking into the stove too often. The heat should be tested, before the cake is put in, which can be done by throwing on the floor of the stove a tablespoon of new flour. If the flour takes fire or turns a dark brown color, the temperature is too high and the stove must be allowed to cool. If the stove is a proper temperature, the flour will turn a light brown. Hickory rods for egg beating are to be had at the wood turners or woodenware shops. For stirring butter and sugar together, nothing is equal to a wooden spaddle. It should be about a foot long and flattened at the end like that of a mush stick, only broader. Spoons are very tedious and inconvenient, either for beating eggs or stirring sugar and butter, and do not produce the proper lightness.)

Bride's Cake

Cream together one scant cup of fresh butter and three cups of powdered loaf sugar, add one cup of fresh sweet milk, then the whites of twelve eggs; sift three teaspoons baking powder into one cup of cornstarch mixed with three cups of sifted flour and beat in gradually with the rest. Flavor with rose water or orange flower water. Beat all thoroughly, then put in buttered tins lined with white, letter paper, well-buttered; bake slowly in a moderately hot stove. A beautiful white cake. Ice the top and ornament as desired.

Rainbow Cake
Very Special

Prepare favorite pound cake straight-sided and about the circumference of a large dinner plate. Cut horizontally in slices, or bake in a twelve-inch loaf pan. Cool twenty-four hours. Cut into slices more than a half inch thick. Spread each slice thickly and smoothly with marmalade of peach, raspberry, strawberry and orange. The marmalade or jelly should be a different sort on each slice. Lay the slices nicely and evenly, one upon the other, taking care that none of the marmalade oozes down between the slices and between the edges. Then make a thick icing of white of egg and powdered loaf sugar and flavor it with rose or orange flower water (meringue). Spread it smoothly. Heap a large portion of it on the center of the cake and, with a broad knife (dipped in cold water), spread the icing all over the top and sides of the cake. Then set it away to harden. Decorate the cake with a border of candied violets and candied mint leaves. When the cake is to be eaten, cut it down into triangular pieces; each including a portion of the different layers of marmalade.

(This is an elegant cake and very simple to prepare. For a short cut, use a baker's pound cake. Whipped cream may be used in place of the meringue. Ornament with candied violets as above.)

Rose Meringues
(1852)
Very Unusual

Beat to a stiff froth the whites of six eggs and then beat in, by degrees, a spoonful at a time, a pound or more of finely powdered loaf sugar, until it is of the consistency of very thick icing or meringue. Have ready a quantity of freshly gathered rose buds, about half grown. Having removed the stalks and green leaves, take as many buds as will weigh three ounces. With a pair of sharp scissors, clip or mince the rose buds as small as possible into the pan of meringue; stirring them in very gently with a wooden spoon. Then stir the whole very hard. Have ready some sheets of white, letter paper, laid on baking tins. Drop the meringues on it, in heaps all the same size, and not too close together. Smooth them with the back of a spoon or a broad knife dipped in cold water. Set them in a moderately cool stove and bake about twenty to thirty minutes. If not thoroughly done, continue them longer in the stove. To heighten the red color of the meringues, color with a few drops of fresh beet juice.

Note: Moisten underside of paper. Remove rose meringues with the flat side of a silver knife.

Poor Man's Fruit Cake
(1890)

One pound fat salt pork, three cups of hot coffee, four cups of powdered loaf sugar, one cup each of currants, of figs and of stoned raisins, one tablespoon cinnamon, one teaspoon of powdered cloves, seven-and-a-half cups of sifted flour. Chop the fat pork very fine and pour over it the boiling coffee; let the coffee cool slightly and add the sugar. Chop the figs coarsely, chop raisins, wash and dry currants; then put the fruit altogether and sift over it a little of the flour. Add the spices and the rest of the flour and stir the latter into the coffee and sugar. When the mixture is well beaten, add the fruit and bake in buttered loaf pans lined with the buttered paper for an hour.

1, 2, 3, 4, Cake

One cup fresh sweet butter, one cup fresh milk, two cups powdered loaf sugar, three cups sifted flour, three teaspoons baking powder and four eggs. Put the ingredients together the same as you would a loaf cake. Place the batter in buttered loaf tins and bake until done. Cool cake. Sprinkle with a thin layer of cocoa, then sprinkle on top a cloud of powdered loaf sugar, or ice cake with favorite white icing, top with fresh grated coconut.

Huckleberry Slump

One-and-a-half quarts fresh picked huckleberries, one-and-a-half cups powdered loaf sugar, one table-spoon fresh butter, one cup sifted flour, pinch salt, two tablespoons melted butter and one-half cup light cream or milk. Put huckleberries in the bottom of a well-buttered baking dish, mix in sugar, dot with butter and sprinkle with cinnamon or grated nutmeg. Make a batter of the flour, salt, baking powder, sugar, butter and milk, mixing all ingredients until smooth. Spoon over berries. Bake in a moderate stove for forty-five minutes or until the top is golden brown. Pass a pitcher of thick sweet cream.

Old-Fashioned Country Cherry Cobbler

Four cups fresh, red, sour cherries, one-and-a-half cups loaf sugar, powdered and sifted, four table-spoons cornstarch, few grains salt, one cup cherry juice, few drops of fresh beet juice for color, one tablespoon butter, one teaspoon grated lemon rind and juice of a lemon. Drain cherries thoroughly from all juice. Combine sugar, cornstarch and salt in a saucepan, gradually stir in cherry juice. Add beet juice and bring to a boil. Cook gently for ten minutes, stirring constantly until thickened and clear. Remove from heat. Add butter, lemon rind and juice. Stir in the drained cherries. Pour cherry mixture into a two-inch deep baking dish. Bake in a moderately hot stove for twenty minutes.

Biscuit Topping

One-fourth cup butter, two cups sifted flour, two tablespoons powdered sugar, one tablespoon baking powder, one-half teaspoon salt, three-fourth cup sweet milk. Combine flour, sugar, salt and baking powder into a bowl; cut in butter until the mixture is mealy; add milk all at once; stir until the dough forms a soft ball. Roll out one-half inch thick; flute edges; place on a baking sheet; bake in a hot stove for fifteen minutes until the crust is golden brown. Place baked biscuit on top of the cherry filling and serve topped with vanilla flavored whipped cream or homemade vanilla ice cream.

Note: To obtain enough cherry juice, cover stoned cherries with half the sugar, add one-fourth cup white or good red wine; cover and let stand for two hours. If not enough, fill cup with any good, red, fruit juice.

Boiled Sponge Cake

One cup loaf sugar, crushed and powdered, one-half cup water, the yolks of five eggs, the grated rind and juice of half a lemon, one cup sifted flour, the whites of five eggs. Boil the sugar and water to a thread stage and pour, in a fine stream, on the yolks of the eggs, beaten thick and lemon colored. Beat constantly for some time, then set the dish in cold water and continue beating until the mixture is cold, adding, while beating, the juice and the rind of the lemon. When cold, fold in half the whites, beaten to a stiff froth, and the flour, then the rest of the egg whites. Bake in an ungreased tube pan until golden (about one hour). Let cool in inverted pan.

Lady Fingers

Six eggs, one-and-one-fourth cups powdered sugar, one cup sifted flour, a grating of lemon or orange rind, the juice of half a lemon. Mix and then press mixture, in portions an inch wide and five inches long, through a tube onto a baking sheet covered with paper. Dust with powdered, sifted sugar and bake ten minutes, without browning. Remove from paper, brush the white of an egg over the flat surface of one biscuit and press the underside of a second biscuit upon the first.

Finger Biscuit with Pistachios

Press the lady finger mixture onto paper in oval shaped strips, two inches long by two inches wide, dust with powdered sugar and, when baked, cover the tops with meringue (boiled frosting) and sprinkle with chopped pistachios.

Africans or Othellos

Press the lady finger mixture on the paper in rounds, an inch-and-a-half in diameter. When baked, spread the flat of the biscuit with jam or jelly, cover with the remaining biscuit. Dip in chocolate fondant or any favorite frosting. Dry on oiled paper.

Ladies' Vanilla Sponge Cake

Take the white, *only*, of twelve eggs (reserving the yolks for some other purpose) and beat these whites to a stiff froth. Then beat in a pound of powdered loaf sugar and a tablespoon of vanilla syrup, as to flavor it highly. Stir the whole well together and, at the last, stir in *slowly* and *lightly* a quarter pound of sifted flour. Transfer the mixture to a square pan, greased with fresh butter. Sift powdered sugar over the top; set it directly in a quick stove and bake well. It is best to cool the cake well, ice it when cold, flavoring it with a little vanilla syrup. It is important to make the vanilla syrup yourself. Much of the vanilla extract sold in the shops has a disagreeable taste, instead of a pleasant one.

A favorite cake with the ladies whenever they gathered for a quilting bee or an afternoon tea.

Fine Little Honey Cakes

Mix a quart of strained honey with a half pound of powdered loaf sugar, a half pound of fresh sweet butter, and the juice of two oranges or lemons. Warm these ingredients slightly, just enough to soften the butter. Then stir the mixture very hard, add a grated nutmeg. Mix in, gradually, two pounds (or less) of shifted flour. Make it into a dough just stiff enough to roll out easily. Beat well, all over, with a rolling pin. Then roll out, half an inch thick, into a large sheet. Cut it into round cakes with the top of a tumbler dipped frequently in flour. Lay them in a shallow tin pan (slightly buttered) and bake them well.

Chocolate Cake
(1885)

One cup fresh sweet butter, three of brown sugar, one of fresh sweet milk, four of sifted flour, yolks of seven eggs, nine tablespoons grated chocolate, three teaspoons of baking powder. Bake in buttered layer tins until done. Put together with frosting or whipped cream. If desired, make a white cake of the whites of eggs, beaten to a stiff froth, and put together, alternating with the chocolate layers and chocolate frosting.

Mix ingredients in the order given, creaming the butter and sugar until very creamy, add the milk alternating with the flour, then the eggs and chocolate. Sift the baking powder with the flour. Mix well.

Dark Fruit Cake

One cup fresh sweet butter, one of brown sugar, half a pint dark molasses, two eggs, one cup sour milk, a teaspoon soda, a pound of sifted flour, one pound of currants, one-and-a-half pounds stoned raisins. Mix in order given. Flavor with good brandy. Bake in buttered loaf tins, lined with buttered brown paper, in a moderate stove. While fruit cake is still warm, pour brandy over top. Wrap and store in a cool place.

Hard Money Cake

Gold Part: Yolks of eight eggs, scant cup sweet butter, two of powdered loaf sugar, four of flour, one of sour milk, teaspoon soda, tablespoon cornstarch; flavor with lemon. Mix in order given.

Silver Part: Two cups powdered loaf sugar, one of butter, four (scant) of flour, one of sour milk, teaspoon soda, tablespoon cornstarch, whites of eight eggs beaten to a stiff froth, flavor with almond or peach. Mix. Put in buttered pans, alternating one spoonful of gold and one of silver until the pans are three-fourth full. Bake in moderate stove.

Ice Cream Cake

Stir together, till very light, a quarter pound of powdered loaf sugar and a quarter pound of fresh sweet butter. Beat six eggs very light and stir them into a half pint of rich milk. Add gradually, the eggs and milk to the butter and sugar, alternately with a half pound of sifted flour. Add a glass of sweet wine and some grated nutmeg. When all the ingredients are mixed, stir the batter hard. Then put it into small deep pans or cups that have been well buttered, filling them about two-thirds full with the batter. Set them immediately into a brisk stove and bake them a golden brown. When done, remove them from the cups and place them to cool on an inverted sieve. When quite cold, make a slit in the side of each cake. If very light and properly baked, they will be hollow in the middle. Fill up this cavity with ice cream, carefully put in with a small spoon, and close the slit with your fingers to prevent cream from running out. Spread them on a large dish and send to the table at once.

Sweet Potato Huff
Golden Cake

Half boil some fine sweet potatoes; peel them and, when quite cold, grate as much as will weigh half a pound. If cooked long enough to become soft, it will render the cake heavy. Stir together, in a deep pan, half a pound of fresh sweet butter and half a pound of powdered sifted loaf sugar, till quite light and creamy. Then add a teaspoon mace, nutmeg and cinnamon, all mixed together; add the juice and grated rind of two large lemons or oranges. Beat, in a shallow pan, six eggs until thick and fluffy and stir them into the pan with the butter and sugar, in turn with the grated sweet potatoes, a little of each at a time. Then stir the whole very hard. Butter a deep tin pan with straight sides. Pour in the mixture and bake it well. Ice it when it is cold, adding lemon or orange juice to the icing. In spreading the icing, begin by heaping it on the center of the cake and then gradually bringing it all over the top and sides, dipping the knife frequently in a bowl of cold water.

Sour Milk Gingerbread

One cup good molasses, one cup sour milk, two cups sifted flour, one egg, two teaspoons ginger, two teaspoons soda, one-half teaspoon salt. Mix and sift dry ingredients, add rest of ingredients, beat well, pour into buttered pan and bake twenty to thirty minutes in a moderately hot stove. A delight when frosted with chocolate icing flavored with a little ginger.

Ginger Snaps

One cup molasses, one-fourth to one-half cup butter, three cups sifted flour, one-half teaspoon soda, one tablespoon ginger and two small teaspoons salt. Boil shortening and molasses two minutes. Add remaining ingredients, mixed and sifted. Beat well. Chill overnight. Roll out very thin. Cut out with a knife or cookie cutter. Bake on a buttered pan, in a quick stove, eight to ten minutes.

Country-Boy Gingerbread

Three-fourth cup fresh butter, one-and-a-half cups sifted flour, five eggs, one-and-three-fourths cups powdered loaf sugar, one tablespoon yellow ginger, one teaspoon baking powder, few grains of salt. Cream butter and add flour. Add remaining ingredients and beat ten minutes. Bake in a buttered bread pan forty-five to sixty minutes. Combine whipped cream with a few tablespoons applesauce. Sweeten and flavor to taste. Serve as a sauce.

Sea Voyage Gingerbread

Sift two pounds of flour into a pan and cut up in it a pound-and-a-quarter of fresh sweet butter; rub the butter well into the flour, then mix in a pint of good dark molasses and a pound of the best brown sugar. Beat eight eggs till very light. Stir into the beaten eggs two glasses of brandy. Add also a teacup of ground ginger to the egg, and a tablespoon of powdered cinnamon, with a teaspoon of soda melted in a little warm water. Wet the flour mixture with this mixture till it becomes a soft dough. Sprinkle a little flour on your pasteboard and, with a broad knife, spread portions of the mixture thickly and smoothly upon it. The thickness must be equal all through; therefore, spread it carefully and evenly as the dough will be too soft to roll out. Then, with the edge of a tumbler dipped in flour, cut it out into round cakes. Have ready a square pan, slightly buttered; lay the cakes in them, sufficiently far apart to prevent their running into each other when baked. Set the pans in a brisk stove and bake the cakes well, seeing that they do not burn. You may cut them, with the lid of a canister (or something similar), the usual size of gingerbread nuts. These cakes will keep during a long sea voyage and are frequently carried to sea.

Many persons find highly-spiced gingerbread a preventive to sea sickness. This, perhaps, accounts for the large amount of ginger used in this recipe.

Icings And Fillings:

Almond Icing

Whites of four eggs, one pound of sweet almonds, one pound of powdered loaf sugar, a little rose water. Blanch almonds by pouring boiling water over them, then stripping off the skins (they slip off very easily). When dry, pound to a paste in a mortar, moistening with rose water as you go on. When beaten fine and smooth, beat gradually into icing; put on very thick and, when nearly dry, cover with plain icing. This is a very fine-flavored icing.

Chocolate Frosting

Whites of two eggs, beaten to a froth, one cup of powdered sugar, one-fourth pound of grated chocolate, wet with one tablespoon cream and one teaspoon vanilla. Beat the sugar into the whipped whites, then add the chocolate. Whisk hard for three minutes before adding the vanilla. Let the cake get quite cold before you spread it. Spread between layers and beat more sugar into this to form a firm icing for the top.

Whipped Cream Coconut Topping and Filling

One cup fresh sweet cream, whipped stiff, three tablespoons powdered sugar, one-half cup grated fresh coconut, stirred in lightly at the last, one teaspoon of rose water. A very delicate and delicious white cake topping. Should be eaten soon after it is made, since the cream will sour or stale after twenty-four hours. Keep it in a cold place.

Crab Apple Meringue Frosting

Whites of four eggs, whipped stiff, heaping cup of powdered loaf sugar, two heaping tablespoons of crab apple jelly beaten into the meringue after it is stiff. Use as a filling between layers, reserve enough to pile on top of cake. Must be eaten the same day. For a very pretty icing, cut crab apple jelly into small cubes, fold gently into the meringue.

Baked Icing

Two egg whites beaten to a stiff froth, one cup brown sugar, pinch of cinnamon, nuts, coarsely chopped. Beat the whites stiff, add sugar gradually, beat well and pour the topping over the cake batter, season with spices as desired. Sprinkle with the nuts. Bake until the cake is done and the top golden in a not too hot stove.

Pecan Butter Frosting

One-half cup fresh sweet butter, one cup powdered loaf sugar, two teaspoons of cream, few drops of vanilla or almond flavor. Cream the butter thoroughly with the sugar until light and fluffy, make smooth with the cream. Add the flavor and spread on top of favorite layer cake, sprinkle with toasted, coarsely-chopped pecans. This is a delicious icing.

Black Walnut Filling

One cup of powdered loaf sugar, one-fourth cup water, one egg white beaten to a stiff froth, one-half cup stoned raisins, one-half cup black walnuts broken into coarse pieces, one teaspoon vanilla. Boil sugar and water until it threads from the spoon and then pour over the beaten white. Beat until thick, add the raisins, nuts and vanilla. Spread between layers. Dust top thickly with powdered sugar, or spread with whipped cream. Can be used for any favorite cake.

Pink Frosting

Beat whites of two eggs to a stiff froth, add, gradually, half a pound of best pulverized sugar, beaten in a mortar until well powdered, sift, then beat with egg whites for at least a half hour, flavor with a few drops of lemon juice or rose water. Use strawberry, currant or cranberry jelly or syrup to color a delicate rose. A few drops of beet juice will do.

Fig Filling

One-half pound figs, one-fourth cup water, two table-spoons sugar, juice of half a lemon, three teaspoons of sherry wine. Chop the figs very fine, cook, with the sugar, water and lemon, to a smooth paste; add wine; then spread between layers of cake. Cooked less thick the mixture may be used with powdered sugar as a filling and frosting for a sponge layer cake.

Gold Frosting

Beat the yolks of four eggs for ten minutes over warm water, stir in enough powdered loaf sugar, sifted twice, until stiff enough to spread, not to run. Flavor with a little white wine.

Mocha Cream Butter Icing

One cup sweet butter, the yolk of one egg, two-and-a-half cups powdered loaf sugar, strong coffee to taste. Use only fresh sweet butter; if salt butter is used, wash it first in cold water to free it from salt, pat it to remove the water. Beat butter to a cream; add the beaten egg yolk and gradually the sugar and enough strong coffee to desired flavor and color. Beat well until smooth. Use the filling between layers and for piping on the top.

White Mountain Cream

One-and-a-half cups of powdered loaf sugar, one-fourth teaspoon cream of tartar, one-half cup boiling water, the whites of two eggs, one-half teaspoon vanilla. Stir the sugar, cream of tartar and water over the fire until the sugar dissolves and the mixture reaches the boiling point. Then wash down, cover, let boil three minutes. Uncover and cook, without stirring, until the syrup threads when dropped from the spoon. Pour the syrup in a fine stream over the beaten egg whites, beating constantly meanwhile. Add the flavor and beat until cool enough to spread. This frosting is made to perfection when it has a thin, glossy crust upon the outside and is soft and creamy inside.

COOKIES

Bow Knots

Two eggs, one-third cup powdered loaf sugar, sifted, one tablespoon thick sweet cream, one tablespoon sweet butter, melted, one-half teaspoon cream of tartar, few grains of salt, pinch of mace, flour enough to make a stiff dough and one-eighth teaspoon of soda. Beat the eggs, separating the whites and yolks; add the sugar, cream and butter, then the flour sifted with the other dry ingredients. Roll small pieces of the dough into strips the size and shape of a pencil, tie in a bow or single knots, fry in deep hot fat and roll thickly in powdered sugar. Often served for tea.

Candy Cookies

One cup fresh sweet butter, two-and-a-half cups of good, dark molasses, few grains of salt, two cups of sifted flour, a pinch of powdered cloves. Boil butter and molasses together until thick, but not quite candied; when cooled a little, add the flour, salt and cloves; if more flour is required, add just a little. When thoroughly cold, roll out and cut into square or round cookies. Bake in a slow oven until golden brown.

Soft Caraway Cookies

One-half cup sweet butter, one cup powdered loaf sugar, one beaten egg, one-half cup sour cream, two-

and-a-half cups sifted flour, one-half teaspoon soda and one teaspoon caraway seeds. Mix in order given; drop from a teaspoon on a buttered pan; bake in a slow stove.

Chocolate Cookies

One square chocolate (one ounce), two cupfuls of powdered loaf sugar, one cupful fresh sweet butter, flour to thicken, two eggs, one teaspoon soda, one-half cupful sweet milk. Melt the chocolate and butter together over warm water, add the sugar, eggs well beaten, and the milk, in which the soda has been dissolved. Beat well. Add flour, to roll out thin, and cut into small cookies. Bake in a moderate stove. Frost cookies with chocolate or vanilla icing.

Coconut Cones

One pound powdered loaf sugar, sifted, one-half pound grated coconut, whites of five eggs, one teaspoon best arrowroot, whip the eggs as for icing, add the sugar as you go on, until it will stand alone, then beat in the coconut and arrowroot. Mold mixture with your hands into small cones and set these far apart, not to touch, upon buttered paper in a baking tin. Bake in a very moderate stove.

Cornmeal Doughnuts

A teacup and a half of boiling milk poured over two teacups of cornmeal; when cool add two cups of flour, one of sweet butter, one-and-a-half of sugar, three eggs, flavor with nutmeg. Let rise until very light, roll about one-half inch thick, cut in diamond shapes and boil in hot lard until golden on both sides.

Gingerbread Nuts

One-and-a-half pounds of sifted flour, three-quarters of a pound powdered and sifted loaf sugar, and the same of sweet butter, one ounce of ginger, the same of cloves, cinnamon and allspice, the grated rind of an orange, and a half teaspoon of mace. Mix all together, then stir in molasses until a stiff dough. Let it stand an hour, then make into small balls the size of walnuts. Press them flat with a nut in the center and lay them, not to touch each other, in a buttered cookie tin. Bake in a moderately hot stove for ten minutes; avoid burning.

Ginger Drop Cakes

One cupful of molasses, one cupful of powdered loaf sugar, one cupful of hot water, one-half cup of fresh sweet butter, four-and-one-half cups of flour, one egg, one tablespoon of ginger, one tablespoon soda. Dissolve the soda in hot water and add it to the molasses, place the butter and the sugar together and stir them into the molasses, add the ginger and enough flour to roll out. Drop the mixture, by spoonful, onto a buttered baking pan and bake in a rather quick oven, avoid burning.

Lemon Snaps

A large cup powdered loaf sugar, sifted, two-thirds cup fresh sweet butter, half teaspoon soda dissolved in two teaspoons hot water, flour enough to roll thin; flavor with lemon juice and grated lemon rind. Roll out, cut into fancy shapes and bake in a quick oven.

Mother's Jumbles

Three eggs, one cupful of powdered loaf sugar, sifted, two-thirds cupful of sweet butter, flour to thicken, three tablespoons milk, two teaspoons of baking powder, one-half teaspoon of ginger or nutmeg (if liked). Cream the butter and the sugar together and add in their order the beaten eggs, baking powder, nutmeg and flour. Sprinkle some sugar over the sheet of dough just before cutting the jumbles out, passing the rolling pin lightly over all. Bake quickly in a moderately hot stove ten to fifteen minutes.

Place one-half cup of crushed loaf sugar in a mortar, pulverize coarsely with pestle. Sprinkle on jumbles.

Pepper Nuts

One pound of powdered loaf sugar, sifted, five eggs, half a pound of sweet butter, half a teacup milk, two teaspoons baking powder, flour enough to roll. Cream sugar with eggs and butter until very smooth. Add milk, add baking powder and flour to form a soft dough. Turn out onto a floured board. A nice finishing touch can be given by sprinkling the dough with granulated sugar and rolling over lightly with a rolling pin, then cutting them out and pressing a large raisin in the center of each; or, when done a nice, light brown, brush over with thick sugar syrup, sprinkle with currants and return to stove a moment. Bake in a quick stove until golden brown.

To granulate loaf sugar; crush loaf sugar, place in a mortar and pulverize lightly with the pestle.

Little Railroad Cakes

Two cups of powdered loaf sugar, two cups flour, sifted, six tablespoons soft, fresh, sweet butter, two tablespoons of milk, six eggs, one teaspoon of soda, two teaspoons cream of tartar, one teaspoon grated lemon rind, and one teaspoon of lemon juice. Cream sugar with butter, add milk and eggs. Beat well with a wooden spoon. Add flour, soda, cream of tartar, grated lemon rind and juice. Mix well. Turn mixture into a buttered shallow pan, bake in a quick stove for twenty-five minutes or until golden brown. Cool. Sprinkle top thickly with powdered sugar. Cut into two-inch squares.

Sand Tarts

One cup of fresh sweet butter, two cups powdered loaf sugar, two eggs, well-beaten, three cups of sifted flour, pinch salt, one teaspoon baking powder. Cream butter and sugar with a wooden spoon, add eggs, and sifted dry ingredients. Mix well and set aside in a cool place for one hour. Turn out onto a floured board, roll out thin and cut into square cakes with a knife; brush tops with slightly beaten egg white. Sprinkle with cinnamon sugar and press a blanched almond in the center. Place on buttered cooky tins. Bake in a moderate stove, (350° F.) for ten to fifteen minutes.

Sponge Cake Drops

Beat three eggs to a froth, add a teacup of powdered loaf sugar. Stir into this one heaping coffee cup of sifted flour, in which one teaspoon of cream of tartar and a teaspoon of soda are thoroughly mixed. Flavor with lemon or rose extract. Butter tin baking sheets with sweet butter and drop mixture by teaspoonful about three inches apart. Bake instantly in a very quick stove. Watch closely as they will burn easily. Serve with ice cream.

Macaroons

Blanch a pound of almonds by pouring boiling water over them and, when the skin becomes loose, slip them off; then dry them thoroughly, (this should be done some hours before using them). Then pound them, a few at a time, in a mortar, adding a little rose water as you pound them to prevent them from oiling. When you have them all in a smooth paste, beat the whites of eight eggs, gradually adding a pound of powdered, sifted loaf sugar and a tablespoon of flour. Add the almonds and two more whites of egg, stiffly beaten. Drop them with a spoon onto buttered white paper on baking tins. Bake quickly. Moisten underside of paper. Remove maracoons with the flat side of a silver knife.

Sugar Cookies

Eight tablespoons powdered loaf sugar, sifted, six tablespoons melted sweet butter, four tablespoons sweet milk, two eggs, two teaspoons baking powder, flour to thicken. Stir the butter and sugar, mixing well with a wooden spoon; then add the milk. Sift the baking powder with a little flour and stir this in, adding enough flour to roll out the dough. Place the batter on a well-floured board and roll it thin; then cut out the cookies with a cutter. Dip each in powdered sugar as soon as cut and bake on a buttered cooky tin in a quick stove.

If cookies become moist in keeping, put them on a baking tin, place in stove and, when heated for a few minutes they will be crisp.

Tea Cookies

Cream half a pound of sweet butter and the same of powdered loaf sugar; add a wine glass-and-a-half of cold water, ten drops of essence of lemon, a few caraway seeds, more if you like, and one pound of sifted flour; roll out as thin as paper. Bake on buttered tins. Cut into squares.

Tommies

Boil one cup pulverized loaf sugar and a half cup water until it threads. Remove to the back of the stove and drop in five marshmallows cut into small pieces. Let stand until the mallows dissolve, then gradually pour onto the whites of two eggs, beaten until frothy. Add two tablespoons shredded coconut and one-fourth teaspoon vanilla. When partially cool, add one cup of English walnut meats, broken up. Spread on thin crackers and brown slightly in a hot stove. Delicious for afternoon teas.

PIES

A Note on Pies
(1880)

Your husband may admire your grace and ease in society, your wit, your schoolday accomplishments of music and painting, but all in perfection will not atone for a badly made pie, sour bread, muddy coffee, tough meats, indigestible pastry and the whole train of horrors resulting from poor housekeeping. However, success in the culinary arts wins gratitude, and adds luster to the most intellectual accomplishments.

—Marion Harland

Pie Pastry

Butter intended for pastry should be fresh and sweet; if salted, wash carefully to extract salt, then wipe it dry and lay in cold place until ready to work it in. 'Keep cool' is a cardinal motto for pastry makers. A marble slab is a good thing on which to roll out paste. The next best is a hard-wood, clean board, used only for this purpose. It is much harder rolling out good pastry in the summer than when it is cold on account of the tendency of the butter to oil, and thus render the crust heavy. Few people know how to make a good pastry crust, and it often has a resemblance to putty or leather. It should be light, flaky, goodly to behold, goodlier to taste. Since pies are eaten freely all over the countryside, let us make them as palatable as possible. Handle as little as possible.

Plain Paste with Butter

Sufficient for a two-crust pie. Two cups of sifted flour, two-thirds cup fresh sweet butter, one-half cup ice water, one teaspoon sugar and one of salt. As in puff paste (see p. 225), have everything cold as possible; and in warm weather place the butter and flour in the icebox for several hours before using. Sift the flour and measure it, and put it in a large mixing bowl; add the salt and sugar, and then place the butter in the center of the flour and, with a sharp knife, cut it quickly into small pieces, at the same time mixing it with the flour. Now gradually add the ice water; lift with the knife that portion of flour which has been moistened first, push it to one side of the bowl, wet another portion of the flour, and so continue until all is moistened. Add the water very carefully wetting only the dry flour and never stirring twice in the same place. Then cut and mix all together until the mixture can be lifted from the bowl with the knife. Dredge the baking-board lightly with the flour and roll the paste lightly and quickly away from you into a long thin sheet. Fold first the sides, then the ends, turn the paste around and roll it from you again; then fold it and stand it on ice until wanted. In order to make this paste a perfect success, the materials should be *very cold*, the mixing and rolling should be quickly done, and as little flour as possible should be used for finishing.

Flaky Pastry

Three cups sifted flour, one-half teaspoon salt, one-half cup fresh sweet butter, three-eighths to three-fourths cup cold water, and one-half cup washed or sweet butter. Keep butter cold. With a knife, or the tips of the fingers, work the half cup shortening into the flour and salt. When the mixture looks like meal, add the cold water gradually, and, with a knife, mix to a paste as in plain pastry (see above); knead slightly, cover and let stand five minutes, then pat with the rolling pin and roll out into a rectangular sheet. Fold in the butter as in puff paste (see below). and give the paste two or three 'turns', allowing it to stand five minutes between each turn. This pastry may be used at once.

Puff Paste
#1

One pound sifted flour, three-fourths pound fresh, cold sweet butter, one egg, use yolk only, ice water. Chop half of the butter into the flour; stir the beaten yolk in a half cup of ice water and work the flour into a stiff dough; roll out *thin*, baste with one-third of the remaining butter, fold closely, roll out again, and so on, until the butter is used up. Roll very thin and set the last folded roll in a very cold place for ten to fifteen minutes, before making out the crust. Wash with beaten egg white while hot. This puff paste is recommended for pastries and for fruit pies.

Puff Paste
#2

One pint sifted flour, one-half pound fresh sweet butter, one egg yolk, well-beaten, one-half cup ice water. Mix the flour, a tablespoon of cold water, the beaten egg and ice water into a paste with a wooden spoon. Flour your pastry board and roll out the crust very thin. Put the butter in the center of the sheet, in a flat cake. Turn the four corners of the paste over it and roll out carefully not to break the paste. Should it give way, flour the spot, that it may not stick to the roller. When very thin, sprinkle lightly with flour, fold up, and roll out four times more. Set in a cool place for an hour, roll out again, and cut into tartlet shells or top crust for pies. The bottom crust of pies may be made of plainer pastry.

Country Apple Big

Pare, core and slice ripe, tart, winter apples: Pippins, Greenings or Baldwins. Line your dish with a good crust, put in a layer of apples, then sprinkle thickly with brown sugar, add a few cloves here and there, lay on more apples, and so on, until the dish is filled. Cover with the crust and bake until done. Sift powdered sugar over the top before sending to the table. Serve with wedges of country-aged, store cheese.

Apple Sauce Pie

Stew green or other ripe, juicy apples, pared and cored. Mash to a smooth compote, sweeten to taste and while hot, stir in a teaspoon of sweet butter for each pie. Season with grated nutmeg and a pinch of cinnamon. When cool, fill your crust. Either crossbar the top with strips of paste or bake without a cover. Eat cold, with powdered sugar sprinkled thickly on top.

Apple Custard Pie

Three cups stewed apples, nearly a cup of sifted, powdered sugar, six eggs, and one-quart fresh sweet milk. Make the stewed apples very sweet and let cool. Beat the eggs separately until very light and mix the yolks with the apples, seasoning with grated nutmeg. Then stir in gradually the milk, beating as you go on; lastly add the beaten whites. Fill your crust and bake without a cover.

Apple Butter Custard Pie

Beat together four eggs, one teacup apple butter, one of powdered loaf sugar, one level tablespoon allspice, one quart fresh sweet milk and a pinch of salt. Bake in three pies, with a good undercrust.

By the way, never omit a pinch of salt in custard and lemon pie; in fact, many kinds of fruit pies, such as green apple, currant, gooseberry, and pie-plant (rhubarb) are improved by it.

Brandied Carrot Pie

One large, boiled carrot, or two medium ones, one tablespoon grated orange rind, one tablespoon orange juice, one-fourth cup powdered sugar, pinch grated nutmeg, three eggs, beaten lightly, pinch ginger, one pint light cream, one tablespoon clotted cream, three tablespoons good brandy. Press carrot through a fine sieve into a bowl, mash with the brandy, add sugar, orange juice and rind, nutmeg, eggs, ginger, and stir well with a wooden spoon. Add cream, beat well and pour into a pie tin lined with pie paste. Flute rim high to hold filling. Bake in a hot stove for ten minutes, reduce the heat and bake until the filling is set in the center. Test with a silver knife, if it comes out clean, not milky, the pie is done.

Cherry Pie

The common red cherries are the best for pies. Stone the cherries, line a deep pie plate with good, plain paste, nearly fill it with the cherries. Sprinkle four large tablespoons of sugar over each pie and dredge lightly with flour. Cover each pie with an upper crust, which should be rolled as thin as possible; make a vent in the center and press the edges lightly together so that the juice will not escape during baking. Serve the pies the same day as they are baked, else the undercrust will become heavy. Sprinkle powdered sugar over each pie just before sending to the table.

Chocolate Pie

One coffee cup of sweet milk, one-half cup of powdered loaf sugar, vanilla to flavor, two tablespoons of grated chocolate, three eggs, salt to taste. Beat the yolks of the eggs light and add to them two tablespoons of milk. Heat the chocolate and the rest of the milk together, put in the salt and sugar, and, when scalding hot, add the yolks of the eggs, beating constantly. Let the mixture cook two minutes, remove from fire and, when partly cooled, add the flavoring. Line a pie plate with crust, turn in the cooled filling and bake twenty minutes in a quick stove. Beat the whites of the eggs to a stiff froth, sweeten with a tablespoon of powdered sugar and spread over the pie; then brown the egg white slightly in the stove. Serve cold.

Coconut Custard Pie

Two eggs, one pint fresh sweet milk, pinch nutmeg, one-half cup powdered sugar, one cup of coconut, few grains of salt. Beat the eggs and sugar together until light; then add the milk, nutmeg, coconut and salt. Line a deep pie plate with crust, pour mixture in, stirring well, and bake thirty to forty-five minutes, in a moderately hot stove. There should not be enough heat to cause the custard to boil, for this will make it appear watery and very uninviting; the stove should, in fact, be a little moderate for most pies. At the end of the time, insert the point of the knife in the custard and, if it comes out clean (not milky), the pie is done. If the spice is well stirred into the sugar, it will not accumulate in an unsightly manner on top of the custard. Do not cut the pie until quite cold.

Whipped Cream Pie

Sweeten, with powdered white sugar, one teacup of very thick sweet cream, made as cold as possible without freezing. Flavor with lemon or rose water to taste. Beat very light and fluffy and keep very cool until the crust is ready. Make crust moderately rich, prick well with a fork to prevent blistering and, bake until golden brown. Cool shell. When quite cold, fill with the whipped cream. Dot with bits of jelly over the top. Keep cold. Must be eaten the same day.

Grape Pie

Pop the grape pulps out of the skins into one dish, and put the skins into another. Simmer the pulps over the fire to soften them; remove them and rub them through a colander to separate them from the seeds. Then put the skins and the pulps together. Fill the pie tin, lined with pie paste. Bake in a moderately hot oven, cover with meringue made with two egg whites beaten to a stiff froth and three tablespoons sifted sugar. Spread over the top, return to oven and bake a few minutes until lightly colored.

Good, Old-Fashioned Gooseberry Pie
(1890)

Top and tail the gooseberries. Put into a porcelain-lined kettle with just enough water to prevent burning, and stew slowly until they break. Take them off, sweeten well, and set aside to cool. When cold, pour into a pastry shell and bake with a top crust of puff paste (see p. 225). Brush all over with beaten egg while hot, and set back in the stove to glaze for a few minutes.

Fresh Strawberry Pie

Cap and pick over fresh picked strawberries, arrange in layers, besprinkle with a *good* sprinkle of sugar, in a shell of good pastry. Fill it very full, as strawberries shrink very much in cooking. One teaspoon of cornstarch wet with a little juice may be mixed in to thicken. Cover with a good crust and bake until golden brown. Eat cold with a good sprinkle of powdered sugar.

Banana Pie

Slice raw bananas, add butter, sugar, allspice, and a little vinegar or boiled cider, diluted with jelly; mix together, bake with two crusts in a moderately hot stove until the crusts are golden brown. Sprinkle top thickly with powdered sugar. Very nice.

Huckleberry Pie

Select the pie tins that are to be used and fill them evenly with berries, to determine how many will be required. Throw the berries into a pan, look them over carefully, remove all the stems, and wash berries. Drain off all the water from them and let them dry in a towel. Wipe pie dishes clean, dust with a little flour in the bottom of each, line them with a good paste. When ready for the berries, drain them once more and sift flour over them until each berry becomes a *little white ball*, but being careful not to leave surplus flour in the bottom of the pan containing the berries.

Allow a scant cup of sifted powdered sugar to each pie, stir it well into the fruit, and turn the latter into the pie plates. Cover each pie with an upper crust and press the edges well together, for much of the richness of the berries will be lost if the juices escape in baking. Bake (about one hour) and serve cold. Sift powdered sugar thickly over the top. Flouring berries in this way, while still a little wet from the washing, will make just enough thickening to counteract the excessive amount of juice these berries are capable of giving off.

Lemon Custard Pie

Three eggs, separated, two small, fresh lemons, one-and-a-half cups of powdered loaf sugar, one-half cup water, one-and-a-half cups milk, one tablespoon melted butter. Separate the yolks from the whites; rub the sugar with the yolks to a cream and add the water and the milk. Stir all well together and put in the melted butter. When everything is ready to put the filling into the crust, add the juice and grated rind of the lemons. If added this way, the acid will not break the milk. Bake three-quarters of an hour. Whip the whites to a stiff froth, add four tablespoons of powdered sugar, spread the whites on top of the pies. Return them to the stove to brown slightly. These pies should be eaten cold.

Mincemeat Pie

Four pounds (two-thirds apple, one-third meat), three pounds stoned and chopped raisins, two pounds currants, washed and dried, three quarts good cider, one pint brandy, one heaping teaspoon cinnamon, one of nutmeg, one of cloves, one-half teaspoon mace, one-fourth pound citron, cut up very fine, one-half wine glass of sherry. The meat should be a good piece of lean beef, boiled the day before it is needed. Half a pound of raw suet, chopped fine, may be added. Chop the meat, clean out the gristle and bits of skin, and mix with twice the quantity of fine, juicy, chopped apples; then put in the fruit, next the sugar, (make very sweet with brown sugar) add spice, lastly the brandy and wine. Mix very thoroughly, cover closely, and let stand together for twenty-four hours before making pies.

(Keep in a very cool place. Place mincemeat mixture in stone jars, tied over with double covers. Add a little more brandy or sherry wine (if the mincemeat seems dry). Lay strips of notched paste, crossbar pattern, upon top of pie, instead of top crust. Be sure to wash your currants in warm water several times, then in cold water, to remove all foreign matter.)

Peach Pie

Line a pie tin with puff paste (see p. 225), fill with pared peaches in halves and quarters, well covered with sugar. Put on upper crust and bake. Or make as above without the upper crust, bake until done, remove from stove, and cover with a meringue made from two egg whites beaten to a stiff froth with four tablespoons sifted sugar; return to stove and brown lightly.

Country Garden Tomato Pie

Peel and slice green tomatoes; add four tablespoons vinegar, one of sweet butter, three of sugar; flavor with a grating of nutmeg; bake slowly with two crusts. This tastes very much like green apple pie.

Pineapple Pie

A cup of sugar, half a cup fresh sweet butter, one of heavy sweet cream, five eggs, one ripe pineapple, grated. Beat butter and sugar to a cream, add beaten yolks of eggs then the pineapple and cream, and lastly, the beaten whites whipped lightly. Bake with the undercrust only. Keep in a cool place.

Mashed Potato Pastry

Two cups sifted flour, two teaspoons of baking powder, half teaspoon salt, one-half cup fresh sweet butter or other shortening, one cup cold, mashed potatoes, milk or water. Sift flour, baking powder and salt; work in the butter with the tips of the fingers, add mashed potatoes; and just enough fresh sweet milk or water to make a soft dough; turn out onto a floured pastry board, pat out and roll out to fit pie pan. Handle dough as little as possible, too much handling will toughen it. Brush with egg white. Place in a hot stove for five minutes. Fill with chopped meat mixture for meat pie, chicken or fish.

Very Good. If desired, cover top of the pie with rolled out crust. Prick with a fork.

Pumpkin Pie

One quart fresh pumpkin, stewed and strained, one quart fresh sweet milk, one cup powdered loaf sugar, seven eggs, beaten very light (about ten minutes), one teaspoon of powdered ginger, the same of mace and cinnamon. Beat all together and bake in crust with cover.

Sweet Potato Pie

Parboil, skin and slice crosswise firm sweet potatoes.
Line a dish with pie paste, put in a layer of sliced
sweet potatoes, sprinkle thickly with brown sugar,
scatter a few cloves among them and cover with more
slices of sweet potatoes. Fill the dish in this order, put
a tablespoon of butter in each pie, pour in a little
sherry wine or water, cover with crust and bake. Eat
cold or warm.

Grated Sweet Potato Pie

One pound mealy sweet potatoes. The firm yellow
ones are best. One-half cup fresh sweet butter, three-
fourth cup powdered loaf sugar, one tablespoon cinnamon, one teaspoon nutmeg, four eggs, whites and
yolks beaten separately, one cup fresh sweet milk, one
of lemon, juice and rind, and a small glass of brandy.
Parboil the potatoes, and grate them when quite cold.
If grated hot, they will be sticky and heavy. Cream
the butter and sugar; add the yolks, spices and lemon;
beat the potatoes in by degrees until all is light; then
the milk, then the brandy, stir in the whites gently.
Bake in dishes lined with good paste, without a cover.
Cool before eating.
NOTE: The reader will note that countryfolk in the
'old days' used a greater amount of spices and seasonings in pie fillings, cakes, cookies, puddings, etc. than
normally used in everyday cooking and baking.
Reduce amount to suit own taste.

Sunday Supper Mashed Potato Pie
(1875)

One pound mashed potatoes, rubbed through a
cullender, one-half cup fresh sweet butter, creamed

with the sugar, two cups powdered loaf sugar, six eggs, whites and yolks beaten separately, one lemon squeezed into mashed potatoes while hot, one cup fresh sweet milk, one teaspoon nutmeg, the same of mace. Mix all ingredients, fold in stiffly-beaten egg whites. Bake in open shells of pie paste. To be eaten cold.

This is a delicious pie, light and fluffy, and may be made according to directions given above. Its spicy taste and aroma may be reduced by using only one-fourth the amount of spices. Its souffle-like texture, puffed high and baked a light golden brown, may be eaten hot as well as cold.

Rhubarb Pie

Peel or string tender, young rhubarb by breaking off each stem end and stripping down the thin skin that will be found clinging to the broken portion. Break the rhubarb into small pieces, and measure it in a pie dish to ascertain the quantity needed. Place the pieces in a pan, flour them until they are quite white and add a cupful of sifted sugar to each pie. Line a pie dish, put in the rhubarb, with the sugar stirred into it, cover with the uppercrust, and bake one hour. Serve cold. Sprinkle top thickly with powdered sugar.

Supper Pie

Line a pie tin with good pie paste, saving some for the top crust. Put into this a layer of cooked rice, cooked soft, dot with small pieces of crisp, broiled bacon, next a layer of cooked chicken or turkey meat, cut in pieces, then a layer of fresh cooked sweet corn, (scraped off the cob). Repeat until the pie dish is full.

Season with salt and pepper to taste. Cover with top crust, prick with a fork and bake until done. A fine supper or Sunday breakfast dish.

Squash Pie
(1880)

Stew fresh picked squash till dry, press through a colander; to each pint of this, allow one tablespoon sweet butter; beat in, while warm, one cup of brown sugar or dark molasses, a little salt, and one teaspoon of soda; a little allspice may be added, but it darkens the pie. Roll a few crackers fine and add a handful to the batter, as the thickening property of the squash varies, some judgement must be used in adding the milk or cream. This is an eggless pie. For a richer pie, add egg yolks; beat whites to a stiff froth, fold into mixture gently. Pour into a pie plate lined with a good pie paste. Bake until the filling is firmed.

BREAD AND ROLLS

Good bread baking was an accomplishment which every housewife strived for, and her proudest moment came when she placed her beautiful, plump, golden loaves on display at country fairs. There were many blue ribbon winners and neighbors vied with each other to purchase the prize winning loaves. Recipes were rarely used as most of them baked by 'ear.' Many of the countryfolk had their own millstones to grind their wheat and corn with a hand crank. Barrels of golden corn meal and wheat flour were stored in a 'cold' room until aged and ready to use.

In the following chapter there are many old and interesting bread recipes, some dating back to the very beginning of the nineteenth century.

Grandma's egg bread is a treasured, early 1880 recipe; with variations, strictly holiday fare. During the Christmas holidays, the bread was slightly sweetened and filled with a variety of dried fruits and nuts.

Grandma's Egg Bread

One-pound-and-a-quarter sifted flour, one teaspoon salt, one cake yeast, one heaping tablespoon sugar, one-half cup fresh sweet butter, four eggs, half a cup of milk-warm water (lukewarm), one tablespoon honey, one egg yolk beaten with a teaspoon of warm water, and flour for the breadboard. Soften yeast in half a cup lukewarm water, sprinkle with tablespoon of sugar. Cover, set aside in back of stove for five minutes, until it begins to foam. Stir in enough flour in a large, warm, dough pan to make a stiff dough; knead well until smooth, then drop ball of dough into a small saucepan of lukewarm water or milk and let stand covered, in back of the stove, until doubled in bulk (about fifteen to thirty minutes). Put the rest of the flour in a clean, warm, dough pan, add salt, honey, butter, softened but not melted, and the four eggs. Mix to a paste, then beat thoroughly with the hand or a large wooden spoon, until the mixture is smooth. When the sponge is light and doubled in bulk, carefully pour off any excess water, or remove with a slotted spoon. Place the sponge in the center of the egg mixture, fold the egg mixture over the sponge and continued to mix until well blended. Turn dough out onto a floured breadboard; if dough is sticky, work in a little flour. Knead for ten minutes. Place in a warm, buttered bowl, cover. Set in a warm place, free from drafts, until doubled in bulk, or set in a cold place for several hours or overnight. The dough will have risen to double its bulk. Turn dough out on a floured breadboard, knead for a few minutes, shape into loaves. Place in two buttered and floured bread tins. Cover. Place in a warm place until the dough reaches the top of the pans. Brush with beaten egg yolk. Bake thirty to forty-five minutes in a rather moderate stove. When golden brown, tap with fingers; if the bread sounds hollow, it is done. Cool five minutes, remove from pans, tilt bread, on side, across bread tins until cold. If a good crust is desired, remove bread from tins and return to stove for five to ten minutes. When bread is cold, return to tins; it will keep fresh and moist longer. (Do not open door of stove for first half hour.)

Grandma's Egg Bread
(1966)

This is an old recipe of Grandma's egg bread streamlined for modern use. It is fragrant, golden and delicious and may be baked in bread pans or braided into twists. Brush lightly, before placing in oven, with egg yolk beaten with one teaspoon of warm water. Sprinkle with poppy seeds if desired. The following recipe, using almost the same basic ingredients grandma used, fills us with pleasure as we pass this on to collectors of time-honored and cherished recipes. It is certain to have the same exquisite aroma and taste as the one grandma used long ago. The addition of a half teaspoon of baking powder results in a lighter and more delicate bread.

Two packages active dry yeast, one-half cup lukewarm water, one-half cup softened butter or margarine, three eggs, one egg yolk, beaten with one teaspoon water for top, one teaspoon salt, one cup hot potato water, one medium mashed potato, three-and-a-half to four cups sifted flour and one-half teaspoon baking powder.

Soften yeast in lukewarm water, sprinkle with one tablespoon sugar. Cover, set aside in a warm place until it begins to foam. Combine softened butter with eggs, salt, potato water, mashed potato and one tablespoon of honey, if desired, in a large mixing bowl. All ingredients and bowl must be at room temperature. Add yeast mixture. Add gradually, about three cups of flour, then enough flour to make a soft, pliable dough. Turn out onto a floured board, and knead for ten minutes.

When dough is smooth and elastic, place in a warm buttered bowl. Cover with a clean cloth. Place in a warm place, free from drafts, until doubled in bulk, about one to one-and-a-half hours. Turn dough out onto a floured board, knead a few minutes. Cut into two parts, shape into loaves and place into buttered and floured bread pans. Cover. Let stand in a warm place until doubled in bulk. Brush with egg yolk (room temperature). Bake in a preheated oven at 400° F. for ten minutes, reduce heat to 375° F. and continue to bake thirty-five to forty minutes longer, or until the loaves are golden brown. Tap with fingers, when they sound hollow, they are done. Cool five to ten minutes. Tilt bread on side across bread pans until cold. Keep away from drafts.

More Egg Bread
(1875)

Three cups fresh sweet milk, one heaping tablespoon fresh sweet butter, two eggs, beaten well, three tablespoons good yeast, or one cake compressed yeast, one tablespoon sugar or honey, one teaspoon salt, one-fourth teaspoon soda, and flour, sifted, to make a pretty stiff batter. Make all the ingredients, except the eggs and soda, into a sponge, and set to rise overnight. Half an hour before breakfast, add the eggs and the soda (dissolved in hot water); beat all together hard; turn into buttered bread pans or muffin tins (for rolls); let them stand on the hearth for ten minutes and bake twenty-five minutes in a brisk stove until golden brown.

The Bread of Our Forefathers
(1885)

Put in a pan two quarts of cornmeal and half a pint of flour, sifted; stir up well; pour in the center a pint of boiling water, stir up enough of the meal to make a thin batter; cool. Put in a cup of yeast, a teaspoon of salt and enough warm water to make a thick batter; let rise. Then place in well-buttered pans, cover with another pan, and place in a moderate stove. When nearly done, remove cover and bake slowly until done. Excellent when cold.

(All baking pans for bread should have covers, made of the same material, and high enough to permit bread to rise to its full size. If pan is not deep enough to permit bread to rise without touching the cover, a flat piece of tin may be inverted over the bread. The office of the cover is to prevent the crust from browning hard before the expansion of gases has made the bread porous and light.)

Anadama Bread

Anadama bread is an old New England recipe, originated by a fisherman who had a lazy wife and often had to do his own cooking. There are several versions of this true story; the most famous one is that his wife always gave him corn meal mush and molasses for dinner. One day she left the house in the midst of preparing the mush. The husband, desperately, mixed the mush with flour and yeast and set it to bake as bread, saying to himself, "Anna, damn her." The bread was so delicious that the neighbors begged for the recipe. For the sake of polite society, the bread is now known as Anadama Bread.

Two cups water, one-half cup corn meal, two tablespoons butter, one-half cup good molasses, two teaspoons salt, two cakes yeast, one-half cup lukewarm water, seven to seven-and-a-half cups sifted flour. Boil the water and gradually add corn meal in a slow stream, stirring constantly; add the shortening, molasses and salt; let stand until lukewarm. Add crumbled yeast cakes to one-half cup lukewarm water and let stand five minutes. Add to corn meal mixture. Stir in the flour gradually to make a stiff dough. Knead well for ten to fifteen minutes. Place in a warm buttered bowl, cover, and let rise in a warm place until doubled in bulk. Cut through the dough several times with a knife, cover, and let rise again for about forty-five minutes until doubled in bulk. Toss onto a lightly floured breadboard. Mold into loaves and place in buttered bread pans. Cover, and let rise again until doubled in bulk. Bake in a hot stove for fifteen minutes, then have heat moderate. Bake forty-five minutes or until done. Brush bread with warm melted butter, turn on sides to cool.

Soft Corn Bread
(Parkersburg, West Virginia)

One cup rice well-boiled, one-half cup corn meal, two eggs, one quart fresh sweet milk, salt to taste. Mix well. Turn into a buttered baking dish, bake in a moderate stove. Serve hot in the same dish in which baked.

Buttermilk Corn Meal Muffin Bread
(Governor's Mansion, Atlanta, Georgia, 1840)

Eight tablespoons white corn meal, three eggs, one cup cold, boiled rice, three small cups of fresh buttermilk, one good teaspoon soda. Beat eggs light, separately; to the yolks add part of the milk, and four tablespoons of the meal and the rice; then more milk and meal, and lastly the whites of eggs beaten to a stiff froth and the soda. Bake in buttered tins with a quick fire.

Molasses Corn Bread
(1882)

One heaping cup flour, two teaspoons baking powder, one-half teaspoon salt, three-fourth teaspoon soda, two to three heaping tablespoons molasses, one cup corn meal, two eggs, well beaten, one-and-a-half cups sour milk or buttermilk, and three tablespoons soft sweet butter. Sift dry ingredients, add corn meal and mix well. Combine eggs, molasses, sour milk and butter. Add to dry ingredients, mixing well. Bake in a buttered pan, in a hot stove for thirty-five to forty minutes or until golden brown. Cut into squares when cool.

Golden Corn Bread

Take a quart of fresh buttermilk, and one heaping pint corn meal, one teaspoon soda, one of salt, one tablespoon sugar and three eggs; mix well. Have the stove hot, do not bake in a deep pan. The batter seems thin, but bakes very nicely.

Plain Corn Bread

One well-heaped pint corn meal, one pint of sour milk or buttermilk, one egg, one teaspoon soda, one of salt. Mix. Bake in a buttered, dripping pan or gem pans. If preferred, one heaping tablespoon sugar may be added.

(To keep rolls or bread moist after baking, spread top and sides with warm, melted sweet butter. To keep crust soft, wrap in flannel breadcloth while warm. If raisins harden, keep in bread box.)

Brown Bread

Two-and-one-half cups sour milk, and one-half cup molasses; into these put one heaping teaspoon soda, two cups corn meal, one cup Graham flour and one teaspoon salt. Use buttered coffee cups. Steam three hours; afterwards brown in a hot stove.

Country Crumpets

Take one-and-a-half pounds flour, one quart warm water, one cup yeast, one tablespoon melted butter, one tablespoon maple syrup, one teaspoon salt; mix all together. Set at night, or six hours before baking. Beat well at the time of mixing, and also before baking.

Snow Cakes
(Woodbine, N. J., 1882)

This is an interesting, old recipe using freshly-fallen, dry snow in place of water. Take one part Indian meal, and two parts dry, clean snow; or if the snow be moist, use equal parts of meal and snow. Mix well in a cold room. Fill the pans rounding full, and bake immediately in a very hot stove. This makes an excellent quick bread.

(New snow contains ammonia which causes the batter to rise quickly.)

Oatmeal Bread

Four cups boiling water or fresh milk, two cups oatmeal, one teaspoon salt, two tablespoons soft sweet butter, two-thirds cup dark honey or molasses, one cake yeast, nine to nine-and-a-half cups sifted flour.

Pour boiling water or scalded milk over the oatmeal and butter. Cover and let stand for one hour to soften oats. Add salt, honey and veast, dissolved in the luke-warm water. Add flour gradually, beating it in well. Cover, let rise in a warm place, free from drafts, until doubled in bulk. Cut down several times with a knife. Knead well, shape into loaves and cover. Again, let rise in a warm place until doubled in bulk. Place in buttered and lightly-floured bread pans, let rise until the dough reaches top of pans. Bake in a moderate stove for forty-five minutes, or until the loaves are golden brown and crusty. Tap bread with fingers, if they sound hollow, they are done. Turn out of pans, let them rest on sides on top of pans, or on a wire rack. Cool.

To Prepare Homemade Seasoned Bread Crumbs:

Save all crusts and pieces of stale bread. Place in a pan in a warm stove until the bread is dry and toasted. Remove from pan, place toasted bread in a heavy, brown, paper bag. Crush with a rolling pin until reduced to a powder. Season crumbs with salt, pepper and favorite herbs. Store in tightly closed glass jars until ready to use.

Milk Bread, Simplified
(1899)

Here is a recipe dating back to the late 1800's. This bread is easier to prepare than the earlier ones, being simpler and not as time consuming; and the ingredients required are easy to obtain.

One pint milk (two cups), scalded and cooled, one tablespoon sweet butter, one tablespoon honey, one teaspoon salt, one-half cup yeast or one yeast cake dissolved in one-third cup warm water, five to six cups sifted, unbleached flour. Measure milk after scalding, and place in a large mixing bowl; add the butter, honey and salt. When cool, add yeast dissolved in warm water, then stir in the flour gradually, using only enough to make a soft dough. Start with five cups, that it may not be too stiff. Knead for ten minutes on a floured bread board until smooth and elastic. Place in a warm, buttered bread pan, cover with a clean cloth, set aside in a warm place, free from drafts, until light and doubled in bulk. Cut it down several times with a knife; divide into three parts; shape into loaves or rolls. Place in buttered bread pans, cover, let rise again until the dough rises to the top of the pans. Bake in a hot stove for forty to fifty minutes. Brush with warm, melted sweet butter, if desired.

YEAST: one fresh yeast cake dissolved in one-third cup warm water, add one tablespoon sugar, cover, set aside for five minutes, until it begins to foam, add to ingredients.

Poor Man's Bread
(1880)

One pint buttermilk or sour milk, one level teaspoon soda, pinch salt, and flour enough to make a stiff dough. Cut into three pieces, handle as little as possible, roll out one-inch thick. Place in a buttered, dripping pan, or round cake tins. Bake twenty or thirty minutes in a hot stove. When done, wrap in a breadcloth. Eat while warm with butter; breaking open like a biscuit. Each bread will be about the size of a pie.

(Breadcloth: A soft flannel cloth used only to wrap bread in. Never used for any other purpose.)

(If brown sugar hardens, put in a warm oven for a few minutes.)

White Bread
(1885)

He took bread, and giving thanks to God in the presence of all, he broke it and began to eat.   Acts 27:35

To make three loaves of white bread, warm and lightly butter the baking pans; sift three quarts flour into the bread pan; press down in the middle and, into it, put two small tablespoons of fine salt; pour one quart of *milk-warm* (lukewarm) milk slowly into the flour, while constantly stirring with the other hand, until a thin batter is formed; add a pint or more of potato yeast or one teacup of hop yeast. If compressed yeast is used, one yeast cake dissolved in warm water is sufficient. Mix thoroughly, adding more flour until dough is stiff; place on a floured bread board, knead vigorously for twenty minutes or more, flouring the bread board frequently to prevent dough from sticking to it. Divide dough into loaves of the size to suit pans, mold into a comely shape, place in pans. Rub over top a light coating of sweet, drawn butter. Set in a warm place, not too hot, to rise. Cover lightly to keep off dust and air, watch occasionally. Turn pans around when necessary to make loaves rise evenly; when risen to about double in size, draw across the top of each lengthwise with a sharp knife, making a slit half an inch deep. Place them in a moderately heated stove and bake one hour, watching carefully, after the first half hour to make certain that the proper degree of heat is kept. Before browning they will rise to double the size loaf than was placed in the oven. Put in pans deep enough to retain their shape. Bake until done and nicely browned. Nothing adds more to sweetness and digestibility of wheaten bread than thorough baking. When done, remove from pans immediately, to prevent sweating and softening of the crust. Place tipped on edge of pan, or on soft flannel cloth, resting on side to cool.

Summer Bread
(1885)

In summer, take three pints of cold or tepid water, four tablespoons yeast, one teaspoon salt; stir in flour enough to make a thick sponge. Let stand until morning, then add more flour until stiff. Mix well and then knead ten minutes; place in a pan, let rise until light, knead another ten minutes. Mold into four loaves and set to rise, but do not let it get too light. Bake in a moderate stove for one hour. If bread is mixed at six-o'clock in the morning, the baking ought to be done by ten o'clock.

Winter Bread
(1885)

In winter, take one pint buttermilk or sour milk; let it scald (not boil); make a well in the center of the flour, into it turn the hot milk; add one teaspoon salt, enough flour and water to make a sufficient sponge, and one teacup of yeast; let stand until morning, then prepare the bread as in summer (see above). This is more convenient to make in the winter, since a hot fire is needed to heat the milk.

Popovers

Old time cooks took special pride in the excellent popovers they made. Puffed high and light as a feather, they made the plainest meal a luxurious feast. Unexpected company could always count on popovers. Their tops were firm and golden brown, the centers filled with a dab of fresh sweet butter, jam or pale golden maple syrup. Often served as dessert with afternoon tea, or as a main dish, topped with mounds of creamed chicken or fish. Every country housewife had her own favorite recipe, usually given to her by her mother or grandmother, but the rule remains the same. The batter is prepared and poured into sizzling-hot, buttered, iron popover molds, and baked in a hot oven with the door tightly shut; and heaven forfend if anyone dared open the door. Many of the countrywomen were noted for their baking skill; for although popovers were simple to prepare, they had to wear their tops proudly as limp and fallen tops would have been a culinary disaster. Two tea-cups of sweet milk, two cups of sifted flour, two eggs, one tablespoon of sugar, one teaspoon salt (scant), and two teaspoons of butter. Rub the butter into the flour; add the eggs beaten light, separately, then together; then add the salt and milk. Bake them in sizzling-hot, iron popover molds in a hot stove. Fill only half full. Eaten with butter and jam for breakfast or tea.

Mile-High Popovers
(1966)

One tablespoon melted butter, two eggs, one cup milk, one cup sifted flour, half teaspoon salt. Blend with a spoon until the eggs are well mixed. Do not overmix, disregard lumps. Fill six well-buttered, glass custard cups three-fourth full. Set cups in muffin tin for easy handling. Place in a cold oven, set heat at 450° F. Do not open oven for thirty minutes. Popovers should be firm and golden brown. Remove from oven, puncture a few times around the neck of popover to release steam. Return to oven for ten to twelve minutes with heat turned off, for a beautiful golden crust. To reheat left-over popovers, place on a cookie sheet in a 350° F. oven until hot and crusty, five to eight minutes.

Squash Biscuits

One-and-a-half cups of cooked golden squash, well drained, one cup scalded milk, one-half cup light brown sugar, firmly packed, pinch cinnamon or nutmeg, one-half teaspoon salt, four tablespoons fresh sweet butter, one cake yeast, dissolved in one-third cup warm water, four-and-a-half to five cups sifted flour, chopped nuts. Place drained squash in a large mixing bowl, add milk, sugar, cinnamon, salt and butter. Mix and cool to lukewarm. Dissolve yeast in the warm water, sprinkle with one tablespoon sugar. Cover, set in a warm place, free from drafts, for five minutes, until yeast begins to foam. Add yeast to squash mixture, add about two-and-a-half cups sifted flour. Beat well with a wooden spoon, gradually add enough flour to make a soft dough. Turn out onto a lightly floured bread board, and knead for ten minutes until smooth and elastic. If the dough is sticky, add a little more flour, knead well. Place the dough in a warm, buttered bread pan, turn dough until the top is covered with the melted butter. Cover with a clean cloth. Set in a warm place, free from drafts, overnight, or for several hours during the day, until doubled in bulk. Turn out onto a lightly floured bread board, knead and shape into biscuits. Arrange on buttered baking pans, cover and let rise again until very light. Brush gently with warm, melted butter, sprinkle with nuts, and bake in a hot stove until golden brown, about fifteen to twenty minutes. Top with favorite jelly.

White Mountain Bread

Two pounds of sifted flour, with a quarter of a pound of fresh sweet butter and the same of lard rubbed through it, a teaspoon of sugar, add a little salt, mix it with a pint of sour milk, and stir through it a teaspoon of soda. Roll out very thin, bake on buttered tins. Mark with a knife into squares. Break up and serve hot.

Saratoga Bread

Warm two tablespoons of butter in a pint of sweet milk, stir it gradually into a quart of sifted flour, add half a teaspoon of salt and four tablespoons yeast; let rise all night if for breakfast. If for tea, set it at noon. Before baking, add half a small teaspoon of soda; pour into a buttered shallow pan, and bake half an hour in a good stove.

Maryland Beaten Biscuits

Two pints of flour, two tablespoons of lard rubbed through it, a little salt and one egg; rub all well together. Mix with cold milk into a stiff dough, and beat two hours with a rolling pin until snow-white. Mold into little balls rather larger than a walnut, flatten them a little, prick with a fork, and bake fifteen minutes in buttered pans.

Pocket Book Rolls

Take, at noon, one pint of morning milk, a piece of butter the size of a walnut, a tablespoon of sugar, and a little salt; boil all together; when cool, add a half teacup of yeast, two quarts flour, sifted; knead as you would bread, and set in a warm place to rise. It will be light by tea-time. Then knead it again; at bedtime knead it again, using as little flour as possible. In the morning, roll out without kneading, about one-half inch thick. Cut out, spread with soft butter; fold them over, put in a buttered pan; let rise a few minutes and bake until nicely golden brown.

Bread Cakes

Put to soak, overnight, a quart bowl full of broken stale bread in cold water to cover it; in the morning, strain through a clean cloth and squeeze out all the water. Mash bread in a basin with the back of a large wooden spoon. Add three beaten eggs, a little salt and a pint of milk, and enough flour to make a batter; bake as you would buckwheat cakes (see p. 51).

Potato Rolls

Boil two pounds of potatoes, mash them with two ounces of sweet butter, add a pint of milk, a little salt, one-half cup yeast, and flour enough to make a soft dough. Set aside in a warm place, covered. When light and doubled in bulk, roll out, cut in cakes like biscuits, using as little flour as possible. Set them in a warm place to rise, and bake ten minutes, or until the rolls are golden brown.

Very Fine Rolls

One pint new milk poured over two large boiled and mashed potatoes, two ounces of butter and two of lard stirred into the potatoes and milk, a teaspoon of sugar, one of salt, two pounds of sifted flour, and half a teacup of yeast; knead all together for twenty minutes after breakfast for tea; when very light, roll them out an inch in thickness; put in buttered pans, let rise again until very light, and bake in a hot oven.

Bread Muffins
(1854)

Take four thick slices of baker's bread and cut off the crust. Lay them in a pan and pour boiling water over them; but barely enough to soak them well. Cover the bread and, after it has stood an hour, drain off the water and stir the soaked bread until it is a smooth mass; then mix in two tablespoons of sifted flour and a half pint of sweet milk. Having beaten two eggs light, stir them gradually into the mixture. Butter some muffin rings; set them on a hot griddle, and pour into each a portion of the mixture. Bake them brown; send them to the table hot; pull them apart or open with your fingers; spread with fresh sweet butter. They will be found an excellent sort of muffin; very light and nice.

Country Fair Johnny Cake
(1862)

Two cups of sour milk, one cup of sifted flour, two cups of Indian meal, three tablespoons of melted butter, two tablespoons of sugar, one teaspoon soda, and two eggs. Place the milk, and sugar in a mixing bowl, and beat the eggs until very light. Dissolve the soda in a little cold water, and stir it into the mixture in the bowl. Then add the flour and meal, sifted together, the melted butter and the eggs, stirring these ingredients in the order named. Pour batter into well-buttered tins, bake thirty minutes in a quick stove; or before the fire on a board.

Johnnie Cake

A quart of Indian meal, a pint of warm water, a level teaspoon of salt. Sift the Indian meal into a pan. Make a hole in the center and pour in a pint of warm water, adding the salt. With a wooden spoon mix the meal and water gradually into a soft dough for a quarter of an hour. Stir hard, till it becomes light and spongy. Then spread the dough, smooth and evenly, on a stout, flat board. A piece of the head of a flour barrel will serve this purpose. Place the board upright, and set a smoothing iron or a large stone against the back to support it. Bake it well. When done, cut it into squares and send it hot to the table, split and buttered with fresh-churned sweet butter. You may eat it with molasses.

BEVERAGES

Note: When a guest was being paid a particular honor his cup was filled to overflowing. Hence the joy in the biblical phrase, ". . . my cup runneth over!"

Making Fresh Tea

If the kettle boiling be,
Seven minutes makes the tea.

Fresh-drawn, filtered water, just at the boiling point, is the first needful item when a cup of tea is desired. The second item is a clean, dry, heated teapot, preferably of chinaware. Never leave tea leaves and the liquid left over in the teapot for a cup mid-way between meals. Never drink the tea that has stood longer than five or six minutes upon the tea leaves. At the first boiling of the water, rinse the cleaned pot and let stand a moment on the hot stove to dry; put in the tea leaves and pour over the furiously boiling water; put on the cover and let stand five minutes on the hot stove without boiling. If made at the table, cover the pot with a 'cozy.' After standing more than five minutes the flavor of the tea is impaired.

Iced Tea

Make the tea by the first receipt, strain it from the leaves and keep it cool. When ready to serve, put two cubes of loaf sugar in a glass, half fill with broken ice, add a slice of lemon and a clove, fill the glass with the cold tea. If desired, add a sprig of fresh mint.

Tea Nectar

Make a quart of strong tea, pour it into a deep skillet, and set over the fire; beat the yolks of four new laid eggs, and mix with them a pint of good white wine, a grated nutmeg, and powdered loaf sugar to sweeten. Put all together; stir it over the fire until it is very hot, then drink in china dishes.

An Excellent Substitute for Milk in Tea

Allow four new laid eggs to four cups of tea. Beat up the whole of the eggs in a basin, pour over it the very hot tea. These should be added very gradually, and stirred all the time, to prevent eggs from curdling. In point of nourishment the tea is much improved by the addition of eggs.

Saloop

Take a quart of fair water, and let it boil one-quarter hour; then put in one-fourth ounce of sassafras finely powdered. Let boil one-half hour longer, stirring all the time, then add one-half cup good white wine, and the juice of two small lemons. Sweeten to taste. Drink it in china tea cups. 'Tis a great sweetener of the blood.

Roasting Coffee

Put one pound of *raw coffee* in a small frying pan. Place it on the stove, shake and stir occasionally for fifteen minutes, or till yellow. Then cover it, increase the heat, and shake until the kernels are a deep cinnamon or chestnut color and have an oily appearance. Be careful that none are burned. Keep covered and, when still warm, not hot, add one egg and its shell. Beat and stir until every kernel is coated with the egg. The egg will dry quickly. It helps preserve the flavor, is the cheapest form in which to use egg for clearing, and does not interfere with the grinding. Coffee should be kept in air-tight tin cans and ground only as required. The finer the ground the stronger will be the extract.

Coffee

Common Coffee Pot

One heaping tablespoon ground coffee, one egg shell, one cup freshly boiling water. Scald coffee pot. Put in the coffee and the egg shell. Add the boiling water. Cover the spout and boil just five minutes. Stir it well. Set the pot back off the stove, where it will keep hot, but not boil. Add half a cup of cold water. Pour out a little of the coffee and pour it back again to clear the grounds from the spout. Let it stand at least ten minutes. If served from the pot, be careful not to roll the coffee by shaking the pot, or by careless pouring. A tablespoon of caramel mixed with the ground coffee gives additional flavor and color.

Breakfast Cocoa

Two cups of scalded milk, two cups boiling water, two tablespoons cocoa powder, two tablespoons sugar. Scald the milk in a double boiler; mix the sugar and cocoa, stir in the boiling water, gradually, and let boil five minutes. Turn the liquid into the hot milk, and beat with a whisk for five minutes. Serve with additional sugar and cream, if desired.

Chocolate

Two ounces chocolate, four tablespoons powdered loaf sugar, one cup boiling water, three cups scalded milk. Break chocolate into pieces and melt over hot water; add the sugar and boiling water, and stir until smooth and glossy; let cook five minutes, beating meanwhile with a whisk to make frothy and prevent a skin from forming.

Cream and Flavoring

On occasion a flavoring of vanilla or cinnamon, one or both is a pleasing addition to a pot of hot chocolate or cocoa. If cinnamon bark be used, let it steep in the milk while scalding the latter. Add ground cinnamon to the sugar and cocoa powder, or to the melted chocolate. Whipped or frothed cream may be added to the liquid just before removing from the fire and also to each cup as it is served.

Wine Nogg
(1873)

Beat in a bowl the white of an egg to a stiff froth, then add the beaten yolk to the white. Sweeten a glass of good white wine with loaf sugar, which has been powdered fine. Beat it into the egg mixture and top with a few grains of freshly ground nutmeg.
(A strengthening and ideal refresher, and a great nineteenth century favorite.)

Camomile Tea

Steep one heaping tablespoon of Camomile flowers in a glass of boiling water. Cover tightly. Let stand one-half hour. Strain through a very fine sieve. Sweeten with honey or white sugar. Drink hot or serve on shaved ice with a paper-thin slice of lemon pierced with a clove.

(Very soothing and refreshing, and considered a real tonic. The hot water will release the delicate perfume of the Camomile flowers.)

Mead

One quart boiling water, one-half pint good molasses, two-and-a-quarter pounds brown sugar, one-half ounce of flavoring extract, two ounces tartaric acid. Put the water, sugar, molasses and acid together; add the extract, which may be sassafras, or any other kind used for such a purpose. Bottle and set away in a cold place.

To Make Mead: place two tablespoons of the syrup in a glass of ice water, stir until well mixed, add a quarter of a teaspoonful of bicarbonate of soda to render the drink effervescent. This is a most refreshing drink.

Nectar of the Gods
(Salisbury, N. C., 1893)

Beat up one strictly fresh egg in a glass and add, by degrees, one cup of fresh coffee prepared with cream and sugar to taste. Drink it while hot and you will find it so delicous that you will be willing to forgo any other coffee concoction.

Mother's Harvest Ginger Drink

One egg, one quart of very cold water, one-half pint of good vinegar, one scant tablespoon of ginger, three tablespoons of sugar. Beat the egg well, add to it the sugar and the ginger. Stir until perfectly smooth and put in the water. When the sugar is dissolved, add the vinegar, using this, however, according to its strength, only enough being required to give the drink piquancy. A very cooling summer refresher.

Currantade

One quart currants, one-half pint red raspberries, one quart syrup, two quarts water, juice of one lemon. Crush the currants and the raspberries, add the water and filter the whole through a jelly bag. Add the syrup, cold, to the filtered juice, turn into jars, close tightly, and let stand on the ice for two hours before serving. One quart of water and one pint of sugar boiled rapidly for twenty minutes gives about one pint of syrup at 35° on the syrup gage.

Pineapple Lemonade

Two cups sugar, one pint cold water, the juice of three or four fresh lemons, a freshly grated pineapple; let stand two hours, add a quart of water (cold charged water preferred) and serve at once.

Raspberry Shrub

One quart cider vinegar, six quarts red raspberries, one pint crushed loaf sugar to each pint juice. Put three quarts of the berries in an earthen jar, and pour over them the vinegar; let stand about twenty-four hours then strain through a jelly bag, pressing out all the liquid; pour this liquid over a second three quarts of fresh berries and let stand again twenty-four hours; again strain through the jelly bag expressing the juice. Add the sugar as above and boil twenty minutes. Store as canned fruit, or in bottles. To serve, use one-fourth cup of shrub to three-fourths cup cold water or charged water.

Grape Wine

Wash and stem the grapes and squeeze through a coarse cloth. Allow one quart of soft water to each three quarts of juice, and three pounds of brown sugar to four quarts of juice. Let stand six weeks in an open vessel, covered with a light cloth to exclude dust, and then bottle.

Claret Cup

One quart of claret wine, one quart of charged water, and one pint water or tea, the juice of six lemons, one-half cup good brandy, sugar syrup to sweeten, mint leaves, if liked, strawberries or pieces of pineapple or both. Mix all ingredients, except the charged water, the mint and the fruit; chill on ice. At serving add the other ingredients.

Hot Claret Punch

Heat a bottle of claret with half a cup of sugar, a piece of stick cinnamon, half a dozen cloves, and the juice of two lemons; stir the sugar to dissolve. Strain and serve.

Refreshing Mint Punch

Shake together, in a wide-mouth glass jar, one cup water, one cup of powdered loaf sugar, and the leaves of fresh picked mint. When the sugar is dissolved, add the juice of six fresh lemons and one cup currant juice. Fill the jar with cold water and chill on ice. Shake well and, when ready to serve, add one pint of chilled carbonated water.

Egg Punch

Beat together the yolk of one fresh egg and a tea-spoonful of honey for a few minutes; then add two teaspoons of sherry, brandy or port wine, stirring well. Beat the white of an egg into a stiff froth, stir into the egg yolk mixture, beating well. Serve at once. This will fill the glass. If desired, sprinkle lightly with grated nutmeg.

For egg milk punch, stir the egg yolk mixture into a glass of fresh cool milk, then beat in the frothy egg white.

PRESERVING

Jellies, Marmalades, Fruits
and
Sweetmeats

Preserves, Jellies and Marmalades

The preserving kettle was one of the most important utensils in the country kitchen. During the long, hot summer and in the early fall, the kettle bubbled constantly with the fresh fruits and berries which the surrounding land yielded. And since the country housewife would have to make sufficient quantities of preserves to last all through the winter, she was not only extremely diligent in her labors at the preserving kettle, but also regarded this otherwise laborious task as the one time in which she could be especially creative.

As a result, she included in her array delicious, jewel-toned jellies, marmalades, jams, old-fashioned apple butter; preserved whole fruits, brandied peaches and pears, and pickled fruits, fragrant with exotic spices. In some jars she even tucked in a fresh geranium leaf so that its heady perfume would further stimulate eager appetites.

Century-old recipes were handed down, from generation to generation, by word of mouth until each housewife—improving upon them as the years went by—swore they were her very own, original recipes.

At summer's end the countryfolk took prideful

pleasure in showing off their well-stocked preserve cellars, and many visiting folk would cluck their tongues in admiration at the great number and variety of preserves; each jar so neatly labeled and dated. At the country fairs the tables, which displayed the preserves, were as popular as those which displayed the cakes.

The country housewife labored long and hard at this task, but she found her reward in the loving appreciation heaped upon her by her family. More than any other woman in America at that time, it was the country housewife who could truly boast, "Man's work is from sun to sun, but woman's work is never done".

SOME RULES FOR PRESERVING

To a rural housewife, the making of her preserves was important not only as a family mealtime necessity but also because it reflected upon her ability as a cook —especially among her neighbors. Therefore, she was most careful to observe some time-honored rules, when preserving, which had been passed along from mother to daughter. Chief among these was to select only the very finest, firm and ripe fruits and vegetables for preserving. Then each pickle, vegetable or fruit was carefully wiped with a damp cloth before going into the big kettle; her rules forbade her washing them with dripping or running water which would often cause sogginess. Likewise, only the choicest, homemade cider vinegar was to be used. The muslin spice bags were prepared beforehand and kept in tightly covered jars, ready for use at a moment's notice. Grated horseradish or nasturtium leaves were placed in jars, to prevent mold from forming, and fresh, green, grape leaves were tucked amidst the pickles to keep them green.

Such were only a few of the dozens of 'homey rem-edies' handed down from generation to generation. In reading them over today, some may sound so terribly 'old-fashioned' but actually our generation is discovering that a great many of them are so practical to use, and so efficient in result, that more and more we are drawing upon these old 'receipts" and claiming them real culinary 'finds!'

GENERAL INSTRUCTIONS

Overripe fruit should never be used, all fruits with imperfections should be discarded; fruit must be dry and free from morning dew or rain. Do not touch the jelly bag while the fruit is dripping, squeezing will cause the jelly to be cloudy.

A New Way of Keeping Fruit

It is stated that experiments have been made in keeping fruit in jars covered only with cotton batting, and at the end of two years the fruit will be sound. The following directions are given for the process: Use crocks, stone butter jars or any convenient dishes. Prepare and cook the fruit precisely as for canning in glass jars; fill the jars with the fruit while hot, and immediately cover with cotton batting, securely tied on. Remember that all the putrefaction is caused by invisible creatures in the air. Cooking the fruit expels all these and thus protected will keep an indefinite time. It will be remembered that Tyndall has proved that atmospheric germs cannot pass through a layer of cotton.

(The above was written in 1896).

To Preserve Fruit Without Sugar
(1896)

Cherries, strawberries, sliced pineapple, plums, apricots, gooseberries, etc., to be used the same as fresh fruit, may be preserved in the following manner: Gather the fruit before it is very ripe; put it into wide-mouth bottles made for the purpose; fill them as full as they will hold, and cork them tight; seal the corks; put some hay in a large kettle, set in the bottles, with hay between them to prevent touching; then fill the kettle with water to the necks of the bottles, and set it over the fire until the water is nearly boiling, then take it off; let it stand until the bottles are cold. Keep them in a cool place until wanted, when the fruit will be found equal to fresh.

A New Method of Preserving Fruit

A new method of preserving fruit; take pears, apples and other fruits, reduce to a paste by jamming, which is then pressed into cakes and gently dried. When required for use, it is only necessary to pour four times their weight of boiling water over them, and allow to soak for twenty-four hours, and then add sugar to suit the taste. The fine flavor of the fruit is said to be retained to perfection. The keeping qualities are excellent, so that they may be had at any time of the year, and bear long sea voyages without detriment. No peeling or coring is required, so there is no waste. (As the above instructions, written in 1896, indicate, the countryfolk unknowingly dehydrated and then rehydrated fruits. Often certain foods were prepared, for their excellent keeping qualities, and packed and taken on long trips and sea voyages.)

Cherry Jelly
(1890)

Two cupfuls of apple pectin, two cupfuls of cherry juice, two cupfuls of powdered loaf sugar. Combine pectin and cherry juice and bring to a boiling point. Skim and add sugar gradually. Simmer gently until the jellying stage is reached. Pour into jelly glasses and cool.

1966 VERSION

An easy and simple way to make cherry, orange, apple and pineapple jelly, and have fun doing it, is to purchase natural cherry, apple, orange or pineapple Gel, which may be found in the baby food section in most markets. Add two cups of cherry juice to two cups of cherry fruit Gel and two cups of super-fine sugar. Cook according to directions above. Pour into sterilized jars, or small jelly glasses. Pronto! And so simple to prepare.

Currant Jelly

Pick the currants when fully ripe, strip them from their stems, and put them over the fire in a large kettle. When they commence to cook, mash them with a potato masher; when broken and boiling hot, put them a few at a time in a jelly bag or thick cloth, squeeze out all the juice, and to every pint allow a pound of sifted, powdered loaf sugar; put the juice over the fire in a preserving kettle, let it come to a boil, skim it well, put in the sugar, stir until dissolved, then lift it from the fire and fill the glasses. Paste up the next day with letter paper, lay a piece on top of the jelly to fit inside of the glasses before you cover and paste.

Four Fruit Jelly

Take equal quantities of ripe strawberries, raspberries, currants and red cherries. All should be fully ripe and the cherries must be stoned, taking care to save all the juice that comes from them in the stoning. Add it, afterwards, to the rest of the fruit. Mix the fruit together and put it into a large, linen bag. Squeeze it well into a tureen placed beneath. When it has ceased dripping, measure the juice; and, to every pint, allow a pint and two ounces of the best double-refined loaf sugar, finely powdered. Mix together the juice and the sugar. Put them in a porcelain preserving kettle. Set it over the fire and let it boil a half hour, skimming it frequently. Try the jelly by dipping out a spoonful and holding it in the open air. If it should congeal readily, it is sufficiently done. Put the jelly, warm, into tumblers or wide-mouth glasses. Take double tissue paper, it must be white and cut exactly to fit the surface of the jelly, and dip in brandy. Lay it nicely and smoothly inside the top of the glass, pressing it down with the fingers all around the edge. Then paste white paper over the top, and a little way down, notching it round with scissors to make it fit the better. Set the jelly away in a cool, dry closet.

Fine Orange Jelly

Take four large calves feet, singed, but not skinned. Boil them in a gallon of clear, soft water, until the liquid is reduced to one quart and the meat has dropped from the bones. Strain it into a pan, cover it, and let it stand until the next morning. It should then be a firm cake. Take a knife and carefully remove the fat from the top of the cake, and all the sediment from the bottom. Press some clean, soft blotting paper upon it, to clear from all remains of greasiness. Then cut the cake of jelly into slices and put them into a porcelain-lined preserving kettle. Add to them a-pound-and-a-half of loaf sugar, broken up, a pint of strained orange juice, and the yellow rind of four oranges, pared thin and cut into strips. Beat slightly the whites of six eggs and add them to the mixture, with three of their shells, crushed small. Set the kettle over a clear fire and stir until you see all indications of scum begin to rise. Then cease stirring immediately, or the jelly will be cloudy. After it has come to a boil, simmer it ten minutes, then pour the whole into a clean jelly bag; place a white pan beneath for the jelly to drip into. Take care not to squeeze the bag, or the clearness of the jelly will be irrecoverably destroyed. If it is not clear at the first running through, empty the bag, wash it clean, and return the jelly to it, and let it drip again. Repeat this, if necessary, till it is quite bright and transparent. When it has congealed and has become firm, put it into a glass bowl and break it up. If you wish it in molds, put the jelly into them while it is still liquid; but not until it is quite clear. The oranges should be ripe, highly colored, and rolled under the hand to increase the juice. (A very old recipe and quite unusual. Calves feet were probably used instead of pectin or gelatine to congeal the jelly and clarified with egg whites and egg shells to form a beautifully golden jelly.)

Calf's Foot Jelly

Take two calves' feet; add one gallon of water; boil down to one quart; strain well and, when cold, skim off fat; add to the whites of six eggs, well beaten, one pint white wine, one-half pound broken up loaf sugar, the juice of four lemons; mix well; boil the whole for a few minutes, stirring constantly, and then strain through a flannel. This forms a very nutritious article of diet for the convalescent.

Red Rose Petal Jam

Four cups red rose petals, four cups warm water, three cups powdered sugar, sifted, one tablespoon lemon juice, one to two teaspoons red beet juice. Cut off the white part of rose petals. Place petals in a deep porcelain-lined kettle with the water. Simmer gently until tender. Put through a fine sieve to drain. Combine rose petal liquid with sugar and three tablespoons clear orange blossom honey. Cook gently until the syrup spins a thread when dropped from a spoon. Add drained rose petals and beet juice and continue cooking until nice and thick. Pour into jelly glasses, cover with tissue paper dipped in brandy, tie up, and set aside in a cool place until needed. *Delicious served with afternoon tea. Spread thinly-sliced sponge cake or fresh baked popovers with the exotic rose petal jam.*

(Most everyone in the country raised flowers, especially beautiful red roses; when the roses reached full bloom the petals were used for lovely syrups and jam. They were poured into little, white stoneware pots and were proudly offered as gifts to friends; to a new mother, or a convalescing friend or relative. Nothing can taste more delicious than this delicately perfumed jam; it is true poetry and the nectar of the Gods. Recipes using flowers; violets, orange blossoms, nasturtiums, pink and red roses, date back to the old days, when perhaps great-grandmother conceived the idea. A rare delicacy. Perhaps only a jar or two was made and treasured, and served only on special occasions.)

Harvest Apple Marmalade

Break up four pounds of loaf sugar. Put it into a porcelain-lined preserving kettle and pour on a quart of clear, cold water. When the sugar has melted; stir it, and set the kettle over the fire and, after it has come to a boil, let it boil for a quarter of an hour, skimming well. Have ready some fine pippin or bell-flower apples, pared, cored and sliced. There must be enough apples to weigh four pounds when cut up. Put them into the syrup, adding the grated rinds of four lemons. Let it simmer, stirring it well, until the apples are all dissolved and forming a smooth mass. Then add the juice of the lemons, boil it fast, and continue boiling and skimming until it becomes a thick marmalade. It will generally require simmering an hour-and-a-half, and boiling fast half an hour more. When it is done, put it warm into deep, white-ware jars; cover it closely and paste white paper over the top, or tie a piece of bladder closely. Put it away in a dry cool place. For immediate use, put some in a handsome mold and, when cold and firm, turn it out onto a glass dish; first dipping the mold into warm water.

Fine Orange Marmalade

Quarter some large ripe oranges and remove the rind, the seeds, and the strings; taking care as you do so to save all the juice. Put the pulp and the juice in a porcelain saucepan, and mix it with an equal quantity of strained honey. If not sweet enough, add some powdered loaf sugar. Boil them together slowly, stirring frequently. Try, if it is done, by taking a spoonful and placing it in the cold air. If, in cooling, it becomes a very thick marmalade, it is sufficiently boiled. Put it into wide-mouth glass jars, and cover it closely; first, with a double tissue paper, cut exactly to fit the surface of the marmalade, and then with thick, white paper, pasted down carefully over the top of the jar. A cover of bladder, washed well, soaked in water, and then put on wet, to contract when drying, is still better.

Grandma Bertha's Prune Marmalade
(1874)

Two pounds prunes, one-and-one-half cupfuls of fine vinegar, two-and-a-half cupfuls of loaf sugar, broken up and powdered, one teaspoon cinnamon, one teaspoon powdered cloves. Soak prunes overnight in cold water and cook the next morning in the same water in which the prunes were soaked. After cooking slowly for forty-five minutes, drain well, saving the juice. Cut the prunes into small pieces and discard the pits. Place the prunes and the juice in an enameled saucepan with the vinegar, sugar and spices and simmer slowly for forty-five minutes, until the marmalade is thick. Place in small, white, stone jars or jelly glasses. Place one whole clove on top of the jelly before sealing.

(This beautifully spiced and aromatic prune marmalade brings back nostalgic memories of the very same marmalade my grandmother used to make. Dark, smooth and thick; the scent of cloves delicately perfumed the air as the little jars were opened. The prune marmalade was always spread on crusty slices of home-baked rye bread.)

Quince Marmalade

Pare, core and slice quinces; stewing the skins, cores and seeds, in a vessel by themselves, with just enough water to cover them. When this has simmered long enough to extract all the flavor and to break the parings into pieces, strain off the water through a thick cloth. Put the quinces into a preserve kettle when this water is almost cold. Pour it over them and boil, stirring and mashing the fruit with a wooden spoon as it becomes soft. The juice of two oranges to every three pounds of fruit imparts an agreeable flavor. When you have reduced all to a smooth paste, stir in a scant three-quarters of a pound crushed and powdered loaf sugar, for every pound of fruit; boil ten minutes more, stirring constantly. Take off and, when cool, put into small jars, with brandied papers over them.

A delicious quince cheese may be made by boiling down the marmalade until very thick. Pack into small pots. It will turn out as firm as cheese, and can be cut into slices for luncheon or afternoon tea.

(In the 'good old days' quince jelly, preserve or conserve was an important addition to the preserve closet. Its delicate perfume and distinctive flavor graced many a tea table. Today quinces are not readily available in most city areas, but the preserve may be found in fine gourmet food stores.)

Raisin Marmalade
(1879)

This recipe is particularly valuable in seasons when fruit is scarce. Take six fine, large, cooking apples, peel them, put them over a slow fire, together with a wineglassful of Madeira wine and a half pound of powdered loaf sugar. When well stewed, split and stone two-and-a-half pounds of raisins, put them to stew with the apples, and add enough water to prevent burning. When all appears well dissolved, beat it through a strainer, and lastly through a sieve. Mold it, if you like, or put it away in small preserve jars, to cut in thin slices for the ornamentation of pastry, or to dish up for eating with cream.

(The above recipe is a delightful change from some of the present day marmalades. Use plump, seedless raisins and, if desired, add a breath of your favorite spice for added aroma and flavor.)

Rhubarb Marmalade

Three pounds rhubarb, three-and-a-half pounds powdered loaf sugar, two lemons, four ounces almonds, finely ground. Select rhubarb that is pink and tender, (early spring rhubarb). Cut into one-inch-lengths, but do not peel. Place in a porcelain-lined or enameled kettle, with the sugar. Simmer slowly until the sugar is dissolved, then add grated rind and juice of two lemons. Add chopped almonds to the mixture, stir well and boil for thirty-five to forty minutes. Pour into small jars or jelly glasses; seal when cold.

Tomato Marmalade

Five pounds firm, ripe tomatoes, two fresh lemons, about two teaspoons grated ginger root, and four pounds of loaf sugar, broken up and powdered. Peel and slice tomatoes; cut lemons in paper-thin slices; add grated ginger root; put in a porcelain-lined preserve kettle and simmer gently for one hour. Add sugar and cook until thick and smooth; watch carefully so the bottom does not scorch. Cool. Pour into jelly glasses; seal.

A delicious *tomato butter* may be made by taking two pounds of tart, juicy apples, five pounds of firm, ripe tomatoes, one cup good cider vinegar, six cups of loaf sugar, broken up and powdered, juice of one small fresh lemon, a small, muslin spice bag, containing three sticks cinnamon, broken into one inch pieces, one slice ginger root, three blades mace, one dozen whole cloves. Place peeled and sliced apples together with peeled and cut up tomatoes in a porcelain-lined kettle with the sugar. Add the spice bag. Simmer slowly for three-and-a-half to four hours until the mixture is smooth. Discard spice bag. Pour into sterilized jelly glasses, seal. Set in a cool place until needed.

(Tomato butter, marmalade and preserves were a great favorite with the countryfolk. Usually served with a meat course, its sweet, tangy smoothness, laced with exotic spices, was a superb relish to serve at tea or supper; and always a prime favorite with the menfolk.)

Preserved Fruits

Measure an equal amount of white sugar with good, white vinegar into a stoneware crock, and let stand for two or three days. Add fruits in season, such as firm ripe peaches, small pears, cherries, figs, apricots, cubed melon, purple plums and some dates, if available. Fruit must be ripe and dry, and free from all moisture and imperfections. Keep in the cool part of the cellar or a cold closet, well covered, for six to eight months. It will then be ready. A delicious preserve, served either hot or cold with meats or fowl.

Preserved Cantaloupe

Peel and measure three pounds of sweet cantaloupes. Discard seeds, and cut into one inch cubes. Pour boiling, salted water over them. Strain well. Place in cold water, strain again. Place one cup good vinegar into a porcelain-lined kettle, bring to a boil. Add cubed melon, cook two minutes. Place in a deep tureen and keep in a cool place for two days. Strain well. Cook vinegar with one pound sifted, crushed and powdered loaf sugar, add six cloves and one small stick cinnamon, broken into small pieces. Boil fifteen minutes. Pour into a cleanly rinsed tureen. Cover and let stand overnight. Next day, put into little pots, cover, set aside in a cool place until ready to use.

Preserved Cherries

Stone the cherries, saving every drop of juice. Weigh the fruit, allowing a pound for a pound of sugar. Put a layer of fruit for one of sugar until all is used up; pour over the juice and boil gently until the syrup begins to thicken. The short-stem, red cherries, or the Morellas are best for preserves. Sweet cherries will not do.

Wild Cherry and Currant Jelly

Two-thirds wild cherries, stone and all, and one-third of red currants. A pound of crushed loaf sugar to a pint of juice, and make as you would plain currant jelly (see p. 267). This besides being very palatable and an excellent table jelly, is highly medicinal, good for coughs and any weakness of the digestive organs. (This recipe was first put up as an experiment, now many of the countryfolk would not pass a winter without it.)

Preserved Figs

Pound for pound of ripe figs and sugar. Peel of one lemon and the juice of two. A little ginger. Cover the figs with cold water for twelve hours. Then simmer them in water enough to cover them until tender, and spread out upon a sieve or tray to cool and harden. Make a syrup of the sugar and a cup of cold water for every pound. Boil until clear of scum, put in the figs and simmer for ten minutes. Take them out and spread upon dishes in the sun. Add the lemons and ginger; boil the syrup thick; give the figs another boil for fifteen minutes, and fill the jars three-quarters of the way to the top. Fill up with boiling syrup, cover. When cold, seal up.

(Preserved figs was one of grandma's great favorite recipes and only served when the ladies gathered for a quilting bee or at the annual church supper. Often a good dash of brandy or sherry wine was added, together with coarsely chopped nuts and a bit of spice. It was considered a special delicacy, and passed along with small squares of pound cake or fresh baked egg loaf. Daughters begged for the recipe; usually it was inherited, along with grandma's collection of hand written recipes, but never given or passed along promiscuously.)

Preserved Ginger

Prepare the roots of fresh green ginger and lay them in cold water for fifteen minutes. Boil in three waters, changing hot for cold every time, until very tender; drain and lay in ice water. For the syrup, allow a-pound-and-a-quarter of sugar for every pound of ginger, and a cupful of water for each pound of sugar. Boil and skim until the scum ceases to rise. When the syrup is cold, wipe the ginger dry and drop it in. Let it stand twenty-four hours. Drain off and reheat the syrup. This time put in the ginger when blood warm (lukewarm). Do not look at it again for two days. Then reboil the syrup and pour over the ginger boiling hot. In a week, drain off once more, boil, and add again, while hot, to the ginger; cover closely. It will be fit for use in a fortnight.

Ripe Tomato Preserves

Seven pounds of round, yellow or red egg tomatoes, skinned. Seven pounds crushed loaf sugar, and the juice of three lemons. Drop tomatoes into hot water for a few minutes, remove skin. Let them stand together overnight. Drain off syrup and boil it, skimming well. Put in the tomatoes and boil gently for twenty minutes. Take out the tomatoes with a perforated skimmer and spread upon dishes. Boil the syrup down until it thickens, adding, just before you take it up, the juice of three lemons. Put the fruit into jars and fill up with hot syrup. When cold, seal or tie up.

Preserved Pineapples
(1854)

Take six large, fine, ripe pineapples. Make them very clean, but do not pare off the rind or cut off the leaves. Put them, whole, into a very large and very clean pot or kettle. Fill it up with cold water and boil the pineapples till they are so tender that you can penetrate them all through with a twig from a broom. Then take them out and drain them. When cool enough to handle them without inconvenience, remove the leaves and pare off the rind. The rind and leaves, left on while boiling, will keep in the flavor of the fruit. Cut the pineapples into round slices, about half an inch thick, extracting the core from the center, so as to leave a round hole in the middle of every slice. Weigh them, and to each pound allow a pound of double-refined loaf sugar, broken up and powdered fine. Cover the bottom of a large dish, or dishes, with a layer of sugar. On this, place a layer of pineapple slices; then a layer of sugar; then another of pineapple; and so on until all the pineapple slices are covered; finishing with a layer of sugar. Let them stand twenty-four hours. Then drain the syrup, and lay them in wide jars. Put the syrup in a clean preserving kettle, and boil and skim until the scum ceases to rise. Then put it hot upon the pineapple. While still warm, cover the jars closely, and paste paper over them. They will be found very fine.

(This unusual recipe for preserving pineapple, is reprinted above in the original text, dating back to the early 1850's. Only porcelain-lined preserving kettles were used. They were scoured clean with sand and dried in the hot sun. Although the countryfolk lacked our modern detergents they made use of natural substitutes; when sand was not available, ashes were used in its place. The preserves were sealed with rounds of tissue paper dipped in brandy, then covered with a bladder, which was washed and soaked in water and put on wet, that it may contract in drying. This method was often used to keep the jars airtight.)

Fruit Chutney

Take five pounds tart apples, three small onions, one small, sweet red pepper, four small, sweet green peppers, one cup white raisins, juice of two small lemons, two cups good cider vinegar, one cup cooked cranberries, strained, two cups brown sugar, two pieces preserved ginger, chopped, pinch cloves, pinch cinnamon. Chop apples, onions and peppers well, add vinegar and strained cranberry jelly. Cook gently over medium heat for one-and-one-half hours, stirring frequently with a wooden spoon to prevent scorching. Add raisins, spices and sugar, continue to cook gently

for one hour longer or until the mixture is smooth and
thick. Pour into jars and seal. Keep in a cool place until needed.

Watermelon Conserve

Six cupfuls of watermelon rind, with a slight pink
tinge to it, five cupfuls of apples, four oranges, four
to five small lemons, six cupfuls of crushed loaf sugar,
powdered and sifted, and five cupfuls of water. Chop
the rind into small cubes, discarding the green rind.
Peel the apples and remove the cores and seeds, chop.
Chop oranges, peeling and all, removing seeds. Use
the juice of the lemons. Mix all the ingredients and
boil slowly, stir up occasionally with a wooden spoon
to prevent scorching; simmer for three hours. Put in
jars and seal as directed for preserves.

Pear Honey

One peck of pears, four cupfuls of grated pineapple,
three-fourth pound sugar to every pound of fruit.
Pare and core ripe pears and put through a food chopper. Measure and add the sugar. Cook, without adding any water, over low heat until the mixture is
thick and the color of rich preserves. Add the pineapple, simmer for three to five minutes and place in
sterile jars.
(The farms all along the countryside yielded an
abundance of fruit in the late summer and early autumn; peach, apple and pear orchards were always
heavy with ripe fruit. Baskets of fruit were constantly
being brought into the kitchen; and the busy housewife had to use her imagination to preserve the fruit
in many different ways, adding a bit of preserved ginger, a stick of cinnamon, or a few whole cloves in order to change the flavor or aroma in each batch of

fruit. The preserves were labelled with the different spices and they knew at a glance which contained their favorite. The taste and the scent differed slightly, but the variety of flavors added a little interest and zest to their meals.)

Brandied Grapes

For this purpose the grapes should be in large, close bunches and quite ripe, but not bruised or soft. Remove every grape that is in the least shrivelled, or in any way defective. With a needle prick each grape in three places. Have ready a sufficiency of double-refined loaf sugar, powdered and sifted. Put some of the sugar in the bottom of the jars, then put in a bunch of grapes, and cover it thickly with sugar. Then another bunch, then more sugar, and so on till the jar is nearly full; finishing with a layer of sugar. Then fill the jar up to the top with the best white brandy. Cover the jars as closely as possible, and set them away. The grapes should be of the best quality, either white or purple or both; the varied colored grapes in the jars makes a very attractive addition to the preserve closet.

Brandied Peaches and Pears

Four pounds of fruit, four pounds of loaf sugar, crushed and powdered, one pint of the best white brandy. Make a syrup of the sugar and enough water to dissolve it. Let this come to a boil; put the fruit gently into the syrup and let boil for five minutes. Having removed the fruit carefully, let the syrup boil for fifteen minutes longer, or until it begins to thicken quite well; add the brandy and take the kettle at once from the fire. Pour the hot syrup over the fruit and seal. If, after the fruit is taken from the fire, a reddish liquor oozes from it, drain this off before adding the clear syrup. Put up in sterilized glass jars. Peaches and pears should be peeled before brandying.

Brandied Fruit Compote

Place one pound each of large, plump dried prunes, dried apricots, dried peaches, stoned grapes, and dried, sliced apples, in a large stoneware crock or bean pot. Slice one small, fresh lemon, very thin, add to pot. Dribble one pint fine orange blossom honey over the fruit. Add three to four cups of boiling water. Cover, set aside in a cool place for twenty-four hours. Pour over all one-half to three-fourth cup good white brandy. Let stand two or three days longer until the syrup is thick and the fruit is puffed and tender. Serve as a side dish with fowl or as a dessert.

Baked Fruit Compote: Place plump prunes, apricots, dried peaches, dried apples and stoned grapes in a large crock or bean pot; add enough boiling water to reach the top of the fruit; add one small, thinly-sliced lemon and orange, four to six whole cloves, one inch piece of cinnamon stick, one small piece candied ginger. Dribble dark honey over all. Cover bean pot or crock. Bake in a slow oven for three to four hours, or until the syrup is dark and thick. Cool. Set aside in a cool place until needed. Serve topped with fresh, thick, sweet or sour cream. Beautifully spiced, this may be served as a side dish or as a dessert topped with heavy sweet cream.

(Many of the fruits in season grew in such great abundance that the countryfolk dried them either on frames, in the hot sun, or in a very slow oven; the process was repeated for days, until the fruit was sufficiently dried. These were stored between layers of fresh leaves and served later as sweetmeats, or used in fragrant compotes.)

Brandied Fruit Sauce

One pint good brandy, one pint alcohol, four cups loaf sugar, broken up and powdered, dark red, sweet cherries, strawberries, blackberries, currants, firm, ripe, cubed melon, cubed pineapple, raspberries and white cherries. Add two cups of sugar to every two cups of fruit. Place fruit in a wide-mouthed stone crock; add the brandy, alcohol and sugar. Keep adding fruits and berries all summer, if necessary, add a little more brandy from time to time. Cover, place in a dark, cool place in the cellar; the syrup will thicken as it stands. The brandied fruits will be ready for a delicious dessert sauce for ice cream and cakes during the winter months.

Dried Peach Butter

One pound dried peaches, one cupful of loaf sugar, broken up and powdered, one-and-three-fourths cupfuls of water, one-fourth cupful of sherry wine and one teaspoon lemon juice. Wash the dried peaches carefully and soak overnight in cold water. Cook in the same water the next day until the fruit is very soft. Rub through a sieve with the back of a large, wooden spoon, add the sugar, sherry and lemon juice. Simmer gently until the peach butter is thick and smooth. Pack in small pots, seal and keep in a cool place.
Note: Dried peaches may be purchased in most food stores or health food stores.

Golden Autumn Pumpkin Butter

Eight cupfuls of pumpkin puree. Four cupfuls of broken up loaf sugar, powdered fine, one-and-one-half teaspoons cinnamon, one of ground ginger, one-fourth teaspoon ground cloves, one-fourth teaspoon ground nutmeg, four lemons. Pare pumpkin, cut into pieces, steam in a large perserving kettle until very soft. Drain and put through a sieve, rubbing it through with the back of a large, wooden spoon. To eight cupfuls of pumpkin puree add the spices and the juice of four lemons. Cook slowly in the oven until the pumpkin butter is thick and smooth. Pour into wide-topped jelly glasses. Cool and seal.

(During the month of October golden pumpkins in every size and shape dotted the entire countryside. The housewife's imagination ran riot. She produced luscious pumpkin muffins and bread, cooked delicious, creamy pumpkin soup, and made high, fluffy souffles with hot, mashed pumpkins, laced with molasses, spices, brandy, and puffed high with clouds of beaten egg whites and rich with fresh, heavy, sweet cream and fresh-churned, sweet butter. Some pumpkins were, of course, stored away for the Thanksgiving pies.

The younger members of the family pared and cubed the golden vegetable for the preserving kettle, to be made into fragrant pumpkin butter. As a reward for their labors, they were permitted to select a pumpkin of their choice for Halloween lanterns, which, with candle light flickering from their eyes, were placed on the porches, in the windows and in the fields, to add to the spookiness of the night.)

Crystallized Grapes

Take large bunches of fine, ripe, thin-skinned grapes and remove any that are imperfect. They must be ripe. Tie a string in a loop to the top of the stem. Strain into a deep dish, three whites of eggs, beaten lightly with a whisk. Dip the bunches of grapes into it, immersing them thoroughly. Then drain them

well and roll them about in a flat dish of finely powdered loaf sugar till they are completely covered with
it, using your fingers to spread the sugar into the
hollows between the grapes. Hang the bunches by
the strings till the icing is dry. They should dry in a
warm place. Send them to the supper table, or for tea,
on fine glass dishes or china plates. Decorate with
fresh picked mint leaves.

Dried Fig Cakes

Take your ripest figs and remove the acrid juice of
the skin by plunging them in boiling water. Remove;
sponge dry; cook in a rich syrup; boil down until
thick enough to dry on earthen platters or plates in
the sun or oven. Nice for eating as a sweetmeat, or
for using in cakes or puddings. A delicious fig marmalade may be made by taking your ripest, softest
figs and peeling them as for preserves; make your
syrup with three-fourths of a pound of crushed loaf
sugar to one pound of fruit and cook all together,
slowly, till it becomes a thick pulp, stirring constantly;
when it becomes thick, great care is needed not to let
it burn; this can be prevented by placing your preserve kettle in water. Add a fresh, thinly-sliced lemon,
with seeds extracted, to the pulp, or a piece of
minced, preserved ginger for a piquant flavor.

Red Rose Petal Syrup

Four cups rose petals, two cups water, two cups loaf
sugar, broken up and powdered, four whole cloves.
Place cleaned rose petals, with the white part cut
away, in a deep porcelain-lined kettle. Add just
enough water to cover petals; add sugar and cloves.
Cover and simmer gently for one hour until the syrup
thickens. Add a few drops of red beet juice for a

deeper color. Strain through a fine sieve. Bottle syrup. Use rose petal syrup to flavor hot tea or chill and use to flavor lemonade, desserts or cakes.

Carrot Sweetmeats
(1880)

Boil very small, firm, fine-grained, fresh-picked carrots in water until tender; add sugar, some slips of citron, assorted fragrant spices, if preferred, a little good white wine; simmer slowly together until thickened; put away in little stone jars.

PICKLING
Pickles, Relishes, Fruits and Vegetables

Pickles and Relishes
Sweet and Sours

Every farmhouse along the countryside could proudly boast of having numerous jars of pickles, relishes, preserves, jams and jellies stacked high on shelves in cellars scrubbed as clean as their kitchens. Since the countryfolk raised an abundance of fresh vegetables and fruits, their large, old-fashioned kitchens were filled all summer long with the fragrance of good things cooking slowly in huge kettles on the back of the big, old stove. And lined up in rows, like so many small, transparent soldiers, were glass jars all ready to be sterilized in huge wash boilers.

The bubbling goodness of pickled cauliflower, chow-chow, piccalilli, tomato relish, catsup, vinegars, sweet pickles, spicy watermelon rind, pink cantaloupe rind, and an assortment of pickled plump peaches, plums, pears and cherries filled the air for weeks on end. From time to time the cook would dip the enormous ladle, used to stir the heavy ingredients, into the kettle and spoon out some of the spicy, taste-provoking syrup to sample on her tongue. Or again, she might dribble a little stream of syrup into a saucer to see if it was thick enough, or if it jellied properly when cooled.

Bumper crops of string beans, pickled, were eaten out of the jars long before they ever reached the table, and it was the rare cook indeed, or her helpers, who could resist 'sampling' the pickled walnuts—from an old, old sweet and sour recipe—which set their taste buds tingling with its pungent flavor of cloves and cinnamon stick. Barrels of sourkrout, (or sauerkraut) with apples and celery stalks nestling in its snowy whiteness, kept company with kegs of pickles 'drinking in' the dilled brine. These would be ready and waiting to 'set' upon the table in the dead of winter.

The countryfolk did not have to go to the country store for their 'sweet and sours'. Their storerooms, deep in the cold cellars, contained everything necessary to keep the household well supplied with these, plus many an additional 'surprise' which the diligent housewife would bring forth and set on the table for special occasions.

Celery Pickles

Put together in a porcelain-lined kettle two quarts chopped, white cabbage, two quarts chopped celery, three quarts fine vinegar, half an ounce of crushed white ginger root, and a bit of turmeric, one-fourth pound white mustard seeds, two tablespoons salt, five tablespoons of sugar; cook slowly several hours, until cabbage and celery are tender. The addition of chopped, sweet red peppers is good.

Piccalilli

One large, white cabbage, fifty small cucumbers, five quarts small strong beans, eight small carrots, one dozen sticks celery, five sweet red peppers, three green bell peppers, two heads of cauliflower. Chop fine, soak overnight in salt and water, then wash well and drain thoroughly. Pour over them hot vinegar spiced with mace, cinnamon and allspice; take off the vinegar and scald until safe to leave like common pickles; or seal while hot.

Chow Chow Pickles

Let two-hundred small cucumbers stand in salt and water, closely covered, for three days. Boil for fifteen minutes in half a gallon of best cider vinegar, one ounce each of white mustard seed, of black mustard seed, of juniper berries, and of celery seed (tying each ounce separately in swiss bags). Add one handful of small green peppers, two pounds of loaf sugar, broken up, a few small onions, and a piece of alum half the size of a nutmeg; pour the vinegar, while hot, over the cucumbers, which have been rinsed well with cold water. Let stand a day, repeating the operation three or four mornings. Mix one-fourth pound of mustard with the vinegar, pour over cucumbers, and seal up in wide-mouthed jars.

Green Tomato Pickle

One peck green tomatoes, sliced, six large onions, sliced, and one teacup of salt. Let stand twenty-four hours, then drain well. Scald in one pint of vinegar and one quart water for fifteen minutes, then drain. Take two quarts of vinegar, two pounds of brown sugar, one-fourth pound of white mustard seed, one tablespoon each of cinnamon, cloves, and allspice, one teaspoon dry mustard, one-half teaspoon cayenne pepper. Boil thirty minutes.

(This green tomato pickle recipe was found tucked away, written on a scrap of paper, yellowed with age, between the leaves of a very old book. One had to use one's own imagination as to what to do after the pickle was cooked. Probably, taking for granted that all country housewives were experts in canning and preserving, they trusted their own good judgment and skill, and were able to get their own delicious and satisfying results. Each cook had her own secret spice bag to nestle between layers of relishes. Although they used the same basic recipe, each had her own 'special' ingredient to add; thus there are dozens of variations upon the basic recipe.)

Stuffed Pickled Red Peppers

Take large red ones (the best variety of sweet pepper), make a small incision at the side, take out the seeds, being careful not to mangle the peppers; soak in brine that will float an egg, for two days, changing the water twice. Stuff with chopped cabbage, chopped tomatoes, seasoned with spice as for pickled mangoes (see p. 300) (omitting the cayenne pepper), or stuff with a mixture of nasturtium seeds, chopped onions, red cabbage, chopped, grapes and cucumbers, seasoned with mustard seeds and a little mace. Cover with spiced vinegar. Cover the jar closely. Keep in a cool place until done.

Pickled Red Cabbage

Cut a good, firm, red cabbage into quarters; spread it on a flat platter or large dish and sprinkle thickly with salt; set it in a cool place for twenty-four hours; then drain off the brine, wipe it dry and lay it in the sun for two hours. Cover it with cold vinegar for twelve hours. Prepare a pickle by seasoning enough vinegar to cover the cabbage with equal quantities of mace, allspice, cinnamon, black pepper, a cup of sugar to every gallon of vinegar, and a teaspoon of celery seed. Pack the cabbage in a large stone jar; boil the vinegar and spices five minutes and pour on hot. Cover and set away in a cool, dry place. It will be good in a month. A few slices of fresh beet root improves the color.

Pickled Eggs

Pickled eggs are very easy to prepare and are an excellent accompaniment with cold meats. Boil hard three-dozen eggs, drop them in cold water and remove the shells, and pack them, when entirely cold, in a wide-mouthed jar, large enough to let them out without breaking. Take as much vinegar as will cover them entirely, and boil in it white pepper, allspice, a little root ginger; pack them in a stone jar, or wide-mouth jars, occasionally putting in a tablespoon of white and black mustard seeds, mixed, a small piece of garlic, if liked, sliced horseradish, whole cloves and very little allspice. They will be fit for use in eight or ten days. Color with beet juice and use as a garnish for salads.

Pickled Nasturtium Seeds

Take the green seed after the flower has dried off. Lay in salt and water for two days, in cold water one day. Pack in bottles and cover with scalding vinegar; season with mace and white peppercorns, and sweeten lightly with white loaf sugar. Cork and set away four weeks before you use them. They are an excellent substitute for capers.

Pickled Button Onions

Take small button-onions; remove outer skin and lay the onions in dry salt for twenty-four hours. Then soak off the salt in several waters; wash them well and put them into a porcelain-lined kettle with equal quantities of vinegar and water. Simmer them until tender. Then take them out and drain them. Return them to the kettle and scald them with fresh vinegar boiled in another kettle. When cold, take them out, drain them again, and put them in wide-mouthed jars. Fill them up with cold vinegar. Place among them thin muslin bags with mace and broken nutmegs. On top of each jar, put a tablespoon of sweet oil. Cover them tightly.

Country Fair Pickled Purple Plums
(1890)

The fruit must be large, fine, fully-ripe, and with no blemishes. To every quart of plums allow a quarter of a pound of loaf sugar, powdered and sifted, and a pint of the best vinegar. Damsons being more acid will require a half pound of sugar. Put the fruit with the sugar and the vinegar in a preserving kettle, add little bags of broken pieces of cinnamon and blades of mace, and, if you choose, a few cloves. Give them one boil, and skim them well. Put them in warm stone jars and cover them closely at once. By winter they will be fit to eat.

Pickled Sauerkraut with Green and Rosy Red Apples

The real pièce de résistance amongst the countryfolk were the small, wooden barrels of sauerkraut which they prepared in the early autumn. Between layers of tangy, snowy whiteness nestled red and green apples, green tomatoes tinged with red, and small ribs of celery with the leaves on; all home grown. The apples, tomatoes and celery marinated in the sauerkraut brine until they were soft and juicy, and one bite of the apple would release a stream of winy goodness; it was like both eating apples and drinking cold apple cider at the same time. An old, old recipe.

Core, wash and shred enough firm white heads of cabbage very fine. Line the bottom and sides of clean crocks or wooden kegs with cabbage leaves. Place in the bottom of the kegs a layer of shredded cabbage about three inches deep, sprinkle over about four ounces of salt. Alternate layers of shredded cabbage, with salt, apples, tomatoes and celery. Cover with a large plate, then with a clean cloth, and then place a large clean rock on top to weigh it down. When fermentation begins, the cabbage will sink to the bottom of the keg and the brine will come to the surface. Skim off the scum. Place barrels or crocks of cabbage in a cold part of the cellar to ferment for ten to fourteen days. *Uncover, skim off top every day.* Be careful to replace the plate, cloth and stone. (Tomatoes and celery may be omitted if desired, but the apples are a must.)

Pickled Peppers, Small Cucumbers and String Beans

Put all these vegetables together into a strong brine—strong enough to bear up an egg to the surface; and let them stay in it for three days. Then take them out and lay them in cold water for an hour. Change the water for fresh and let them remain another hour. Do this a third or fourth time. Having washed them well in fresh water, put them in a preserving kettle (one lined with delft porcelain is best), and surround and cover them with fresh cabbage leaves, or vine-leaves. Fill up the kettle with cider vinegar mixed with an equal quantity of water and, during four hours, let them simmer without boiling. Then take them off the fire, take them out of the kettle, transfer them to broad pans and pour the vinegar over them. When they are cold, return the pickles to the kettle (having first washed it clean), and scald them four times with fresh vinegar till it reaches the top. Lay among the pickles, mace, nutmegs broken small, mustard seed, and whole white peppercorns, tied up in thin, small, white muslin bags.

(Brine: A strong solution of salt and water)

Pickled Green Beans
(1875)

Pick fresh green beans of the best variety, when young and tender. String, and place in a kettle to boil, with salt to taste, until they are tender when pierced with a fork. Drain well through a colander. Put into a stone crock, sprinkle with a little cayenne pepper, cover with hot, strong-spiced, cider vinegar; add sugar if desired.

Grandma's Pickled Fruits
(1854)

Take a variety of young fruits, freshly picked, and put them into strong salt and water for three days; stirring them well, with a long wooden spoon, night and morning. Then take them out and spread them on trays, or old servers, or large flat dishes; taking care that they do not touch each other. Set them out in the sun every fine morning; and let them remain till sunset; but not if it becomes damp, or even cloudy. Do this until they are perfectly dry. Then wash them well in cold water, drain them, and wipe them separately with a coarse cloth. Put them into large jars. To a three gallon jar, put in half a pound of horseradish, sliced, and two cloves of garlic; half-a-hundred small, white onions, two ounces of mace, one ounce of cloves, two nutmegs, powdered, two pounds of the best crushed sugar, half a bottle of the best ground mustard, one pound of yellow mustard seeds, and half a pound of green ginger, sliced and scraped. Then take half an ounce of turmeric powder; mix it with sufficient vinegar to render it liquid, and pour it scalding hot into the jar, which must be no more than half full. Have ready some boiling vinegar, of the very best cider kind, and pour it scalding hot into the jar, until it is three-quarters full. The fruit will expand to their natural size. When perfectly cold, cover or cork the bottle tightly and seal. These fruits will be fit for use in a month; but improve by keeping. (For this pickle you may use firm purple plums, small peaches, berries, and any other fruit desired. The same recipe may be used for a variety of vegetables; such as button tomatoes, radish pods, beans, cauliflower, sliced white cabbage, sliced small cucumbers, celery, and small lemons or limes. Mixed together in any proportion desired. The turmeric gives a yellow tinge and is indispensable to this pickle. This sounds like a very complicated recipe, and only the brave may attempt it; but, made in small quantities, it is an interesting and an unusual mixture. The syrup is thick and golden, much like the Mustarda fruits imported today from Italy. A rare treat to serve with turkey, chicken or roast duck.)

Cider Mill Apples

Three quarts juicy, sweet apples, pare, core and remove all seeds; one-and-one-half quarts fresh, sweet cider, two cups brown sugar, or sweeten to taste. Put cored and sliced apples in a large porcelain-lined preserve kettle. Simmer gently for four hours until thick and smooth. Store in earthenware crocks in the cellar and use as needed.

Pickled Apples

With the tangy taste of fresh cold cider, these are simple and easy to prepare. An old, old recipe, but just as delicious today as it was in grandma's day. Pick tart, juicy, firm apples, discard ones with imperfections; remove stem and core carefully; do not break apples; do not peel. Stud each apple with three to four whole cloves. Make a syrup of equal parts of powdered loaf sugar and fresh, sweet, apple cider, about two cups sugar to two pounds of apples. Simmer apples gently in the syrup until tender, the *apples must keep their shape*. Cool. Boil down syrup until thickened. Pour over apples. Store in stone crocks in a cold part of the cellar. Pickled apples are delicious served as a garnish with roast goose, duckling or pork.

(See recipe for sauerkraut with pickled apples, p. 292. A real taste-treat.)

Pickled Raisins

Leave two pounds raisins on stem, add one pint good vinegar and half pound of crushed loaf sugar. Simmer over a slow fire half an hour. Cool. Place in widemouth jars. Cover tightly until needed.

Spiced Grapes

Take five pounds of grapes, three of sugar, two teaspoons cinnamon and allspice, half teaspoon cloves; pulp grapes. Boil skins until tender, put in sugar. Cook pulp, strain through a fine sieve, add it to the skins. Put in sugar, spices and vinegar to taste; boil thoroughly and cool.

Pickled Grapes

Fill a jar with alternate layers of sugar and bunches of nice, green and red grapes, just ripe and freshly gathered; fill one-third full of good, cold vinegar, and cover tightly until done.

Pickled Strawberries

Place strawberries in bottom of a large jar, add a layer of cinnamon sticks and cloves, then more berries, and so on. Pour over it a syrup made of two coffee cups of good, apple cider vinegar and three pints of loaf sugar, broken up. Boil five minutes; let stand twenty-four hours and pour off syrup. Boil, pour over berries, and let stand as before. Then simmer berries and syrup slowly for twenty-five minutes, put in jars and cover. The above is for six quarts of berries. Pineapples can be made in the same way, allowing six-and-one-half pounds of fruit to above proportions.

Pickled Watermelon Rind

Six to eight pounds of watermelon rind, four cups good homemade cider vinegar, six cups of brown sugar, three sticks cinnamon, broken into one inch pieces, one large lemon, thinly sliced, three teaspoons allspice, three teaspoons cloves, two pieces preserved sliced ginger. Cut the rind off the sliced watermelon with a bit of pink left on it, cut into uniform cubes. Soak rind overnight in salted water to cover. Drain well, cover with fresh boiling water and cook rind in a porcelain-lined preserving kettle until tender. Drain well. Rinse out kettle. Place vinegar, brown sugar and spices, tied in a little muslin bag, into the kettle. Bring to a boil, simmer ten minutes, add rind and lemon. Cook gently for forty-five to sixty minutes or until the rind is transparent and the syrup is thickened. Discard spice bag. Pour into wide-top, sterilized jars. Seal tightly. Keep in a cool place until needed.

(Watermelon rind was an important addition to the preserve and pickle closet. Its tangy sweetness, crisp and firm, laced with a variety of aromatic herbs and spices, covered with thick and beautifully perfumed syrup, was true company 'fare'; and always graced the table at holiday time. The green rind with a blush of pink on it made the meal a very festive occasion. The cook guarded her recipe jealously, and if asked how it was made, she often left out just a pinch or two of something, which still kept her 'receipt' unique.)

Fine Pickled Peach Mangoes

Take fine, large, freestone peaches. They should be ripe, but not the least bit bruised. The best for this purpose are the large, white, freestone peaches. Having rubbed off the down with a clean flannel, cut the peaches in half and remove the stones. Prepare a mixture, in equal portions, of mace, nutmeg, and root ginger; all broken up small but not powdered. Fill with this the cavities of the peaches whence the stones were removed. Then put together the two halves of each peach (making them fit exactly), and tie them round with coarse thread or fine twine. If you choose, you may stick the outside of the peaches all over with cloves. Put them into stone jars; filling each jar rather more than three-quarters full; and laying amongst them little, thin, muslin bags of turmeric to color them yellow. Fill up the jars to the top with good, cold vinegar of the best quality—real, white wine vinegar, if you are sure that it is real.

If the pickled peaches are to be sent to a distant place, or to a warmer climate, boil the vinegar, and pour it on scalding hot. Close the jars immediately; sealing the corks with red cement and tie a bladder tightly over the top of each. These peach mangoes will be fit for use in two months.

(Most of these pickling recipes date back to the very early and middle 1800's. They are written in the original text and make fascinating reading. These recipes may even be used today, using smaller quantities as desired; they are very simple to follow.

'Necessity was the mother of invention' and, when beef was slaughtered for home use, the bladder of the animal was washed thoroughly and cleaned well and dried. When ready for use, it was dipped in cold water and wrapped around each jar. These were saved and used as we would use wax paper or any plastic wrap.)

Pickled Cherries

Take large, fine, red cherries, perfectly ripe, and cut the stems about one inch long. Put the cherries into jars with layers of powdered loaf sugar between each layer of fruit, interspersing them with little, thin, muslin bags of broken bits of cinnamon stick, mace and nutmeg. The jars should be three-quarters full of cherries and sugar. Fill up with cold vinegar, cover closely.

Pickled Blueberries
(1880)

Nearly fill a jar with ripe berries; and fill up with good molasses. Cover and set away. In a few weeks they will be ready to use.

Pickled Peaches, Pears and Sweet Apples

For six pounds of fruit use three pounds of loaf sugar, broken up, about five-dozen cloves and a pint of very good vinegar. Into each whole apple, pear and peach, stick two cloves. Make a syrup from the sugar and vinegar, when it begins to boil, add the fruit. Cook until tender.

(The above recipe may be prepared exactly as it is written. Use perfect fruit, dry, and free from blemishes. Small pieces of cinnamon stick and preserved ginger may be added for flavor and aroma. Tuck a small sprig of crisp parsley into the stem-end for extra eye appeal when serving.)

Stuffed Green Peppers

Get large, sweet green peppers, bell type are best. Cut around the stem, remove it, and take out all the seeds. For the stuffing, use two quarts chopped cabbage, a cupful of white mustard seeds, three tablespoons of celery seed, two tablespoons salt, half a cupful of grated horseradish. Fill each pepper with part of this mixture and, in each one, place a small white onion and a little piece of cucumber. Tie on the stem with string, put the peppers in a large, widemouth jar, and cover with cold vinegar.

Stuffed Mangoes

Get small, green muskmelons or cantaloupes. Cut a small square from the side of each one and, with a teaspoon, scrape out all the seeds. Make a brine of one pint of salt to a gallon of water. Cover the mangoes with it while it boils. Let them stand for two days. Then drain them, and stuff them with the same mixture as used for the stuffed green bell peppers (see above). Pour boiling vinegar over them, using in it a small bit of alum.

Pickled Butternuts and Walnuts

Gather them when soft enough to pierce with a pin. Lay them in a strong brine five days, changing this twice in the meantime. Drain, wipe them with a coarse cloth; pierce each by running a large needle through it, and lay in cold water for six hours. To each gallon of vinegar allow a cup of sugar, three-dozen each of whole cloves and black peppercorns, half as much allspice, and a dozen blades of mace. Boil five minutes; pack nuts in small jars and pour over them the scalding hot vinegar. Repeat this twice within one week; tie up and set away. They will be good to eat in a month, and very good eating too. (Strong Brine: Very strong salted water.)

Tomato Ketchup
(1846)

Twenty-four nice, ripe, red tomatoes, skinned, four large onions, and six large green peppers, chopped fine; four tablespoons salt, four of brown sugar, four of ginger, one of cinnamon, one of mustard, two nutmegs, grated, eight cups of cider vinegar. Boil all together till thoroughly cooked, about three to three-and-one-half hours, stirring frequently with a large, wooden spoon. Bottle while hot.
(To Skin Tomatoes: Blanch in hot water for one minute, remove skin with a sharp knife.)

Aunt Emma's Raspberry Catsup

Four quarts ripe, plump raspberries, four cups good, homemade cider vinegar, one-half teaspoon white mustard seeds, one slice fresh ginger root, one stick cinnamon, broken into pieces, six cloves, two cups loaf sugar, broken up and powdered. Place berries and vinegar in a porcelain-lined kettle, simmer gently for one hour. Strain well through a fine sieve, rubbing through with the back of a large, wooden spoon. Wash out kettle, return puree to kettle, add mustard seeds and spices. Cook gently for twenty-five minutes, strain again, measure. Add two cups of sugar to each quart of berry puree. Simmer over low heat, stirring constantly until the raspberry catsup is smooth and thick. Pour into bottles when cool.

Tart Tomato Butter

Two pounds of tart, juicy, red apples, about five pounds of large, firm, ripe tomatoes, juice of one small lemon, one cup good cider vinegar, three cups brown sugar, three cups loaf sugar, crushed, two blades of mace, two sticks cinnamon, two slices of fresh ginger root, one-half teaspoon cloves. Place chopped apples, vinegar and sugar into a large porcelain-lined preserving kettle. Blanch and skin tomatoes, chop and add to the apples; tie spices in cheesecloth or into thin muslin bags and place into the kettle. Simmer slowly, stirring constantly with a large, wooden spoon, for three hours or until the mixture is smooth and thick. Remove spice bag, cool, pour into wide-mouth jars, or small stone crocks. Keep in a cool place.

Clover Vinegar
(1881)

Pour a large bowl of molasses into a crock, and pour over it nine bowls of boiling rain water; let stand until milk-warm (lukewarm). Put in two quarts of fresh clover blossoms and two cups of baker's yeast; let stand two weeks. Strain through a linen towel. Nothing will mold in it.

(There was no end to the ingenious imagination of the country-folk. Nothing that grew was wasted. They knew every edible herb that grew wild in the fields, and also the uses for most of them. Clover vinegar is a very old, old recipe, and most unusual. Soft rain water took the place of distilled water (we believe) and that may have prevented mold from forming.)

Mint Vinegar

Put into a wide-mouth bottle enough fresh, clean peppermint, spearmint or garden-fresh parsley leaves to fill it loosely; fill up with good vinegar. Stop closely, leave on for two or three weeks. Strain, pour off into another bottle, and keep well corked for use. This is excellent for cold meats, to season soups and bread dressings for roasts.

Spiced Vinegar

Take one quart of cider vinegar, put into it one-half ounce of celery seed, one-third ounce of dried mint, one-third ounce dried parsley, one garlic clove, three small onions, three whole cloves, a teaspoonful of whole peppercorns, a teaspoon of grated nutmeg, salt to taste, and a tablespoon of sugar; then add a tablespoon of good brandy. Put all into a jar and cover it well; let it stand in a cool place for three weeks. Then strain and bottle it well. Useful for flavoring salads and other dishes.

CANDY

Candy

The fondness for sweets was easily satisfied as the country housewife drew from her imagination and from cherished, old, family recipes candies and tidbits using natural sweetening, dried fruits, nuts, and seeds. Golden honey, molasses, corn syrup, homemade peanut butter, roasted nuts, pumpkin and sunflower seeds were made into taffies, fudge, peanut brittle, bonbons and chocolate sweets. Popcorn, always a great favorite with the children, was either salted, buttered or glazed with syrup and mixed with nuts and raisins—providing a nourishing nibble for the entire family. The sparkle of birthday parties, holidays, and family celebrations seemed gayer when mother brought forth her trays of homemade candies.

Excellent Cream Taffy
Pulled

Two cups powdered loaf sugar, sifted, one-half cup vinegar, one-half cup water, butter the size of a walnut; boil without stirring until the candy will harden when dropped in a little cold water. A small bit dropped off a teaspoon is sufficient. Flavor with vanilla. When cool enough to handle, pull until snow-white. Cut into sticks or break into uneven pieces.

Chocolate Caramels

One cake chocolate, grated, scant one pint sweet milk, one-fourth pound sweet butter, one pound powdered loaf sugar, sifted; boil slowly, stirring to prevent burning. Flavor with vanilla. Try a little in a saucer to determine when it is done. Stir until it begins to thicken. Pour quickly into buttered pans and cut into squares.

Chocolate Fudge

Four cups powdered loaf sugar, sifted, one cup fresh sweet cream, one cup water, one-half cake chocolate, one-half cup sweet butter. Cook until it just begins to hold together, then pour into pans, not buttered; when cool enough to bear a finger, stir it until it no longer runs. It should not grain but be smooth. Cut into squares.

Chocolate Peanut Clusters

Melt one cake of chocolate over hot water (not boiling) until smooth, adding a lump of sweet butter; stir with a wooden spoon. When completely melted, remove from fire at once, stirring well. Add one-and-a-half cups of roasted peanuts. Drop from a teaspoon onto a buttered tin. Let stand until cold. Store in a paper-lined tin.

Chocolate Crisps

Melt a cake of chocolate over hot, but not boiling water, until smooth, adding a lump of butter; stir with a wooden spoon. When completely melted, remove from fire at once. Spread on small, plain, crisp crackers or thin cookies. Sprinkle with coconut or coarsely chopped nuts. Let stand in a cool place until the chocolate hardens.

Almond Hard-Bake

Boil one-and-three-quarter pounds of brown sugar with one-half pint water until brittle. Lay one pound of roasted, split almonds on a buttered tin, over which pour the syrup. Let cool until it hardens. Break into uneven pieces. Store in a tin.

Dried Fruit and Nut Candy

Cut a few figs in two and tastily arrange on a buttered tin, exposing the seeds as much as possible. Add a few raisins, some walnut and almond meats, an occasional date, stoned, brazil nuts cut into lengthwise pieces, a few red cinnamon candies and some thinly sliced coconut. Put in a kettle two-and-one-half pounds powdered loaf sugar, one teaspoon of cream of tartar and three-fourth pint water. Boil until brittle. When tested, pour over fruits and nuts. Do not stir the sugar while boiling, or even scrape from the sides of the kettle when pouring out. When cold, break into uneven pieces.

Roasted Peanut Candy

Into a kettle put one-and-a-half pounds of brown sugar, and one pint water; boil until it snaps when tested. Add two ounces sweet butter, three-quarter pound roasted peanuts. Pour into a buttered tin. When partially cold, cut into sticks with a stiff, sharp knife.

Chocolate Covered Fruits

Melt a cake of chocolate over hot but not boiling water. Stir with a wooden spoon, adding a lump of butter. When completely melted, remove from fire at once, stir well. Have ready some stoned plump prunes and any dried favorite fruits. Place fruit on a fork, dip into the slightly cooled chocolate, covering fruit completely. Place on a lightly buttered sheet of paper until the chocolate hardens. Keep in a cool place. These are very good to serve at afternoon tea.

Mother's Pets

Have ready a few dozen small gingersnaps or very thin butterscotch cookies. Dip into melted chocolate, coating cookies on all sides. Top each with half of a pecan or walnut. Set aside in a cool place to harden. When cookies are not available, toast white baker's bread lightly. Cool, trim off crusts, and cut into four squares. When dry and crisp, dip into melted chocolate and sprinkle thickly with freshly grated coconut mixed with a little powdered sugar.

(These are delicious sweets for the children and can be made in a hurry when out of the usual candy assortment.)

Crystallized Popcorn

One cup powdered loaf sugar, sifted, enough water to dissolve it, and a lump of butter as large as a walnut. Boil until it strings from a spoon, then stir quickly into three quarts of popped corn. Add assorted nuts and raisins. Stir well with a large, wooden spoon until the popcorn and nuts are completely coated. Cool. Break up into pieces.

Peanut Butter Balls

Pulverize loaf sugar in a mortar until it is like flour. Mix one cup with one cup peanut butter. Add one cup grated coconut, one-half cup chopped nuts, one to two tablespoons honey, pinch ginger. Turn mass out onto a board dusted with powdered sugar. Knead until thoroughly mixed. Pinch off pieces the size of a small walnut, roll into balls. Set in a cool place to harden.

Walnut Anna
(Fort Fairfield, Maine, 1896)

Two cups brown sugar, one-half cup fresh sweet cream; boil together for twenty minutes, or until it ropes. Then take from the fire and add one cup broken walnut meats; pour into a shallow, buttered tin. When partially cool, crease in squares with a knife. When cold it will be pronounced delicious even by the most fastidious epicures.

Grandma's Old Fashioned Candy

One quart good molasses, four cups shelled nuts, (roasted) one cup soft brown sugar, and one half cup sweet butter. Combine all ingredients except nuts. Boil for one half hour over a slow fire. Then add the roasted nuts, and continue cooking for fifteen minutes. Drop on lightly buttered cooky tins, or on a piece of marble. Let the candy harden.

THE SAYING OF GRACE

"It is very nice to think
  The world is full of meat and drink,
  With little children saying Grace,
  In every kind of place."
                              —Robert Louis Stevenson

The country housewife arrived at the highlight of her day when the food and the baked goods, on which she had so laboriously toiled all day, were ready and set out on the table, and the entire family was gathered together for the main meal.

Now the time had come to give thanks to God for His bounty, and to beseech His blessing for the well-being of the family. This saying of grace, a family tradition with most of the country folk, was most often spoken by the head of the house. One of the children was sometimes selected for the occasion and more infrequently, the honor was passed to a guest at the table.

While the majority of the passages used in saying grace was culled from the Bible, some were also taken from various poets and others were contrived at the moment by the speaker. The following are just a few examples of the saying of grace in Nineteenth Century rural America.

Dear Father, bless this circle around this table,
Keep it alive with love,
Strong with faith,
And grateful for the
Blessings which enrich it.

—Canon Riley

Father, we thank Thee for love,
We thank Thee for food,
We thank Thee for work,
We thank Thee for understanding,
Keep our hearts humble, please,
That we may never forget
From whence all this comes.

Amen

Dear Heavenly Father, we do pray,
    That You will bless our food today;
Bless our family gathered here,
    And everyone whom we hold dear.

Amen
N.M.D.

It is good to give thanks to the Lord,
To sing praises to Thy name,
O Most High.

Amen
Psalm 92:1

We thank Thee, our heavenly Father,
For Thy care over us,
And pray that Thou wilt bless our food.

Amen

Be present at our table, Lord,
Be here and everywhere adored.

Amen

What God gives, and what we take,
'Tis a gift for His sake,
Be the meal of beans and peas,
God be thanked for those, and these,
All are fragments from His dish.

—Robert Herrick

We thank Thee, O Father,
For the bread on our table,
And for the mother who prepared it with love.

Amen

For food and all Thy gifts of love,
We give Thee thanks and praise.

Amen

We thank Thee, then, O Father,
For all things bright and good,
The seed-time and the harvest,
Our life, our health, our food.

—Matthias Claudius

Blessed art Thou, Lord our God,
King of the Universe,
Who bringest forth bread from the earth.

Amen

God is great, and God is good,
And we thank Him for our food,
By His hand we must be fed,
Give us, Lord, our daily bread.

Amen

We thank Thee, Lord, for our daily bread,
As by Thy hands our souls are fed,
Grant us to grow more like Thee,
Today and through Eternity.

Amen

O God, bless, reward, and keep all mothers
In Thy tender loving care,
Watch over little children,
The little sisters and brothers,
And fathers everywhere.

Amen

We thank Thee, for the food wherewith Thou
dost constantly feed and sustain us on every day,
in every season, at every hour.

Amen

THINGS WORTH KNOWING

Rose Sugar

Spread fresh rose petals on a flat dish and dry them in the oven. Put a pint of the dried petals in a mortar with a half pint of powdered sugar. Pound the whole into a powder, rub the latter through a fine sieve and bottle tightly. One tablespoon of the sugar will flavor desserts.

Orange Sugar

Cut off the thin, yellow rind of twelve oranges, then spread them on a platter, and set in a warm, dry place to dry. When the rind is dry, which will be in about forty-eight hours, put half of it in a mortar with a cupful of powdered sugar. Pound the mixture to a powder, rub through a sieve, return the coarse parts left in the sieve, and pound them once again. When all is through the sieve, put the balance of the peel and another cupful of powdered loaf sugar in the mortar and proceed as before. One tablespoon of the sugar will flavor one quart of custard or cream. Lemon sugar is made the same way.

Vanilla Sugar

Cut an ounce of vanilla bean into small pieces, mix them with a pint of powdered loaf sugar, and pound all in a mortar until the mixture is like flour. Sift through a fine sieve, pound what will not pass through and sift until all is fine. Allow a tablespoon of the vanilla sugar to a quart of cream.

How To Roll Bread

Cut off all crusts from a loaf of fresh, white, baker's bread. Spread a thin layer of butter on one end and cut off this end as thin as possible, using a very sharp knife; then roll up with the buttered side inward, and lay it on a napkin. Continue this way until the requisite of rolls are made. Draw the napkin firmly around them, tie them, and then set them in a cold place for several hours. Rolled bread is nice with raw oysters or at a supper or a luncheon party.

How To Make Tarragon Vinegar

Put bunches of fresh tarragon in a quart preserving jar; fill the jar with white wine vinegar, cover tightly and set it away in a cool, dark place for two or three weeks; then strain and bottle. Fill the jar once more with fresh vinegar and set it away. This will be ready in a month to use, but it need not be strained until the first is used. This vinegar is fine in any kind of salad and in many sauces.

How To Bake A Lemon Or Orange

Bake a lemon or orange twenty minutes in a moderate stove. When done, open up at one end and take out the inside. Sweeten with sugar and molasses. This is an excellent old remedy for hoarseness.

How To Get More Juice Out Of A Lemon Or Orange

Heat in a moderate stove, then roll around between the palms of both hands. The fruit will have twice as much juice when squeezed.

How To Chop Suet

Cut in small pieces and remove any membrane. Sprinkle small pieces with flour and chop in a cold place to prevent it from becoming sticky. Use as desired.

How To Dry Apples

Pare, quarter and core apples. String on a strong cord and hang out on a sunny, warm day. Take in before evening damp. Repeat every dry, warm, sunny day until the drying process is complete. Keep in a dry room at night. These dried apples retain their natural fresh flavor. Store in a cool place. Fine for compotes, pies and stuffings.

How To Blanch Almonds

Shell the almonds and pour boiling water upon them. Let them stand in the water until the skin may be rubbed off, then throw them into cold water. Rub off the skins between the hands and dry the nuts between towels.

How To Salt Almonds

Spread shelled and blanched almonds out on a bright, tin, pie plate, add a piece of butter, and set in a hot oven until they are golden brown. Stir with a wooden spoon until all the almonds are coated with the butter. Remove from the oven, stir well, dredge thickly with fine salt, and turn out to cool.
(Watch carefully so that they do not burn.)

How To Put Out A Grease Fire

Remove food if possible. Sprinkle heavy coarse salt on smoking skillet, stove or broiler. Fire will be snuffed out immediately.

How To Clean A Looking Glass

Divide a newspaper in two, make a square, folding it neatly. Wet in cold water. Rub the glass first with the wet paper, then dry with the other half. Fly specks and all other marks will disappear as if by magic. Use only the best quality paper, such as used by the best weekly papers. Paper which has wood or straw will leave lint on the glass.

How To Clean Silver Easily

Save the water in which potatoes have been boiled with a little salt, and let it get sour, which will be in a few days. Heat and wash the articles with a woolen cloth, rinsing in pure water. Never let a particle of soap touch the silver. For wiping silver, polish with an old linen cloth cut into squares.

How To Make An Old-Fashioned Rose Jar

Gather fresh rose petals on a dry day, after the dew is gone, and place the petals in rose jars, which are vases with lids. Arrange the petals in thin layers, covering each layer with a thin layer of salt. Repeat until the jar is filled. A handful of lavender flowers and rosemary leaves may be added. Add three ounces of pulverized bay salt, one ounce of nutmeg, one ounce of cinnamon, and one ounce of cloves. Keep the jar closely covered except when the perfume is wanted in the room.
(A very attractive addition to old-fashioned bedrooms.)

How To Prevent Hinges From Creaking

Rub with a feather dipped in oil.

How To Make Artificial Coral

Melt together four parts yellow resin and one part vermilion. Dip odd shaped twigs or stones in this. When dry they will look like coral. Very nice.

How To Make Bar Soap

Six pounds of washing soda, three pounds of un-slaked lime, six gallons of water, six pounds of clear fat. Place the soda and lime together, pour over them four gallons of water, and stir well. Let the liquid stand until perfectly clear, then drain it off, place it over the fire, add the fat, and boil until the mixture begins to harden (which will be in about two hours), stirring almost continuously. Meantime, after drain-ing the four gallons of water from the lime and soda, add the remaining two gallons of water to the sedi-ment. Stir well and, when this liquid is clear, drain off also. While the soap is boiling, thin it with this water, adding a little at a time, as the soap puffs up as if to boil over. Try the thickness by cooling a little on a plate, and put in a handful of salt just before remov-ing the soap from the fire. Wet a tub with cold water to prevent the soap from sticking, turn the latter in and, when solid, cut into bars, placing them on a board to dry.

Lard

The best way of preparing 'leaf lard', as it is called, is to skin it carefully, wash, and let it drain; then put it, cut into bits, into a large, clean, tin kettle or bucket, and set this in a large pot of boiling water. Simmer gently. Stir from time to time until melted; throw in very little salt, to make the sediment settle; and when hot (it should not boil fast at any time, but simmer gently until clear), strain through a close cloth into jars. Do not squeeze the cloth as long as the clear fat will run through and, when you do, press the refuse into a different vessel, to be used for commoner purposes.

Most of the lard in general use is made from the fatty portions of pork lying next to the skin of the hog, and are left for this purpose. Scrape the rind, and cut all into dice. Fill a large pot, putting in a teacupful of water to prevent scorching, and melt very slowly, stirring every few minutes. Simmer until there remains nothing of the meat but fibrous bits. Remove these carefully with a perforated skimmer; throw in a little salt to settle the fat and, when it is clear, strain through a colander, sieve or coarse cloth. Dip the latter in boiling water, should it become clogged by the cooling lard; observe the directions about squeezing the strainer. If the family is small, bear in mind that the lard keeps longer in small than in large vessels. Set away the jars, closely covered, in a cool, dry cellar or store-room.

In trying out lard, the chief danger is of burning. Simmer gently over a steady fire, and give it your whole attention till it is done. A moment's neglect will ruin all. Stir it very often, almost constantly at the last—and from the bottom, until the salt is thrown in to settle it, then withdraw to a less hot part of the fire. Bladders tied over lard jars are the best protection; next to these, paper, and outside of this, cloths dipped in melted grease.

(Every country housekeeper knew how unfit the pressed lard sold in stores was for really nice cooking. It was close and tough, melted slowly and was sometimes full of lumps. And even when lard was 'tried out' by the usual process, it was often mixed with much water. Therefore, housekeepers who wanted really fine lard always prepared it at home. It was a necessity, not only for frying and larding meats, but more especially for baking flaky pie crusts. The 'leaf' produces only the finest lard and was never mixed with inferior fat. Thus the directions given above for 'leaf lard' were always carefully followed by the country housewife. And the sizzling sounds of the rendering fat pushed to the back of the stove was a familiar sight in every country kitchen.)

Odds And Ends

A dish of hot water set in the stove will prevent cakes from scorching.

****

Gather herbs when beginning to blossom, keep in paper sacks.

****

Prick nutmeg with a pin, good oil will run out.

****

To remove a tight ring, hold hand in very cold water.

****

If your coal fire is low, throw on a tablespoon of coarse salt, and it will help it very much.

****

Dish water and soap suds poured about the roots of young fruit trees and berry bushes will facilitate their growth.

****

Cranberries will keep all winter in a keg of water.

****

Cover lemons with cold water, changing every week; this will make them more juicy.

To keep parsley fresh and green, place in a large preserve (glass) jar, cover tightly. Keep in a cool place.

****

To keep cake fresh put an apple cut in half in container.

****

To make fresh bread slice easily; place loaf in ice box to chill.

****

To measure molasses or honey; grease cup in which it is to be measured.

****

OLD-FASHIONED REMEDIES AND BEAUTY SECRETS

In the old days, grandma used many old-fashioned remedies, handed down for generations, to alleviate common ills and, in emergencies, doctoring each member of the family. Since the country doctor traveled over the countryside by horse and cart, it took hours, sometimes days, before he was able to reach a patient. Some of grandma's concoctions may not have cured but were harmless, and she knew enough about first aid, from a 'doctor's manual' which was kept close at hand, until professional help arrived. Many of her home remedies and the knowledge and the use of healing herbs has survived the test of time. She read and believed in the Scriptures and found in it many remedies and the use of "herbs for the healing of all diseases." And so the countrywife not only 'doctored' her family, but was also a nurse, midwife and 'jack of all trades.' Her day was long and hard; the following sentiment, written by a nineteenth century *Poor Methodist Woman*, so well expresses her joy and love for a leisure moment, and also her love for God, for her family, and for living.

"I do not know when I have had happier times in my soul, than when I have been sitting at work, with nothing before me but a candle and a white cloth, and hearing no sound but that of my own breath, with God in my soul and heaven in my eyes. I rejoice in being exactly what I am, a creature capable of loving God, and who, as long as God lives, must be happy. I get up and look for a while out of the window, and gaze at the moon and stars, the work of the Almighty hand. I think of the grandeur of the universe, and then sit down, and think myself one of the happiest beings in it."

Daily Strength for Daily Needs (1884)
Mary W. Tileston

PLEASANT AND SOOTHING FOODS FOR THE DELICATE STOMACH OR CONVALESCENT

Beef Tea

Put into a jar, without a drop of water, one pound of lean beef, cut into small bits. Cover tightly. Set in a pot of cold water. Heat gradually to a boil and continue this steadily, for three or four hours, until the meat is like white rags and all the juice is drawn out. Season with salt and a pinch of herbs. When cold, skim. The patient may prefer this cold or hot. Serve with thin, unleavened wafers.

Chicken Broth

One-half lean chicken, one quart water, cold, one tablespoon rice or barley, soaked in a little water, fairly warm. Four tablespoons milk, salt and pepper to taste, and a little chopped, fresh parsley. Boil the chicken, unsalted, in the water, keeping it closely covered, until it falls to pieces. Strain it out, skim, add the soaked barley or rice; simmer half an hour, stirring often. Stir in the seasoning and the milk, simmer five minutes after it heats up well, taking care to skim off any visible fat. Serve hot with cream crackers. (Crack the chicken bones before you put in the chicken.)

Beef And Sago Broth

Two pounds of beef, cut up small, two quarts water, one cup sago, soaked soft in lukewarm water, yolks of three eggs, salt to taste. Stew the beef until it falls to pieces; strain it out; salt the liquid and stir in the sago. Simmer gently for one hour, stirring often. Add the beaten egg yolks slowly, boil up once and serve. This is a strengthening and nice soup.

Calf's Foot Jelly

One calf's foot, one-and-a-half quarts of cold water. One-half cup sherry wine, one-half cup crushed loaf sugar, three whites of eggs with shells, one-half cup cold water, juice of one lemon. Scald and clean the foot thoroughly. Split and cut it into several pieces; add the cold water and heat slowly to the boiling point. Skim and let simmer about five hours, strain and let stand until cold. Remove all fat. Crush shells of the eggs and beat the whites slightly; add the water, lemon juice, about one teaspoon salt (to a quart), the sugar and stir the whole into the jellied liquid. Stir constantly while heating to the boiling point. Let boil one minute, then let stand to settle. Have ready a bowl, a colander in the bowl, holding a napkin wrung out in hot water, and a sieve on the napkin. Turn the hot mixture into the sieve, lift this with the egg shells and let the hot mixture filter through the napkin into the bowl. Strain a second time, if necessary. When cold, add the wine and strain into cups or molds. Considered a delicacy and very nourishing. Serve cold.

Elixir of Life

Butter and honey in the proportion of two parts fresh, melted sweet butter, and one part good, orange blossom honey. Whip up and spread on toast.

(Grandma's and great-grandma's favorite remedy for a sore throat or chest cold. A favorite food for generations, tending to rejuvenate the glands and renew their activity.)

A Tonic

Put in a pitcher two single handfuls of camomile flowers, and pour on them a quart of cold water. It will be ready in twelve hours. Take a wineglassful three times a day to produce an appetite in an invalid or convalescent.

(*Note:* Camomile tea bags are available in all health food stores. Steep in hot water according to directions, then chill. Makes a delicious and fragrant drink.)

Eau Sucré

Dissolve three or four lumps of loaf sugar in a glass of ice water, and take a tablespoonful every few minutes for a 'tickling throat' or a hacking cough. Keep it ice cold.

(A simple, old, but often efficacious, remedy.)

Jelly Water

One large tablespoon currant or strawberry jelly, one goblet of ice water. Beat up well for a fever patient. Wild cherry or blackberry jelly is excellent, prepared in the like manner, for those suffering with summer complaint.

Grandpa's Apple Toddy

Boil one large, juicy, pippin apple in a quart of water and, when it has broken to pieces, strain off the water. While it is still boiling, add a glass of very fine whiskey, a little lemon juice, and sweeten to taste. Take hot at bedtime for a cold or to warm the spirit.

Milk Punch
With . . . Spirit

One tumbler milk, well sweetened with loaf sugar powdered fine, four to six tablespoons good brandy, well stirred in.

(This milk punch has been known to brace a convalescent until nature rallies her forces. Give very cold with ice. An egg beaten in with a whisk until it is frothy, before the brandy has been added, is beneficial.)

Chicken Custard

Fill a buttered custard cup lightly with stale bread crumbs and finely chopped breast of chicken. Beat in a whole egg, or the yolks of two eggs; add a few grains of celery salt and pepper to taste, and half a cup or more of milk. Poach as any custard. Serve hot —very good.

Beef Tea Custard

Beat the yolks of three eggs slightly; add a few grains of salt and, very gradually, a cup of hot beef tea; cook in a double boiler, stirring constantly until the mixture thickens; then pass through a fine sieve or a linen napkin. Serve hot or cold in a custard cup. Very nice.

Egg Nog

Beat the yolk of an egg; add one to two tablespoons of sugar, beat again and, when mixed with the egg, add one tablespoon sherry wine or good brandy; mix again, then add gradually a cup of fresh milk and, lastly, fold in the white of an egg beaten to a stiff froth. A favorite and nourishing remedy for the convalescent.

Arrowroot Wine Jelly

One cup boiling water, two heaping tablespoons arrowroot, two heaping tablespoons powdered white sugar, one tablespoon good brandy or three tablespoons white wine. Wet the arrowroot in a little cold water and rub smooth. Then stir it into the hot mixture, which should be on the fire actually boiling at the time, with the sugar already melted in it. Stir until clear, boiling steadily all the while; add the brandy or the wine. Wet a cup with cold water and pour the jelly in it to form. Eat cold with sugar and cream flavored with rose water. An excellent corrective for the bowels.

Arrowroot Blanc Mange

One cupful of boiling milk, two dessert spoonfuls best arrowroot, rubbed smooth with a little cold water; two teaspoons of powdered white sugar, vanilla or other essence. Boil until it thickens well, stirring all the while. Eat cold with sweet cream flavored with rose water, and sweeten to taste.

Panada

Six Boston crackers, split, two tablespoons powdered white sugar, a good pinch of salt, and a little grated nutmeg. Enough boiling water to cover them well. Split the crackers and pile in a bowl in layers, salt and sugar scattered among them. Cover with boiling water and set on the hearth, with a close top over the bowl, for at least an hour. The crackers should be soft as jelly, but not broken. Eat from the bowl, with more powdered sugar sprinkled over them, if you wish. This Panada is very good.

Toast Water

Slices of white toast, nicely browned, without a symptom of burning. Enough boiling water to cover them. Cover closely and let them steep until cold. Strain the water, sweeten to taste, and put a piece of ice in each glassful.

Apple Water

One large, juicy pippin apple, the most finely flavored you can get. Three cups of cold water, one quart if the apple is very large. Pare and quarter the apple, but do not core it. Put on the fire in a porcelain saucepan with the water and boil, closely covered, until the apple stews to pieces. Strain the liquor *at once*, pressing the apple hard in the cloth. Strain again through a finer bag, and set away to cool. Sweeten with powdered white sugar and ice for drinking. It is a very refreshing and palatable drink.

Herb Teas

Herb teas are made by infusing the dried green leaves and stalks in boiling water, and letting them stand until cold. Sweeten to taste.

SAGE TEA: Sweeten with honey—good for a sore throat; with small bits of alum dissolved in it, it is used as a gargle.

CATNIP TEA: The best panacea for infant ills, in the way of a cold or colic; well known to nurses.

PENNYROYAL TEA: Will often avert the unpleasant consequences of a sudden check of perspiration, or the evils induced by ladies thin shoes.

CHAMOMILE TEA: An excellent tonic taken either hot or cold.

BLACKBERRY ROOT TEA: Said to be good for summer disorders.

GREEN STRAWBERRY LEAVES: Tea from green strawberry leaves is an admirable and soothing wash for a cankered mouth.

PARSLEY ROOT: Tea from parsley root, scraped and steeped in boiling water will often cure kidney and kindred affections, as will tea from dried pumpkin seeds.

MINT TEA: Made from the green leaves, crushed in cold or hot water and sweetened, is palatable and healing to the stomach and bowels.

DAMASK ROSE: Tea made from leaves of Damask rose, dry or fresh, will often subdue any simple case of summer complaint in infants.

Poison Antidotes

For any poisoning, swallow instantly a glass of cold water with a heaping teaspoonful of salt and one of ground mustard stirred in. This is a speedy emetic. When it has acted, swallow the whites of two raw eggs.

To Relieve Asthma

Soak a blotting paper in strong saltpetre water. Dry, and burn at night in your bedroom. An excellent prescription.

To Stop the Flow of Blood

Bind the cut with cobwebs and brown sugar, pressed on like lint. Or, if you cannot procure these, bind with the fine dust of tea. When the blood has ceased to flow, apply laudanum.

Cure for Burns

Take one part linseed oil, and two-thirds lime water, Shake up well; apply and wrap in soft linen. Until you can procure this, keep the part covered with wood soot mixed in a soft paste with lard, or, if you have not these, with common molasses.

Ivy Poisoning

A poultice of cornmeal and hops thoroughly cooked is excellent for oak and ivy poisoning.

Burns

Use common baking soda for burns.

For Chapped Hands

Rub with a mixture of glycerine and honey or apply pure mutton tallow at night.

Sunburn

A cake of brown Windsor soap scraped to a powder, one ounce of lemon juice, one ounce of cologne water. Mix well and form into cakes. Also removes tan and prevents hands from chapping.

To Remove Corns

A piece of lemon or a cranberry, mashed, bound on the corn will remove it readily.

An Excellent Way of Improving the Hair

Once in three days take some rich, unskimmed milk that has been made sour by standing in the sun. Stir it up, so as to mix it all through the cream that has collected on the surface. Wash the hair with this, rubbing it well into the roots. Let it remain on the hair about a quarter of an hour or more. Then wash it off with a lather of white soap and warm water; rinsing the hair, afterwards, with fresh water, either warm or cold, according to the season. This is an Asiatic process and, if continued every third day, seldom fails to render the hair of young people thick, soft and glossy.

Hair Tonic

Cold sage tea makes an excellent hair wash.
A Tonic: Best castor oil, one ounce, French brandy, two ounces, bay rum, two ounces. This may be scented with rosemary or rose geranium.

Antique Hair Oil

This is a fine oil for the hair. Mix together, in a clean vessel, half a pint of sweet almond and half a pint of the best olive oil. Then scent it with any sort of perfume. To give it color and the odor of roses, infuse, in the mixed oil, a small, thin, muslin bag of alkanet and perfume the oil with attar of roses. Put immediately into a bottle and cork it well. For a violet perfume, infuse, in the above quantity of mixed oils, an ounce of the best orris powder. Let stand in a warm place for a week; then pour the whole into a strainer, press out the liquid, and bottle it.

Milk of Roses

Mix together a pint of rose water, and an ounce of sweet almonds. Then add ten drops of oil of tartar. Bottle it, shake it well. It is good for the hands.

Excellent Pomatum

Melt some beef's marrow on a slow fire, being careful not to let it burn; then strain it several times over, that it may well be purified. When partially cool, beat in some castor oil, a tablespoon at a time. The proportion should be two-thirds of melted marrow and one-third of oil. Perfume it, by stirring in as you proceed, any sort of essential oil that is not too pungent. You may give it a fine, red coloring by putting in, after the marrow has melted, some chips of alkanet tied in a very thin muslin bag, letting it remain till the tint is thoroughly infused. Keep in a covered jar. A little rubbed every day, or twice or three times a week, with the fingers among the roots of the hair, will greatly improve its growth and softness.

Good Hair Oil

Of castor oil, ammonia and glycerine two teaspoons each, add enough alcohol to cut the oil and put in a four ounce bottle, filling it with rain water. It should be well shaken before using.

To Make Hair Curl

Olive oil, one pound, oil of organum, one drachm, oil of rosemary, one-and-one-half drachms. Mix well. Bottle. *Note: one drachm equals one-eight ounce.*

Old-Fashioned Toilet Ideas

To remove stains from hands after paring vegetables and fruits, dip the hands in a dish of strong tea, rub well with a nail brush, and rinse in tepid water. Ripe tomatoes, also the juice of a lemon, will remove stains from the hands.

For Rough Hands in the Winter

A bowl of Indian meal is excellent. Keep in the bathroom or near the kitchen sink. If faithfully used, will keep the hands soft and smooth and, when chapped and sore, will often heal them. After washing and drying the hands, dip them in a bowl of Indian meal and rub diligently several times a day. A few drops of olive oil used on the hands occasionally will keep them smooth.

Care of the Feet

1. Lemon juice applied at night is most refreshing to tired feet.
2. A good rub with petroleum jelly and dusted with powder is soothing.

3. Cold feet are helped by putting cayenne pepper in the shoes.
4. Rub the soles of the feet at night; it will act as a tonic and stimulant.

Wrinkles

To cure tired wrinkles, sleep by an open window. White wax, one ounce; strained honey, two ounces; juice of lily bulbs, two ounces. Melt and mix. Apply twice a day for wrinkles.

Freckles

Place some finely grated horseradish in a dish of buttermilk, and let stand overnight. Strain and apply the wash night and morning.

The Complexion

Wash in cool, but not cold water, and attend carefully to the diet and digestion. Blanch one-fourth pound best Jordan almonds; take off skins and mash fine. Rub with them a small quantity of best, white soap, adding gradually one-quart of rain water. Strain through a fine sieve or fine muslin and, after washing with a soft cloth, apply.

MORE: One drachm powdered benzoin gum, one drachm nutmeg oil, six drops of orange blossom tea, or apple blossoms; put in one-half pint rain water and boil down to one teaspoon. Add one pint sherry wine. Mix well. Apply evening and morning.

MORE: One ounce of powdered benzoin gum in one pint whiskey, place a little in the wash bowl and bathe face; allow to dry without wiping. Perfectly harmless.

To Refresh the Skin

LAVENDER WATER: A delightful toilet water is made of white wine vinegar and lavender flowers. Steep handfuls of the lavender flowers in the vinegar. Keep the jar for three days in a warm place in the back of the stove, after which strain and bottle.

JASMINE TOILET WATER: Homemade Jasmine water is very refreshing. To make a gallon, take a quart of spirits of cologne and put it into a gallon jug; add half an ounce of oil of Jasmine. Let it stand two weeks. Fill with the best alcohol, and let stand two weeks more.

HOME MADE TOILET WATER: Use any essence desired; oil of lavender or rose, for instance. About twenty-five drops will perfume five pints of water. Into each half gallon jar put a funnel lined with filter paper; with a bunch of cotton on the bottom. On top of this cotton put some finely powdered magnesia, over which has been poured the perfume essence. It should be divided and half the quantity put in each jar. Pour into each jar some rain water, or ordinary boiled water. This will filter through the cotton, paper and magnesia, and make a soft toilet water with a delightful fragrance.

Lotions

BUTTERMILK AS A COSMETIC: There is nothing better for a tan, freckles, sunburn, or brown spots than fresh buttermilk, applied at night with a soft cloth or sponge. Wash off in the morning and repeat several nights. One application will have no effect. Buttermilk will also keep the hands smooth and soft.

OATMEAL AS A LOTION: Pour boiling water on a bag of oatmeal (fine linen or cheesecloth), let stand a while, press gently, pour off the clear liquid, add bay rum to suit. This is excellent for the face, neck, shoulders and hands. Make little oatmeal bags of fine linen and wash face with it. Cleansing and soothing.

WATERMELON LOTION: The water from the watermelon is most soothing to the face and, it is claimed, that if applied continuously, it will remove freckles.

CUCUMBER LOTION: Mix together, and let stand overnight, three tablespoons of cucumber juice and three of alcohol; the next day, add, slowly, one tablespoon of oil of almonds and ten drops benzoin. Recommended for sunburn and freckles. It is very soothing and whitens the skin. Cucumber water is made by cutting up three large cucumbers, skin and all, and steeping them in half a cup of water over a slow fire till the pulp is soft. Strain well.

WITCH HAZEL JELLY: Three parts witch hazel, one part of benzoin, and one of glycerine, well mixed. A pleasing and soothing lotion.

BEAUTY SECRETS FROM GRANDMA'S GARDEN

Strawberry Lotion

For whitening the skin, this lotion is excellent. Crush ripe strawberries in a saucepan to extract the juice and boil five minutes. Mash them with the back of a wooden spoon during cooking. Strain off the juice and cool. Measure and mix one part alcohol with two parts strawberry juice. Bottle and use to remove tan or yellowness from the skin.

Fresh Berry Lotion

Mash one-half cupful of ripe strawberries and add the same amount of water. Before retiring, after the face, neck and arms have been washed, apply strawberry mixture to the skin. When washed off in the morning, the skin will be nearly white.

Strawberries and Cream for Preventing Wrinkles

If strawberries are nice and ripe, freshly picked, combine with fresh, thick sweet cream. Mash six large, fresh strawberries and add an equal amount of the cream. Pat this on the face with the finger tips, applying liberally under the eyes and where wrinkles are likely to come.

Spring Garden, Lettuce Cream

A delightful cream for bleaching and healing the skin. Select large, fresh-picked lettuce leaves and cover them with boiling water. Let stand thirty minutes; then pour off the water and pound the lettuce with a potato masher. Strain through a fine sieve. Then melt one ounce of spermacetti and four ounces of sweet almond oil in a double boiler or over water. The mixture should not boil, but just melt gently. Remove from the stove and add—drop by drop—the lettuce juice, beating the mixture constantly with a fork until the cream is satin smooth, fluffy and cold. Spoon into little porcelain jars.

Potato Mask for an Oily Skin

For an oily skin subject to blackheads the potato mask is delightful. Wash a nice fresh potato, cut into thick slices. Rub over skin. It removes the oil, cleanses and refreshes and whitens the skin. For a real tonic effect, keep potato cool before slicing.

Onion Tonic for Hair

For very thin hair, cut an onion in half and rub scalp with these vigorously before retiring at night. The juice of onions invigorates the roots of the hair.
(A very drastic and odorous remedy. Evidently the countryfolk, in the old days, believed in its beneficial effects.)

Fresh Cucumber Sachets to Soften and Whiten the Skin

Pick two fresh cucumbers, pare and cut into thin slices. Steep in cool milk for one hour. Fill small, fine, linen or thin muslin bags with sliced cucumbers. Tie tightly with string. Dip bags into the milk. Wash face and hands with the little cucumber bags, allow to dry. Leave on for ten minutes. Wash off with cool water. Dry gently.

A NINETEENTH CENTURY BILL OF FARE AND MENUS

Bill of Fare Table
(1890)

Bills of fare can easily be made by selecting more or less of the dishes mentioned in the following table and serving them in the order indicated.

FIRST COURSE

Raw Oysters   Little Clams   Roman Punch

SECOND COURSE

Soup

THIRD COURSE

Hors d'oeuvres (relishes)   Sardines
Pickled Oysters   Cucumbers   Radishes
Preserved Herrings   Anchovies   Coldslaw

FOURTH COURSE

Fish
Any kind of fish or shellfish

FIFTH COURSE

Hors d'oeuvres (hot)
These are light entrees such as croquettes, all kinds
of hot patties (not sweet), sweetbreads, brains, etc.

SIXTH COURSE

Relevés
For substantial dishes such as roast joints of beef,
veal, lamb, mutton or venison, roast or boiled turkeys
or chickens, fillet of beef, braised meats, etc.

SEVENTH COURSE

Roman Punch

EIGHTH COURSE

Entreés
Cutlets, all kinds of patties (not sweet), sweetbreads,
fricassees, scollops, casseroles, poultry or game *en
coquille*, croquettes. Any of the meats or game made
into side dishes.

NINTH COURSE

Cauliflower   Asparagus   Corn   Spinach
Boiled Celery   String Beans   Peas on Toast
Macaroni   Dressed Eggs   Fritters

TENTH COURSE

Game (of any kind)

ELEVENTH COURSE

Salad (of any kind)
A plain salad is often served with game.

TWELFTH COURSE

Cheese   Macaroni Dressed with Cheese
Cheese Omelet   Cheese Cake
Cheese and salad are often served together.

THIRTEENTH COURSE

Pudding (any kind)   Jellies   Sweet Fritters
Sweet Pastries   Creams

FOURTEENTH COURSE

Ice Cream   Water Ices   Frozen Pudding

FIFTEENTH COURSE

Fruit   Nuts and Raisins   Candied Fruits
Bonbons   Cake

SIXTEENTH COURSE

Coffee
Little Cakes   Biscuits

Menu for Thanksgiving Dinner

Oysters

Noodle Soup

Roast Turkey   Giblet Gravy

Mashed Potatoes   Mashed Turnips

Chicken Pie

Plain Celery   Cranberry Sauce

Creamed Onion

Lettuce Salad

Suet Pudding, with Snow Sauce

Apple Pie   Pumpkin Pie   Mince Pie

Fruit

Coffee

Menu for Christmas Dinner

Oyster Soup

Baked Fish   Tomato Sauce

Potato Balls

Roast Goose, with Apple Sauce

Cauliflower   Mashed Potatoes

Venison Steak

Currant Jelly

Baked Sweet Potatoes   Stewed Celery

Lettuce Salad

Plum Pudding, with Brandy Sauce

Ice Cream   Cake

Fruit

Coffee

INDEX

344

345

348